THE SEXUAL TRAFFICKING IN CHILDREN

THE SEXUAL TRAFFICKING IN CHILDREN

An Investigation of the Child Sex Trade

DANIEL S. CAMPAGNA
Castleton State College

DONALD L. POFFENBERGER
West Virginia Northern Community College

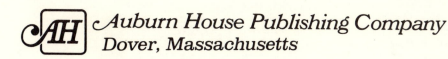 *Auburn House Publishing Company*
Dover, Massachusetts

CB

Library of Congress Cataloging in Publication Data

Campagna, Daniel S.
    The sexual trafficking in children.

    Bibliography: p.
    Includes index.
        1. Prostitution, Juvenile—United States.
    2. Prostitution, Juvenile—United States—Prevention.
    3. Children in pornography—United States.
    I. Poffenberger, Donald L.   II. Title.
    HQ144.C35   1987   306.7´4´088054   87-1242
    ISBN 0-86569-154-1

Printed in the United States of America

To the Victims:
That they may one day know a life free of pain

PREFACE

The purpose of this book is to examine the dynamics of sexual exploitation, including such offenses as child pornography, juvenile prostitution, procuring, pedophilia, sex tourism industry, indenturing, and sex rings. It was written for practitioners in the criminal justice system and in social, youth, and human service organizations, all of whom need practical information about these crimes and about the offenders in child sexual trafficking in order to develop agency policies and programs, to identify resources, and to implement proactive services that can minimize the levels and effects of sexual victimization.

The principal research activity was a five-year, nationwide field study conducted by the authors. Interviews were conducted with juvenile prostitutes, molested children, pedophiles, child pornographers, victims of sex rings, pimps who specialize in procuring minors, madams, brothel owners, members of motorcycle gangs, and adult prostitutes, as well as adults who had been victimized as children. In addition to the field studies, correspondence was carried on with groups advocating intergenerational sexual relationships. (The names of victims and exploiters are fictitious.) Also, interviews were conducted with detectives, juvenile officers, legislators, social caseworkers, directors of youth agencies (private and governmental), district attorneys, judges, representatives of federal agencies that serve youths, and directors of juvenile correctional facilities and emergency shelters. And, finally, we drew on other case studies, talked with informants, and reviewed the existing literature.

Our findings appear throughout the book in the form of observations, case studies, interviews, and contributions by various practitioners. Whenever and wherever possible, information was corroborated through multiple interviews, review of case files, on-site visits, and comparison with survey findings. The final result is, we think, an accurate portrayal of the realities of sexual trafficking in children today. The book is organized into three major parts: (1) Exploited and Exploiters, (2) The Dimensions of Sexual Trafficking, and (3) Addressing the Problem.

THE AUTHORS

ACKNOWLEDGMENTS

A study of this scope and nature would have been impossible without the extraordinary assistance, gracious advice, and guidance of many dedicated individuals. Their generosity of spirit and concern for the plight of sexually exploited children is evidenced in their commitment to ending the markets in child sex. To each of you we extend our gratitude and deepest thanks.

Those who provided encouragement and information include: Michael Jupp, Kenneth J. Herrmann, Jr., Lois Lee, John and Lorraine Cox, Michael Keller, George Haralson, Thelma Milgrim, Stanley Burkhardt, Alexander Lyerly, Thomas McCarthy, Richard Tyler, Craig Love, John Rabun, James Close, Kurt Stakeman, Gordon Railey, Greg Loken, Robin Rushton, Ellen Greensburg, Barbara Wyatt, Charles Williams, Doug McCord, Richard Ruffino, Gregory Christos, Ronald Lane, Larry Ross, Larry Reese, Hank Lane, Christopher Montanino, Aaron Rosenthal, Danny Durham, Thomas Horan, Neil Brown, Joseph Spencer, Thomas Rodgers, Margaret Cahape, Claudette Ladika, Isaiah McKinnon, Thomas Reuscher, Janette Denenkoff, Hal Nees, Mary Murray, Victoria Church, Frank Sacco, Ralph Draper, Chris Corbet, Elaine Surma, Janet Crumm, John Nanny, John Moses, Larry Bragg, Robert Shulenberg, Manfred Holland, John Massey, Paul Hickey, Kathy L., Norman Carlson, and Joseph Collias.

We wish to acknowledge the technical and legal assistance and analysis provided by Lance Levitt (Chapter 7) and Susan Witte. To Ronald Mulholland, the individual who sparked our enthusiasm for this problem five years ago, we extend special thanks.

The names of many other persons have been omitted because of their request for anonymity. The countless juveniles and exploiters interviewed will probably never read this book. We are, nonetheless, indebted to them for their willingness to discuss the dynamics of sexual exploitation.

Finally, we wish to acknowledge the unfailing support and encouragement of our wives, Janet and Yvonne, who were havens of comfort throughout the study.

THE AUTHORS

CONTENTS

Part One

EXPLOITED AND EXPLOITERS

Chapter 1 introduces the topic of sexual trafficking in children by defining the major terms, giving an overview of the various markets, and surveying the range of exploiters of children. Presumption of knowledge is considered as a barrier to understanding, and sources of information are presented. A description is given of how the public and private child sex markets interact so as to ensure a constant level of victimization at both national and international levels. A variety of types of exploiters, such as pimps and pornographers, are identified, with description of how their respective activities contribute to sexual trafficking. The lack of practical knowledge about these offenders and their crimes is discussed in the context of a five-year field study performed by the authors.

Chapter 2 examines the behavioral phenomenon of pedophilia—that is, adult sexual attraction to minors. Various cases demonstrate the diversity of sexual conduct exhibited by pedophiles and explain their behavior as an ingrained sexual orientation which results in the victimization of minors. More elaborate expressions of pedophilia are discussed, including sex rings, groups that advocate intergenerational sexual relationships, and pedophile publications intended to promote the philosophies and interests of exploitive adults.

1

Chapter 1

INTRODUCTION: THE PARAMETERS OF THE PROBLEM

A social service worker in southern California receives startling information about physical and sexual abuse of numerous children by the employees of a popular day care center. A juvenile officer working the backwoods of rural Virginia discovers that several minors in her county are victims of sexual mistreatment, including some being posed for pornographic photographs. The director of an emergency shelter for youths on the East Coast reports an alarming rate of venereal disease among his wards, especially the adolescent males. Further inquiry reveals that these juveniles are part-time prostitutes, selling themselves to men in return for money and drugs. Meanwhile, in the Southwest, a detective learns of a private club that promotes nude dancing by underage girls. The club's owner, alerted to police interest in his activities, leaves town the day before arrest warrants are issued.

These separate cases, occurring in different parts of the country, are integral parts of an elusive criminal subculture so furtive and alien that most people are unaware of its presence. The victims, moreover, represent an isolated stratum of society, and their status as easy prey usually goes unnoticed, unreported, and unchanged. What we are talking about is the sexual trafficking in children. The adage that the more things change, the more they remain the same, seems to apply here: Minors have been, are, and apparently will continue to be the most sexually exploited class of citizens in the United States. Children believed to be involved in sexually exploitive activities here may number as many as 1.2 million.[1] We

believe that approximately 150,000 victims of exploitation participate regularly in child prostitution.[2]

Trafficking in minors, as will be shown, is an enormously lucrative and complex enterprise that shows no signs of declining.
Children are bought, sold, traded, and misused in underground
child sex markets daily. Every state in the United States and most
nations throughout the world contribute in some fashion to the
steady flow of juveniles, customers, and exploiters needed to
sustain this trade. Indeed, few communities are completely immune from sexual exploitation in some form, including child
molestation. Social status, family values, and religious beliefs are
often fragile barriers against the child sex trade, for the victims'
immaturity make them vulnerable to entrepreneurs' manipulation.

In these pages we discuss how and why these activities take
place and examine their long-lasting, devastating effects on the
victims. Our emphasis is on the dynamics of this much-ignored
but volatile issue in terms of its markets, characteristics, victims,
and exploiters. At the same time, we attempt to thrust the subject
of trafficking into the stream of scholarly and general public
awareness, for it is a major premise of our research that the sexual
exploitation of minors is a social problem requiring immediate
attention.

Sexual Trafficking Defined

Sexual trafficking in children can be defined broadly as the sexual
exploitation of a person under the age of eighteen for pleasure or
financial gain. More often than not, such activities contain a
commercial ingredient. The pornographer, for example, expects a
substantial economic reward for his product; a pedophile may use
a bribe or lure to attract a juvenile; a pimp often pays his underage
hustlers with drugs.

The offenses of trafficking, for a variety of reasons, are not
considered here to include intra-familial sexual abuse, although we
view this behavior as a spawning ground of trafficking. Homes in
which sexual abuse takes place produce countless victims, for
minors subjected to sexual abuse at home often run away and
become the subjects of commercial exploiters. Incest, however,
does not involve exactly the same behavioral dynamics and motivations as trafficking. The victim's silent misery is not commercial-

ized, and a web of complicity binds the family in keeping its dreadful secret. Not until the offender looks outside the family in search of similar gratification does the question of trafficking arise.

Sexual trafficking encompasses a multitude of crimes: child pornography, prostitution, sex rings, molestation (outside the family), sex tourism industry, white slavery, bogus adoption schemes, nude dancing or modeling, apprenticeship or recruitment for prostitution, procuring, and indenturing. Each offense represents a specific market which shares several characteristics with the other markets, including an underage victim, one or more adult offenders, and a mixture of sexual pleasure and financial motivation.

When the commercial element is present, the victim is compelled to exchange the use of his or her body for money, food, shelter, alcohol, or drugs, Sex, in other words, becomes the medium by which the victim survives. In less commercial settings, a juvenile may be tricked into accepting sex as part of a relationship with an adult. The relationship is maintained at the victim's expense; it may include pornography sessions, multiple adult lovers, or drug dependency. In all cases, those who are victimized are exploited and eventually discarded.

Types of Child Sex Markets

The number of ways a minor can be sexually exploited is seemingly limited only by the imagination and ingenuity of the offender. The hazards and risks of trafficking encourage exploiters to experiment with innovative methods of operation. As a result, the market dynamics of child sex periodically undergo subtle transformation. The advent of electronic bulletin boards, for instance, eased the burden of communication among pedophiles owning computers. The sheer diversity of demand ensures that someone, somewhere, is testing new ways to guarantee the supply. International traffickers in child pornography use various countries for purposes of production and distribution. Pimps sometimes insulate themselves from detection by shipping their underage hustlers to out-of-state bordellos. Such activities can keep the markets in a relative state of flux as novel techniques for evading arrest and prosecution are devised.

Trafficking is supported by various human desires, including sexual gratification, the pursuit of profit, and a depraved sort of personal fulfillment—as in the case of someone who derives satisfaction from publicly promoting sexual relationships between children and adults (see Chapter 2). These enduring incentives form a bond among exploiters, from the neighborhood molester to the editor of an underground newsletter aimed at pedophiles. Such motivations have their own impetus and are not severely impeded by economic, statutory, cultural, or geographic restrictions designed to prevent sexual trafficking in minors.

The various market entrepreneurs operate on the premise that demand, though it may be periodically restrained by law enforcement, will never disappear. When exploiters are hard pressed by vigorous law enforcement, two things happen in these markets: The price of child sex goes up and exploiters become harder to identify. Some entrepreneurs, such as adult bookstore owners, may choose to leave the trade entirely to avoid unwanted prosecution. Others, like pimps who realize hefty profits from their adolescent prostitutes, are willing to accept the risks.

Commercialized child sex, regardless of the risks, occurs at both public and private levels. Public markets involving juveniles are open to all interested buyers. These activities include prostitution, pornography, nude dancing or modeling, sex tourism, bogus adoption schemes, and procuring. A commercial exploiter working exclusively at the public level is primarily concerned with financial profit, often using technological tools such as the video camera to show the quality of the merchandise and to lessen the possibility of detection (as in the case of mobile photographic developing studios). Advertising and promotion of services are employed at the public level to stimulate trade. A veteran pimp, for example, may decide to display pornographic pictures of his young hustlers to entice new customers. Investments of this type are commonly protected through payoffs, threats, and the blackmailing of customers or hustlers.

At the private market level, the exploitation of minors is most likely to occur when the offender seeks merely sexual pleasure and personal fulfillment. Crimes of this caliber include molestation, recruitment, sex rings, and indenturing. Each centers on the offender's need for sexual gratification at the victim's expense. The organizer of a sex ring, for instance, typically will characterize his functions within the conspiracy as follows: to promote group cohesion and, thereby, minimize the risk of detection; to socialize his victims into appropriate roles within the ring; and to ensure that his own sexual needs are met.

There is a good deal of overlap between the public and private markets, but this is to be expected because mutual interests inevitably coincide. A pimp, for example, may make a marginal investment in child pornography carried on at the private market level, while his prostitutes continue to generate revenue either on the streets or in a sheltered location in the public market. Where child sex is concerned, no preference or pleasure is considered too outlandish by exploiters. The markets, in short, are capable of accommodating—often at exorbitant prices—practically any sort of demand by customers. Skillful exploiters, whether acting privately or for a specific public audience such as the customers of prostitutes, are quick to capitalize on this fact.

Exploiters of Child Sex

Anyone who promotes, perpetuates, or knowingly derives some form of benefit from the traffic in child sex can be considered an exploiter. Certain distinctions should be made, however, in order to separate direct from indirect beneficiaries.

Those directly engaged in sexual trafficking rely heavily on its financial and sexual rewards to the extent that exploitation becomes a life-style. These exploiters include pimps, pornographers, booking agents, hard-core molesters, sex-ring participants or organizers, publishers and printers of child sex newsletters or magazines, and madams and brothel owners who employ juvenile prostitutes. The bulk of their personal income flows from exploitation, and they often invest their profits in other illicit activities. For the professional trafficker, trading in child sex is vital to owning, in the jargon of money managers, a "diverse portfolio."

Indirect beneficiaries, on the other hand, have a limited interest or investment in child sex. They may on occasion act as suppliers or vendors—as in the case of a parent who lends or sells a child to a pornographer for a photograph session—and their rewards take the form of bribes, kickbacks, sex, drugs, commissions, and the exchange of favors. A partial list of these exploiters includes parents, corrupt officials, adult book store owners, club owners who hire underage exotic dancers, certain members of organized crime, motorcycle gangs, motel owners who allow their establishments to be used for prostitution, truck drivers, and a wide range of tipsters, from bartenders to cabdrivers. Although they are in a sense peripheral characters, each may contribute some type of service or fill a specific function within the various markets.

An offender can be both a consumer and supplier of child sex, and it should be noted that female exploiters are appearing with ever-growing frequency. What matters more than fine distinctions, however, is understanding the modus operandi of traffickers and developing techniques for making it harder for them to conduct business "as usual." In the following chapters, all manner of exploiters are introduced. Representative of a wide spectrum of occupational levels, they include physicians, dentists, priests, welders, florists, bankers, judges, politicians, artists, professors, and accountants. The implication is clear: stereotypical views of the exploiter are inaccurate and outdated. Any adult willing to take sexual advantage of a child is an eligible candidate for the role of exploiter. Discouraging as this observation on the human condition may be, it nonetheless appropriately prepares us to approach the subject in a realistic frame of mind.

Presumption of Knowledge: A Barrier

One of the greatest obstacles to the study of sexual trafficking in minors is the popular misconception that a wealth of information about these offenses has already been accumulated. All that remains, according to this view, is to act upon the extrapolated data at hand in order to develop programs, policies, and remedies for the sexually exploited juvenile. The unfortunate fact is that such a foundation of knowledge does not exist. Sexual trafficking is as much an enigma to many criminal justice practitioners as it is to the layperson. Theories and stereotypes abound, but hard facts are woefully absent.[3]

Some crime analysts argue that virtually all types of criminal offenses, from simple theft to treason, can be classified, measured, and understood, and that for every crime, criminal, and victim there is an empirical niche. As a result of this reverent attitude toward official statistics, the rhythms and patterns of crime are presented as fairly predictable events. For example, percentile indexes of national trends show the probability of being murdered in large cities; studies of burglars and their habits give us the odds of having our homes vandalized; and victimization surveys high-light citizen reactions to personal and property offenses.

While it may be comforting to know in an obscure way that statisticians are showing concern for our person and property, however, there remains an enormous volume of illegal behavior connected with sexual trafficking that is, at best, only partially reflected in official statistics. This lack is due in large measure to the jurisdictional limits and legislative mandates of reporting agencies. The FBI, U.S. Customs, and Postal Service record only those cases brought to their attention. No single department or agency at any level of government in the United States is responsible for collecting data on offenses related to sexual trafficking.[4] With the exception of juvenile prostitution, the Uniform Crime Report does not incorporate categories for the majority of trafficking offenses. The three principal methods for keeping a tally of crimes of trafficking are (1) the compilation of reported cases, (2) a head count of the number of juvenile prostitutes working in a given district, and (3) surveys. None of these methods is, by any means, error-free or comprehensive in scope. In short, more is known about the volume and nature of shoplifting in the United States than about any specific offense relating to the sexual exploitation of children.

An unfortunate side-effect of the false presumption of knowledge is the problem of language. Terms are freely tossed about that bear little relevance to the issue at hand, or that lack specificity. Child pornography, for example, is often euphemistically referred to simply as child sexual abuse. This is true in the same broad sense that someone who has been brutally stabbed to death can be said to be the victim of foul play. Neither term, however, expresses the finality of these acts upon the victim; indeed, by becoming part of everyday jargon, inaccurate terms may dilute the perceived seriousness of the offense.

Language defines reality; the words used to discuss crimes reveal something about our knowledge of and attitude toward them. Child pornography, for example, is not simply sexual abuse, per se; it is also the systematic exploitation of a minor for the sake of immediate pleasure or eventual profit. Making this traumatic crime mundane by describing it with a stock phrase creates a barrier to understanding of trafficking in minors. Trafficking is far too serious a problem and abuse too ambiguous a term for the two to be used interchangeably. If, therefore, it appears that the authors are critical of conventional wisdom or attitudes, this is so because they think that the offenses of trafficking deserve greater recognition as crimes against persons than they presently do.

The following case is an example of the consequences of false presumption of knowledge, among other things.[5] An account by a youth caseworker of her experiences with minors involved in juvenile prostitution, it attests to the attitudes of certain agency practitioners who believe that sexual trafficking is either an insignificant or a rare occurrence.

STREET VIEW

I began to notice that a high percentage of the very attractive young girls—those 14 and 15 years old—were wearing new and expensive clothes. In addition to having what appeared to be access to a lot of drugs, like pot and speed, I also noticed that some of these girls would habitually cut school and end up in this one particular house. From my interviews with some of the kids whom I suspected of going to the house, I began to understand what was going on—at least on the surface. They (adult males) were coming on to these kids by providing pot or booze and making them feel beautiful, seductive—you know, important. Given the fact that most of these girls did not have a good self-image to start with, these men undoubtedly began to have an influence. One girl told me, "No one understands me the way they do," referring to several older men who lived in the house.

I found out later that one guy associated with the house made a career of getting close to kids and taking them to other cities for purposes of prostitution. Florida seemed to be the big place. I had two on my caseload who I discovered were in the process of being taken to another city—Akron, I believe—but they panicked and jumped out of the car. The more involved I got, the more I felt I was being placed between a rock and a hard spot. My biggest problem was that after I'd talk to law enforcement to identify the situation, they would go in like gangbusters and everyone would stop talking or disappear.

It took me about a year before people, especially the kids, would trust me. I had to mix with them, relate to them. I found that most of them felt guilty about something. Maybe the kids were involved with drugs, or their parents lied to get extra food stamps or welfare money, or something made them nervous about authority figures. When I tried to get someone who could do something about the situation, the kids were afraid of that person.

Anyway, going back to the house, some FBI people reported that there was no prostitution going on in town. But I know that's because they came in wearing three-piece suits and asking questions point-blank. That approach doesn't work. They did some good though, because once they started asking questions, the people in the house moved out.

I guess my name got around as someone who cared. Whatever the reason, I started getting messages from a local madam or some long-time street hooker expressing concern about kids getting into prostitution. It has been my experience that many of the street people who are heavily involved with prostitution resent and have very strong ethics about children getting involved in their life-style. It is sad, but I found they cared more than the establishment. They certainly knew more. In dealing with the judicial system I found the lengths a court would go to; what they believed to be protection of the young girl was in fact punishment to her. She was taken away from her family and environment, stuck in a group home or foster placement, and forced to live with total strangers clear across the state or even in another state. Not too many kids see that as something for their own good, and I agree. They see that occurring to two or three of their friends and they are not going to tell anybody what is happening to them. It is as though the children are victimized by both sides. They are being used on the street and, by their own perception, the system abuses them.

It is really frustrating when you find out who is involved. I remember taking a girl to the sheriff's department to be questioned one afternoon. I knew she was working the streets, but she was very tough and I thought maybe we could shake it loose. Do you know she was back on the streets before I got home? I received a message telling me I was interfering with someone's bread and butter and to stay out of it. The kicker was that the message was delivered by a so-called friend right in my own living room.

I really got involved out there on the streets. I listened, and learned, and a lot of people talked to me. I just couldn't make others, either professionals or friends, listen. It is a dirty world according to many people, and they don't want to be bothered. School officials, law enforcement people, my co-workers, and the general public all reacted the same: either with disbelief at the existence and extent of such activity, or they didn't react at all. By that I mean they are apathetic.

I did not have much support from my supervisors or peers. There needs to be more teamwork; all the people have to work together. We need to identify the sexually exploited child and follow through with consistency in programming and be more of an advocate. You can't take a child out of all they know and are emotionally tied to and expect them to change behavior patterns. I've had kids on my caseload who have experienced as many as 14 or 15 different placements. How many times can a person make that type of adjustment? The result is that too much of what is supposed to be help turns out to be punishment.

■   ■   ■

The Field Study

Information contained in this book about the sexual trafficking in minors is derived from a five-year field study conducted by the authors and known as the "Meat Rack Report." The term "meat rack" has traditionally been used to describe the site where boy prostitutes, or "chickens" as they are called by their customers, can be found; indeed, juveniles exploited for their sexual value are viewed as flesh in trade. The report focuses on the dynamics of the various child sex markets at the national level. We looked at these crimes through the eyes of the exploiters and their victims in order to see the world as they see it, and to describe it in their own words, based on their own experiences. We also matched their observations against popular assumptions. The truth about trafficking, regardless of what shape it assumes, is not likely to be discerned simply by rehashing outdated materials; rather, these unorthodox crimes require creative investigative skills to interpret. The observations and experiences of exploiters and victims, consequently, are useful in sorting out basic facts from stereotypes about sexual trafficking.

In order to increase the likelihood of rooting out the truth, we adopted a comprehensive multi-tiered approach. In the first tier, several hundred hours of taped interviews were conducted in state and federal prisons, juvenile detention centers, and private agency offices, as well as in numerous street settings. The persons interviewed can be found among three basic categories: victims, exploiters, and agency practitioners.

Within the victim category are juvenile prostitutes (male and female) familiar with life in the streets and in the brothels, minors involved in pornography or sex rings, runaways, children who had been molested or sexually intimidated, and adolescents engaged in nude dancing or modeling. In addition, we sought to identify and interview adults who had first-hand knowledge or the experience of sexual exploitation. These were, in most cases, women who had either endured years of suffering as a child victim or had discovered that their own children were being victimized.

In the second category, the exploiters we interviewed were an assortment of pedophiles, representatives of groups advocating adult sexual relationships with children, child pornographers, pimps who specialize in procuring minors, members of motorcycle gangs, bordello owners, madams, adult prostitutes (male and female), child killers, and various other fringe actors with an interest in trafficking. Each provided useful insights into the commercial sex markets. None of their observations, however, was accepted at face value without some type of corroboration.

The final category, that of agency practitioner, includes a host of professionals within the judicial and social service systems. Among those interviewed were juvenile court counselors, sex crime and juvenile delinquency detectives, social service case workers, directors of correctional institutions for juveniles, judges, district attorneys, and probation and parole officers. In addition, individuals operating private, nonprofit programs serving youths were surveyed, as well as federal judicial officials and legislators. The field data and observations obtained proved helpful in the search for practical solutions and resources that could be used to eradicate trafficking. (See Chapter 8.)

The second tier of information was gathered by a nationwide survey of police departments on the subjects of juvenile prostitution, child pornography, runaways, and missing children. This survey, intended to generate an estimate of the perceived volume of trafficking, yielded responses from 596 departments scattered among all 50 states.

A third level of fact finding was the field observation studies.

These inquiries, ranging anywhere from a few days to several months, involved the surveillance of and talks with juvenile prostitutes and exploiters in different cities such as Wheeling, West Virginia, New York City, Washington, D.C., and Pittsburgh, Pennsylvania. Periodic visits to locations with notorious reputations for prostitution were useful in noting the working habits of juvenile street hustlers. At the same time, we were able to observe the behavior of customers (or "johns") who were in the process of making contact with the underage hustlers, either on the streets or at various truck stops.

Case studies constituted a fourth source of information. These cases were brought to our attention in our roles as consultants or analysts by police and social service agencies. In all but a few instances, they pertain to specific incidents involving sex rings, bordellos, and kiddie porn production. Particular attention in these cases was paid to the victim-perpetrator relationship and the subsequent processing of charges by the judicial system. We were allowed, in many instances, to be present during the interviews with victims and to observe how different prosecutors presented their cases in court.

Informants, either convicted exploiters or offenders on parole, provided a fifth source of information. Although their observations and disclosures were highly subjective, they did prove useful in corroborating certain allegations surrounding the child sex markets.

The sixth and last level of information was an analysis of the relevant professional literature dating back to 1900. While rich in theoretical speculation and clinical reports, the literature is remarkably devoid of practical knowledge in the area of sexual trafficking. With a few noteworthy exceptions, scholarly interest in the subject of child sexual victimization has focused primarily on the family setting, with periodic reference to molesters, therapy for the accused and victim, preparing the minor for testifying, and rebuilding shattered families.[6] Fortunately, research in the last decade indicates a gradual shift toward the equally critical problem of sexual trafficking.

In order to substantiate statements and sift through the various allegations made about sexual trafficking, we relied on a blend of corroborative methods. Case files and records were reviewed to help spot discrepancies in the interview transcripts. Multiple interviews performed over the past five years enabled us to track and cross-reference the lives and experiences of different individuals. Information given by exploiters and minors was matched against law enforcement records made available to us.

Because of the extreme sensitivity of the subject and the vulnerability of the victims, characters presented in this book have been given fictitious names. At the same time, it should be noted that no promises were made, no rewards were offered, and no inducements were used to obtain an interview with either a minor victim or an adult exploiter. As facts were validated, they became part of the final investigative study. Certain areas of concern were omitted because we lacked sufficient corroborative data. These include, for example, the molestation of minors in hospitals and psychiatric clinics, procurement of juvenile prostitutes by gypsies, buying, selling and transporting of underage hustlers by criminal organizations, and the unverified use of minors in various sexual practices pertaining to satanic rites.

Conclusion

Sexual trafficking, the generic term used to describe the crimes of commercial sexual exploitation, remains an unfamiliar concept to those who view the separate offenses as isolated incidents of no direct concern to the juvenile population or as occasional side-effects of sexual abuse within the family. The notion of a minor as a victim of ongoing exploitation is too fantastic or farfetched for many people to accept. Yet, trafficking exists, and it may be as prevalent and destructive as intra-familial sexual abuse. A solitary sex ring composed of two adults and several juveniles, for example, can easily blossom into a group of rings with scores of participants expanding their activities into prostitution and pornography. The victims are taught how to exploit their peers through acquired skills that invariably carry over into adulthood. The potential for harm, enhanced by the amount of personal or sexual gain resulting from trafficking, may surpass that experienced in domestic settings.

Every year an unknown number of juveniles are lost or abandoned because of exploitation. For lack of a better term we call them the "fadeaway children." They are minors whose fates as sexual victims are overlooked by those people and agencies responsible for their well-being and protection. They become invisible, slipping easily through the ever-widening cracks of the juvenile justice and social service systems. As they fade away from the control and restraints of their family and society, these underage victims become casualties, numbers sometimes recorded on the official blotters of juvenile courts, runaway shelters, police arrest logs, and coroner's reports. The more fortunate ones may receive a modicum of treatment, but such services tend to be short-lived and in small supply. After several years of exposure to exploitation, the fadeaways face the prospect of a career as adult criminals, a lifetime of drugs or alcohol abuse, and institutionalization.

The crimes of sexual trafficking persist because a segment of society uses minors for sexual pleasure and profit. All minors subjected to sexual exploitation can be considered victims. In the rush to punish and prosecute the offender, we tend to overlook this critical fact: The underage victims should be entitled to compensation for their injuries, rehabilitation, and protection from further harm. That they are not extended these basic guarantees in a uniform, equitable manner is evidence of failure by the judicial and social service systems to look beyond intra-familial abuse, failure by state and federal legislators to treat the issue of trafficking as a national priority rather than indulge in a political circus, failure by the press and television networks to present a reasoned analysis of the problem instead of a sensational theme, and, last, failure by society to confront the fact that, while most parents love and care for their children, some do not.

It is important to note that some states, such as Missouri and New York, recognize juveniles as adults at ages 17 and 16, respectively. This discrepancy can create confusion in the discussion of a victim's legal status within the context of exploitation, particularly when age of consent is significant. Herein we define a minor as a person under the age of 18, the federal age standard at which a person becomes eligible to vote, be conscripted (in the case of males), and enjoy adult status in all states.

Finally, the language of the various subjects presented in the cases is often extremely frank and brutal. To understand sexual trafficking, however, it is necessary to listen to first-hand information in the language of the streets. While the acts described by victims and offenders will be startling to those unfamiliar with trafficking, they cannot be accurately portrayed in gentle terms, representing, as they do, the routine realities of the child sex markets.

The sexual traffic in minors, like drug trafficking, is an international phenomenon, the details of which have only recently begun to emerge. Furthermore, there is the possibility that all the different types of sexual trafficking crimes have not yet been identified. How many different levels of victimization are there actually? What is the volume of exploitive activity that remains unrecorded in official crime statistics? We trust that others will apply their investigative talents and research expertise to these and other related problems of trafficking.

Endnotes

1. National Legal Resource Center for Child Advocacy and Protection, *Child Sexual Exploitation: Background and Legal Analysis*, Monograph (Washington, D.C.: American Bar Association, 1983).
2. Daniel S. Campagna, *Sexual Exploitation of Children: Resource Manual* (Wheeling, W. Va.: West Virginia Criminal Justice Institute, 1985).
3. This lack of a practical research focus is gradually changing as a result of applied studies by various scholars. For a comparative overview of the diverse quality and texture of these studies, see Ann W. Burgess, "Research on the Use of Children in Pornography," Grant #90-Ca-810, The National Center on Child Abuse and Neglect (1982); Donald M. Allen, "Young Male Offenders: A Psychosocial Study," Archives of Sexual Behavior 9:5 (1980), pp. 399–426; Ann W. Burgess and Marieanne L. Clark (eds.), *Child Pornography and Sex Rings* (Lexington, Mass: D.C. Heath, 1984); and Parker G. Rossman, *Sexual Experience Between Men and Boys* (New York: Association Press, 1976).
4. At the time of this writing, two agencies are attempting to serve as repositories for intelligence data concerning two aspects of trafficking: child pornography and missing kids. They are the U.S. Customs Department and the National Center for Missing and Exploited Children. The former is in the process of developing a central data bank to house child pornography information, whereas the latter, under a federal mandate, is concerned primarily with missing children.
5. The speaker in this case example is a youth caseworker who has requested that her identity be kept anonymous.
6. See Roland C. Summit, "The Child Sexual Abuse Accommodation Syndrome," *Child Abuse and Neglect*, 7 (1983), pp. 177–193; Suzanne Sgroi, "Childhood Gonorrhea," *Medical Aspects of Human Sexuality*, 16:7 (July, 1982), pp. 118–141; David Finkelhor, "Risk Factors in the Sexual Exploitation of Children," *Child Abuse and Neglect*, 4 (1980), pp. 265–273; and Mary De Young, "Counterphobic Behavior in Multiply Molested Children," *Child Welfare*, 63:4 (July/August, 1984), pp. 333–339.

Chapter 2

PEDOPHILIA

> *I've always had lots of adult friends, but I prefer the company of young boys. Sometimes it's hard to get close to them because their parents butt in. Until I got caught with Rob, a really nice kid, nobody ever suspected me. Not even my wife. They told me I need to change my behavior, my attitude towards sex with boys. There's nothing wrong with my attitude, but if changing it will keep me out of jail, okay. I'll go along with their program, but I still insist there's no harm being done. Ask Rob. He refused to cooperate with the police until his parents put a lot of pressure on him. We're still very good friends and I don't hold anything against him.*
>
> AL, A 41-YEAR-OLD PEDOPHILE

Few issues related to sexual trafficking in children incite as much debate as pedophilia. There is even widespread disagreement over the definition of pedophilia, its impact or relevance within the child sex markets, and the effectiveness of statutory penalties against it. For our purposes here, let us define pedophilia in layperson's terms as an adult's sexual preference for, or attraction to, underage persons—that is, a pedophile is a person who derives gratification from engaging in sexual activities with minors. In this chapter we examine the behavioral traits of pedophiles, victim and offender relationships, collecting of pornographic materials by pedophiles, pedophile organizations and publications, pedophile sex rings, and offender therapy.

Evaluating Behavior: The Pedophile Continuum

Constructing a classification scheme for pedophilia is difficult because there are so many different types of pedophile behavior.

Relegating a particular behavior to any given classification can reduce a complex phenomenon to overly simplistic components; also, a restrictive typology may fail to account for the fine shadings and variations in sexual behavior that are common to pedophilia. Rather than attempt to calculate all the possible combinations of conduct, we advocate an alternative approach: the "pedophile continuum." All conceivable variations of behavior exhibited by pedophiles are arranged along a line, one end of which represents the least severe, mildest forms of sexual attraction to minors (such as a fleeting, one-time erotic fantasy involving an underage female) while the other represents the multiple offender whose life revolves around the sexual victimization of minors. It should be possible to locate accurately most forms of sexual deviancy displayed toward children somewhere between these two extremes.

Locating a specific incident on the continuum, of course, requires assessment of the aberrant behavior and its effects upon the victim. The following case provides an example of the diversity of pedophile behavior.[1] Assessing the facts presented by the investigating officers in this case will enable one to estimate the location of the alleged offender on the pedophile continuum.

THE SELF-SACRIFICING PEDIATRICIAN

In November 1984 a postal inspector notified us that a local doctor had been receiving child pornography from Denmark. The inspector said the physician had been formally warned by the post office about the illegality of importing kiddie porn into the United States. The doctor worked in a welfare clinic in a low-income section of town. A background check revealed that he had given up a lucrative private practice in New Hampshire to assume a position with the New Jersey Welfare Department. A 38-year-old white male, the suspect (alias Dr. Hayes) lived alone in a one-bedroom apartment. During the 16 months Dr. Hayes had worked as a pediatrician at the clinic, he had examined approximately 2,000 children for various ailments. Above his office door was a sign which proclaimed, "I am the only house physician who examines children for lead poisoning." In an area where housing had been steadily deteriorating for years, it was not surprising that many mothers brought their children to Dr. Hayes.

Our first step was to build a case by setting up a sting-type operation with U.S. Customs officials, who were very interested in helping with the investigation. We took some of the confiscated literature and placed it in the doctor's post office box. We then requested a superior court judge to issue search warrants for Dr. Hayes' apartment and office. The judge was very impressed with our affidavit but refused to issue a search warrant of the suspect's home. He did authorize a search of the suspect's person and the office.

Dr. Hayes picked up his mail, including the planted pornography. We then confronted him in his office, identified ourselves as police officers, and let him review the search warrant. We opened the material from his mailbox, which turned out to be about 30 three-by-five-inch glossy, borderless photographs of young boys in deviant sexual poses. When questioned about these photographs, Dr. Hayes stated that he had purchased them for research in the field of child abuse and sexual exploitation. I asked him if he was aware that importing child pornography was a federal offense, and he replied that the pictures were for medical purposes. Dr. Hayes did agree to a polygraph test and a search of his apartment, which later uncovered pornographic photographs and periodicals and also sexual devices.

■   ■   ■

The case was brought before the Atlantic County prosecutor's office, which advised us that all we had were postal violations and that we needed to build a stronger criminal case. After months of interviews, the problems of further investigation became insurmountable because of the inability of the juveniles involved to understand or testify as to what had taken place in the doctor's office. We wanted to place hidden video cameras in the office to observe the doctor's examination techniques, but the court refused our request. In the end, Dr. Hayes left our city.

In this case, sexual desire dictated a career change which most individuals would view as a downward move. However, the doctor's new position assured him of a steady supply of child victims. This individual exploited his status as a physician and the repetitious nature of his offenses advanced him toward the more damaging end of the continuum.

Behavioral Aspects of Pedophilia

Although it is usually assumed that most pedophiles or child molesters are males, we have observed an increase in the number of recorded incidents involving female pedophiles. Their behavior has gone unrecognized probably because of inaccurate reporting of such cases, cultural resistance to the notion of women as child exploiters, and a lack of knowledge regarding the behavioral dynamics of female pedophilia. Another factor is the attitude of many people that it is acceptable for an adolescent male to acquire sexual experience with an adult female.

In the following case we can recognize multiple levels of victimization, including pornography, beastiality, and molestation.[2] The crimes were a blend of incestuous behavior and extra-familial exploitation. The offenders were, with a few exceptions, adult females. When compared with other incidents involving female pedophiles brought to our attention, this is not an extreme case. Furthermore, it suggests that female pedophiles are as capable of sexually exploiting minors as male pedophiles.

THE EXPLOITIVE MOTHER

In 1982, officers of the Special Investigation Division of the Tulsa Police Department arrested a woman, Ms. X, for prostitution. Ms. X was the proprietor of a brothel known as the Love Palace, which she operated and maintained from her residence. Also at the house was her 13-year-old son Clark, who was put into the custody of family friends during his mother's detention.

In 1984, officers from the same division received an anonymous phone call. The caller claimed that a teenage boy was being photographed in the nude while being stimulated by a dog, and that he was being abused by customers of his mother (Ms. X), a prostitute.

An immediate investigation began in response to the call. Bits and pieces of intelligence were gathered and reports compiled. After several months, investigators reached an impasse. From all outward appearances, there was no illegal activities taking place at the residence of Ms. X. As a result, the case was left open, pending further leads and additional intelligence.

In 1986, investigators discovered that Clark, now 17 years old, had attempted to commit suicide. He refused to speak with the officers, who, acting on the advice of his physician, did not pursue the matter. Later that year Clark began counseling sessions at the hospital for depression. As part of the treatment program, his mother, Ms. X, also attended. After several sessions Clark was permitted to go home on weekend passes. Upon his return to the hospital it was observed that he had become even more depressed. During one of the counseling sessions, Ms. X arrived, bringing several pictures of Clark and several females in suggestive poses that had been taken in the course of his weekend leave. Writing on the pictures implied that Clark was allowed to be with the adult females as part of a birthday gift arranged by his mother.

In a joint effort involving hospital officials, police officers, and state investigators for the Department of Human Services, more information was gathered and a case was prepared against Ms. X. Clark was taken into protective custody by the state. Using all of the information gathered since 1982, officers obtained a district court search warrant for Ms. X's home. Found during the search were several photo albums containing pictures of Clark and several other children in deviant, sexual poses.

During a police interview, Ms. X refused to comment on many specific matters, but she stated that she had engaged in sexual relations with her son, adding: "Is there nothing sacred between a mother and her son?" Ms. X was committed to the state hospital for the criminally insane. Clark continues to receive extensive therapy.

■   ■   ■

In the above example, the mother disregarded the psychological trauma she induced in her son. The offender perceived her conduct as acceptable and continued her deviant behavior despite outside interference. Even her son's continuing depression and attempted suicide proved ineffectual in bringing the abnormal behavior to an end. Ms. X's place on the continuum is determined by her persistence and her resistance to ending the damaging relationship.

What is the "essence" of the sexual attraction pedophiles feel for minors? Just as a normal heterosexual male would be hard pressed to explain precisely why he is sexually drawn to females, there is no obvious answer to the question of why some adults prefer children. Individuals may know how they are likely to be sexually attracted or aroused, yet not understand why they discriminate in their preferences and reactions.

Nevertheless, once we begin to understand the nature of a pedophile's sexual pathology, a certain logic does emerge regarding their behavior.[3] However deviant the conduct may appear to others, it makes sense when viewed from the offender's perspective.

First, this perspective is determined by the pedophile's own experiences and the ways in which he presents himself to the world. His relationships with other adults, sexual history, family background, personality type, and physical appearance each help to dictate the choice of victim, sexual activity to be pursued, and likelihood of repetition.

Second, juxtaposed with the pedophile's life experiences and background is the victim's sexual history (or lack of one), the cohesiveness of the family unit, the child's personality and physical appearance. Gender and age also help determine what sexual activity the child may be persuaded to endure, as well as the intensity and length of the relationship.

Third, it is important to understand that the actual sexual activity may be a long-term drama between two individuals or an episodic interlude between strangers, with variations depending on the above-identified variables. Of equal importance to understanding of the pedophile's behavior is the fact that the type of sexual activity may vary from subtle seduction to outright assault of the victim.

All too often a discussion of child molestation will focus on dramatic episodes perpetrated by the violent and habitual offender because many people believe that these are the characteristics of all pedophiles. However, implicit in our findings is the fact that pedophiles manifest varying pathologies.

Indeed, a wide range of racial and occupational types are represented in pedophilia. The offender may be married, with children of his or her own, while maintaining a dual sex life involving adults and minors. The ability to ingratiate himself or herself with children means that the offender will always find a way to gain access to minors. This effort may entail sponsoring or working with groups and in activities catering to youths. The offender's interest in minors may be limited, in some situations, to sexual fantasies, but in most cases he or she typically collects adult and child pornography.

Beyond the collecting of child pornography, traits of pedophiles are difficult to isolate. In fact, attempts to do so can raise more questions than they answer. For instance, is an adult male who uses a juvenile prostitute on the assumption she is an adult guilty of molestation? Does an adult woman who finds a teen-age male attractive fit somewhere on the continuum? What of the adult male who marries a minor? All of these and similar situations tend to weaken the value of standard "profiles" of child molesters.

One example of the fallibility of stereotypes surrounding pedophilia is given by the following interview with Carl, a 24-year-old former school teacher who is currently serving a 20-year sentence for kidnapping. Carl has a history of multiple victimizations of adolescent males, including ongoing sexual relationships, assault, and blackmail. His case is a study of cause and effect. Note the amount of methodical planning and the manipulation of victims and the response of the criminal justice system that characterize his exploitive activities. The dialogue, stretching over a ten-hour period on several days, has been condensed into a series of highlighted topics, such as methods of operation, rationalizations, motivations behind behavior, and types of sexual activities.

CARL THE KIDNAPPER

Dan: How did you get here [prison]? What are your charges?

Carl: I was home on a furlough from another institution. I committed a crime against a young man in the neighborhood and was charged with taking indecent liberties with a minor child and kidnapping. I received a sentence of 11 to 33 years.

Dan: What was the nature of the act?

Carl: The first charge was rectal sodomy. I accepted a plea which reduced rectal sodomy to indecent liberties, because it was a lesser charge.

Dan: Can you briefly reconstruct the incident involving the minor?

Carl: It was on a Sunday, no school, in the summertime. I asked this kid to show me where his school was. We got there and I offered him some money to show me where a certain part of his school was, an isolated area I knew about. We went there and he became nervous, said he was ready to leave. I held him, punched him in the nose, and had sex with him a few minutes later.

Dan: Alright, I get the picture. What got you to that spot on that particular day with that particular boy?

Carl: I've been asked that question by a lot of people. You know, there is no real definition or reason why. The only thing I can say is that it was more or less a pattern of behavior. He wasn't the first victim; there was a wide range of victims in different areas. But it was one particular pattern where I approached the victim in a certain area, within one square mile of the school. I'd ask him to show me where a specific area of the school was and the acts were committed there. That was a pattern for over five years.

Dan: But you got caught just for this one incident?

Carl: Right. During the course of those five years there were a number of victims. Most of them were too frightened to tell anyone for whatever reason. No one ever investigated the other acts.

Dan: Any other criminal charges that have occurred in your life?

Carl: The only charges I've ever been convicted of were rape, indecent liberties, sodomy, kidnapping, and arson. All of the crimes I've been involved with, except arson, were against people my own age or younger. I got started at 14.

Dan: How?

Carl: I just used to go out in the neighborhood. When I'd see kids I'd just beat up on them for something to do. And then, you know, it came to my mind that maybe I could take them, use them for sexual purposes. After I was convicted of raping a girl, I went to a special hospital. There I was introduced to homosexuality by other boys.

Dan: Well, that leads to the obvious question: How do you classify yourself now? Do you see yourself as a homosexual, heterosexual, or bisexual?

Carl: I would say bisexual.

Dan: What about these other incidents involving kids for which you were never investigated—that no one knew about?

Carl: Approximately 20 others. Most of these acts were committed in the neighborhood within my ward. I guess the kids are too scared to tell anybody or just didn't know what was happening to them.

Dan: I need those points clarified. What were your basic techniques for getting close to these boys?

Carl: Offering money, I guess. The plan was not to give it to them to keep when it was over. See, I always had five dollars. I was spoiled and my mother always gave me what I wanted. Most young kids get fascinated with five dollars. So you just show it to him and he says, "Wow! How can I get that?" That's all you had to do is show it to them or let them hold it and they'd be glad to take you anywhere you wanted to go.

Dan: So, as you mentioned earlier, they would walk with you over to the school. What then?

Carl: I pretended I was meeting someone there or didn't know my directions. After I got there I may tell the kid my friend said he was going to leave a briefcase for me in a very isolated area of the school, like the window well or basement. I just sent them down to look. When they go down I jump in after them and that's it. Most of the time it wasn't planned or premeditated, just a spur of the moment thing. Go around the neighborhood, see somebody, and say, "I think I'll take him." When I was in the hospital or jail, I used to receive a furlough or home visit. So I went out and committed a crime each time. I once got a furlough for 12 days for Christmas vacation. It was about 8:30 in the evening and I was out walking the neighborhood, enjoying the snow 'cause the next day I was due back at the hospital. The street lights were on. As I was coming up Orchard Avenue, this particular kid got off the bus. He was standing there and when I walked past he asked how to get to Western Street. He had got off the bus at the wrong stop. So I said it was only a 10- or 15-minute walk and offered to show him the way.

At the time it really wasn't in my mind to commit a crime. The street lights were out on the corner and I took him up to the school, the long way around. It was very quiet and nobody was around. We got to the window well, I got him down in it, and made him perform oral and rectal sodomy. Then I let him go.

Dan: How did you feel after it was over?

Carl: It wasn't happy; more like remorse. Each time I committed a crime I would check with a children's hospital, call in 'cause the police always take kids there. I would say my kid was assaulted. I wanted to know if my wife brought him there. I was always able to obtain a name and address from the kid when it happened, so I could pretend to be his father on the phone. That way the hospital would trust me enough to give me the facts. I did that only to see if I should disappear for a while or whether I could walk the streets without having to watch my back for the police. This way I could check to see if the kid reported the incident. Or, I'd call his house so I'd know for sure, tell the kid, "You'd better not tell anybody or I'll kill you. I know where you go to school."

Dan: Would you have carried out any of these threats?

Carl: I doubt it, but I had lots of opportunities and came close to doing it once. Besides, I had friends in school who would take care of the kid for me if I asked them to. But, honestly, these kids trusted me. Like the judge said, "The reason I'm giving you the time I'm sentencing you to is because you were always able to gain the trust of people." I had some kind of appeal to kids, I guess.

Dan: One final question. By assaulting these kids, do you think you may have transformed at least one into a future child molester because of the experience? Do you see any connection?

Carl: Yes. Either a future molester or homosexual prostitute. The reason I say that is because most of the homosexuals I've talked to in jail over the past five years tell me they were molested or somebody in the family did something to them sexually. When they are older, most of them will want to see what it's like for somebody else to be the victim, to use somebody who can't resist or doesn't know what you've got in mind for them until it's too late.

■　　■　　■

Notwithstanding the difficulties mentioned previously, certain behavioral traits of a pedophile can be identified. For example, there is an extraordinarily high probability that the offender was sexually victimized as a minor. Often these individuals indicate that they feel alienated within the adult community. Carl's case also indicates that pedophilia can continue to victimize a person for a considerable period of time, and it makes the point that not all victims of exploitive episodes are identified.

Victim-Offender Relationships

Identifying an ongoing exploitive relationship between a pedophile and a minor is a difficult task. The intense interplay of emotions between a victim and offender is often overlooked. There are,

however, certain signs of molestation. Because many of these
warning signs are ambiguous and could reflect a variety of problems, the key is to look for a cluster of them. If several indicators
are present, a pedophile probably has developed an exploitive
relationship with the minor.[4]

Some of the more revealing indicators include the use of sexual
jargon and sexual role-playing by the youth. Sexual acumen is a
particularly accurate reflection of ongoing exploitation or intra-
familial abuse, as is extreme interest by the juvenile in being with
a particular adult to the exclusion of other adults and youths or in
spending an excessive amount of time at an adult's residence.
Vague or evasive answers by the juvenile when questioned about
the adult may also indicate an exploitive situation, particularly if
the minor passionately defends an adult accused of wrongdoing or
misconduct. In addition, signs of drug or alcohol use by the minor
may be accompanied by such changes as loss of appetite, inability
to sleep, or decline in academic performance. Further behavioral
changes that may occur include loss of friends and frequent requests to stay overnight or spend weekends at the exploitive adult's
home.

The adult involved may discuss his or her child "friends" in
terms normally reserved for intimate companions. Frequent use of
the offender's residence by minors as a congregating site is a
possible indication of exploitation. The adult may be willing—even
anxious—to spend an inordinate amount of money on and time
with a potential victim. The adult often acts as a surrogate parent
by performing a multitude of mundane chores for a child, such as
running errands or babysitting. Often a truly likable individual,
the offender may express genuine interest in a juvenile's welfare,
even to the point of displaying an abnormal amount of anguish or
anger over prolonged absence or separation from the child.

An adult-minor relationship characterized by these basic warning signs may well be an exploitive situation. In the following case
concerning a church accountant, the offender capitalized on the
victims' naivete. The minors' desire to experiment sexually, as well
as the offender's ability to manipulate circumstances, led in this
case to their eventual involvement in a sexually exploitive situation.

A REPENTANT CHURCH ACCOUNTANT

These kids just kind of lived at my house, watching television or
maybe playing Atari games. I bought all of the latest cartridges

for them. They were there, not at my request, but because I let them and they didn't have any other place to play in the neighborhood. They weren't at my house 24 hours a day, but if I was home they could come in any time, with their parents' permission, and play Atari. I enjoyed them being there; they were my friends. This sounds weird for a man 39 years old to say, but I've always been a loner, felt awkward around people my own age. Nothing in common.

One day these two kids, ages 9 and 11, came by while I was outside sunbathing and asked to play Atari. A half hour later I went inside and found them in my bedroom, looking at *Playboy*, with a funny look on their faces as though they had been masturbating. It was no secret that I kept *Playboy* around the house. I also kept a lot of homosexual books locked away in a drawer.

I went back outside after telling them not to look at the magazines. Here comes another boy, a 15-year-old. I didn't want him to go in the house and see them in there, so I kept him outside. We had done something sexually before, in the previous two, three weeks. It was a form of gratification for me and a way of giving him pleasure. He wanted to do it. He saw their bicycles and asked who was inside the house. I told him who and said they were looking at *Playboy*. He wanted to join them so we went inside the house. I told the two younger boys to leave because we wanted to look at the *Playboy* and take our clothes off. Thinking back on it, I really didn't want them to leave. It ended up that we all took off our clothes. We started masturbating ourselves and each other. Finally, it got to the point where we were stretching out on the bed and somebody said it looked like fun to give each other blow jobs. I remember having oral sex with the 15-year-old and he did the same to me. The other two were having oral sex together on the floor. I had to leave the room because somebody knocked on the door. I threw my shorts on and answered the door. It was a mother who had come to get the 11-year-old. He left and I went back to the bedroom, where the remaining two were having oral sex together. That's all we did—no anal sex. Also, I don't think anyone ejaculated.

What I did was wrong because society's moral code says so, because it is against the law, and because I don't want any kid to turn out like me. One reason I let those kids look at the *Playboy* was because, when I was growing up, my parents never talked to me about sex; I wanted these boys to have a healthy idea of what was involved. They wanted to do that stuff; I never forced anybody to do anything. Part of me feels it wasn't wrong and another part knows it was morally wrong. I never thought about doing something against the law. I would never have done anything to harm those children at all.

■   ■   ■

Pornography Collections

The single most distinctive characteristic of a habitual child molester is a compelling interest in collecting adult and child pornography, which can be a valuable source of evidence in the case-building process. The more sophisticated and elaborate a collection, the more probable an offender is involved in long-term, organized exploitation. In addition to pornography, a hard-core pedophile collector will often have in his or her possession a wide variety of erotica and related materials, the most important of which is a diary or journal which typically contains an extensive personal record of sexual experiences with minors. In addition, a pedophile may keep an address book, either on paper or on computer diskette, with the names and addresses of other pedophiles, victimized or targeted children, sources of pornography (local and international), and likely places for meeting children in other areas or cities. To supplement these materials, an offender typically stores personal correspondence from other pedophiles, pornography firms, and names of companies that cater to juvenile needs such as clothing, tickets for athletic events, and toys.

A pedophile's collection of erotic paraphernalia may include a wide range of materials, from sexual devices to all types of adult and child pornography. The pornography is bought, sold, or traded by the offender. Photograph albums which contain both innocuous and pornographic pictures of underage victims are of special interest to pedophiles, as are stored "souvenirs" of an offender's actual or fantasized relationship with a minor, including undergarments, wallets, junior high and high school yearbooks, or ticket stubs from a children's play.

The extent and composition of a pedophile's collection can reveal a great deal about his or her commitment to exploitation. To the pedophile, these possessions are comparable in value to family heirlooms, diaries, and life savings. Because youth is a transitory stage of development, a pedophile's record of sexual conquests serves as a permanent reminder of pleasurable occasions. It is not uncommon for a pedophile to operate a darkroom for processing photographs and films of minors. Processed slides, films, negatives, and videotapes are usually stored at the offender's home or at a secondary site such as a friend's residence, an office, or a rental locker.

A collection, as described above, is one way a pedophile relates his experiences to others' with the same sexual preference. More importantly it will enable the pedophile to show the victim what he wants to do with or to the child, while presenting evidence that other children perform similar acts. The pedophile described in the following case fits this profile.[5]

THE FLORIST

Mr. Trant is a white male in his early forties with an exceptionally high IQ. An only child whose parents (alcoholic mother) were florists, Mr. Trant has a son and daughter by two marriages. He studied photography while serving in the army and later inherited his father's floral business.

Mr. Trant claimed to have engaged in genital fondling with other children as early as age 5 or 6. He participated in various sexual "encounters" with adolescents from roughly age 10 into his late teens. In his early twenties he became a Boy Scout leader. Boys in his troop later admitted to having sexual relations with him. Mr. Trant admitted to sexual relationships with female adults and children during his adult years. He prefers the latter, stating that sex with kids is much easier than with an adult because children do not make value judgments.

The offender became sexually involved with several children from poor families without a live-in father. The youths rode the school bus to a stop outside his flower shop. He would invite them into the shop and give them candy, money, and occasionally flowers for their mothers. Gradually, the children accepted Mr. Trant as a good friend.

After gaining their trust, he eventually took them into the back of the shop. He initially took photographs of the kids with their clothes on. This later led to photograph sessions with them in the nude and progressed to specific sexual acts involving him

with the children. At the time of his arrest, mounds of pornographic literature were confiscated, including films and slides of
his sexual activities with the kids and books on pedophilia.

Mr. Trant was convicted of forcible sodomy and carnal knowledge of a minor. He received a 15-year sentence and was placed
on active probation, with counseling required. Two weeks after
sentencing, Trant molested his 6-year-old son and the paper boy.
Probation revoked, he was sent to prison and released in 1981
on active probation. In 1983 he was again arrested for performing
sexual acts with minors and returned to prison, where he remains to this day. When asked about his intense sexual desire
for children, Trant replied that the only real harm is that it is
against the law. He believes it is a normal, healthy attraction.

                    ■   ■   ■

Methods of Operation

The process by which a minor is manipulated into a state of
victimization is known as a method of operation. During the course
of conversations with various types of pedophiles, we compiled a
fairly standard set of operating methods. Although some offenders
did not admit to premeditation in their activities, an examination
of their experiences reveals that they did indeed influence the
conditions and circumstances that led to an exploitive situation.

"Reconnaissance" is one of the first steps in seeking out a victim.
In order to acquire a "feel" for an area, a pedophile may perform a
careful surveillance of neighborhoods. Places of interest include
day care centers, parks, playgrounds, apartment complexes, shopping malls, roller-skating rinks, arcade game rooms, and recrea-
tional centers. One of the easiest ways to discover where a particular child lives is to discreetly follow his or her school bus.

"Infiltration" entails moving into a neighborhood or a specific
section of a community where, based on the outcome of preliminary surveillance, the pedophile's prospects of encountering children are high. The emphasis at this point is on ensuring both
availability of victims and opportunities to meet and engage them
in conversation without arousing suspicion. Over the course of
several months, an offender may develop friendships with parents
and their children. He will strive to promote a reputation for

himself as a trustworthy, reliable person. At the community level, a molester joins child-oriented groups as well as civic or religious agencies with youthful members. To establish a reputation as an adult who cares for children, the aggressive pedophile will seek employment or volunteer work that results in close contact with youths—for example, as a day care worker, a child photographer, a pediatrician, or a foster parent. The lesson here is that all occupations which involve adult-child contact should require pre-employment screening and background checks of applicants.

Once his reputation has been established, the child molester will begin to wean children away from their families or friends through a variety of methods. Bestowing special favors on a child—lures or bribes—is a powerful enticement and a preliminary step in creating a dependency relationship. In so doing, the offender presents himself to a victim as someone who is truly a supportive, nonjudgmental friend. This tactic is especially effective with minors in disruptive or abusive families. Another technique is to permit juveniles to enjoy greater freedom and liberties, such as smoking and drinking, than their parents would normally allow. The minor who participates in these forbidden pleasures has entered into an implicit bond of agreement with the molester that such activities are best kept secret from parents and other adults in order to avoid punishment. At this stage of complicity, the offender gradually introduces the topic of sex to the victim by showing erotic magazines or films. The friendship is upheld through gifts of money, and the ties between offender and victim become stronger.

After adequate preparation, the offender begins to initiate some type of sexual contact with the child. This may start with a simple kiss or caress, then progress gradually to masturbation and finally to unrestrained sex with the adult and other youths. All the time the pedophile keeps working at lowering the victim's innate resistance and inhibitions toward sex through alcohol, pornography, and value replacement.

To avoid exposure, the molester will bond his underage victims to him by threats, by displays of affection and rewards, by warnings of future punishment from the child's parents, and by making the victim feel responsible and guilty for what has happened. In other words, the pedophile may seek to transfer blame onto the victim. One very effective method for accomplishing this end is to take pornographic photographs of the child and use them for blackmail.

If the molester is ambitious enough, he may decide to broaden the scope of his exploitation to include recruitment. That is, he may be able to persuade his victims to recruit other minors into the relationship on the premise that these children are entitled to "join in the fun." Recruitment is always a necessity, because a pedophile's interest in a specific victim dissipates with time. Although some offenders maintain long-term relationships with their victims (usually out of convenience), they constantly seek new targets upon which to focus their attention. Eventually, a victim is discarded to be replaced by another.

Not all hard-core pedophiles, however, are so circuitous in their efforts to seek new victims. Some take a more direct approach— for instance, offering to babysit for neighborhood parents. Others marry a divorced mother with children, molest the minors, and then either divorce the mother or abandon the family. And, of course, there are those prone to violence as in Carl's case, who prowl communities, randomly select an underage victim, and commit some type of sexual assault. Their method of operation is based on force, bribes and lures, or misrepresentation such as asking for directions or assistance or posing as an authority figure or friend of the family.

The following case illustrates the persistence of pedophiles and the efforts they are willing to make to exploit minors. It involves an individual who successfully convinced other adults and minors, through phone calls, to perform acts of sexual exploitation. Detective Michael Keller, the case investigator, explains how the police became aware of this activity:[6]

TRAFFICKING BY PHONE

On January 11, 1985, I was contacted by Sue, a mother of two young boys. She reported receiving two phone calls from a man who called himself Tom. During the first call, Sue stayed on the line because the conversation sounded like a unique sales pitch. Ten minutes into the dialogue she realized he was not a salesperson and that, in fact, something strange was going on. She encouraged Tom to call again in order to get the police involved. In the second conversation the caller became more explicit and promoted the sexual exploitation of children; he indicated he would call back the following week.

I installed a self-activated recording device on the phone on

January 15th and notified the telephone company to institute a computer trace on all calls. That same day Sue called to tell me Tom had contacted her again. I retrieved the tape and reviewed its contents. The following day I was advised by the telephone company of a successful tap and trace. Our suspect lived in an apartment, and a check of his lease agreement verified his identity.

By February 13, approximately 10 hours of taped conversations between Tom and Sue had been collected. The most frustrating aspect of this investigation was that I could not come up with a suitable charge except telephone harassment, which is a Class "B" misdemeanor and punishable in Texas by 6 months in jail and/or up to a $1,000 fine. However, it was found that his attempts to persuade the complainant to become sexually involved with her two boys constituted criminal solicitation for aggravated sexual assault of a child. Criminal solicitation is a second-degree felony punishable by 2 to 20 years in prison and a fine of up to $10,000.

A search of Tom's residence yielded the predictable share of adult and child pornography. More importantly, we discovered a ledger of approximately 3,000 phone numbers the suspect had called. Beside many of the numbers were various descriptions and a code. When Tom called and received, for example, a favorable response worth a follow-up call, he put the word "Sam" beside the number. At the start of a return call he would ask for Sam. This allowed the recipient the option of not talking by saying that no one by that name was there. He was apparently quite successful, as indicated by the volume of phone numbers with the word "Sam" beside them.

■   ■   ■

Pedophiles like Tom who do not wish to have physical contact with an underage victim are nonetheless capable of promoting sexual exploitation of children by telephone, through computer bulletin boards, and through the mails. A similar case involved a midwestern school teacher who called approximately 100 adolescent males and offered to arrange a sexual rendezvous for them with adult women. After discussing masturbation and genital size with the adolescent, the teacher promised the youth that he would receive payment from an adult woman in exchange for sexual services. He would instruct a potential victim to wait at a specific

time and place for the arrival of a female "customer." The customers were fictitious, but the teacher would become excited by
observing the adolescent (from a safe distance) waiting for his
liaison with an adult female. The teacher was eventually charged
and convicted of promoting the prostitution of a minor. As in the
case of Tom, there was no evidence to show that the teacher had
ever had physical contact with a victim.

Pedophile Organizations and Publications

Organizations and publications that advocate adult-child sex are
relatively few in number but are scattered throughout the world.
They perform an assortment of functions and exist for the following
purposes:

- To recruit and expedite the exchange of information and
  correspondence among pedophiles.
- To act as a medium for advertisers and distributors of soft-core
  child pornography.
- To promote political activism and organization.
- To alert members or subscribers to recent court decisions and
  active criminal investigations.
- To provide a bulletin board news service as to the whereabouts
  of sexually available minors.
- To raise funds for legal representation of accused pedophiles.
- To offer sexual stimulation in the form of erotic fiction or
  suggestive photographs of minors.

All of these organizations and publications strive to justify and
rationalize the illegal behavior of their members or readership.
One, for example, is the North American Man-Boy Love Association (NAMBLA). This organization advocates the cause of adult
males to have sexual and emotional relationships with underage
males. NAMBLA has chapters in Boston, New York, Los Angeles,
San Francisco, and Toronto, with an active membership between
500 and 1,000. NAMBLA publishes a bulletin ten times a year, an
annual journal, and various miscellaneous booklets on the subject
of intergenerational relationships. The bulletins contain information about pending legislation, judicial investigations, and "boys in
the media," along with essays, poems, short stories, photographs,
and occasional sketches of adolescent males. NAMBLA has a

steering committee, five national chapters, and a handful of spokes-persons. A prisoner support committee corresponds with con-victed boy lovers and offers limited funds for legal aid.

NAMBLA's philosophy distinguishes between molestation and man-boy love. Members believe that children and adults can have satisfying emotional and sexual relationships based on consent, that physical intimacy is not bound by age limits, and that minors therefore have the right to select intimate adult companions. An adult male who is attracted to an underage male is, they say, entitled to establish a nuturing relationship based on mutual trust and respect. What is ignored in this particular argument is the question of whether a minor is capable of giving consent; they simply assume that children understand exactly what they are consenting to when they enter into an extraordinarily complex, potentially damaging relationship with a seductive adult.

Another such organization is the Lewis Carroll Collector's Guild. According to its newsletter (*Wonderland*, which is printed four times a year), the Lewis Carroll Guild is "a voluntary associa-tion of persons who believe nudist materials are a constitutionally protected expression and whose collecting interests include pre-teen nudes."[7] *Wonderland* is a collection of articles and advertise-ments, both domestic and international, that promote interest in photographs, artwork, and articles pertaining to nude children on the premise that no exploitation is involved. We have no informa-tion about the subscription or membership size of the guild or its newsletter.

The Pedophile Information Exchange (PIE) is based in Great Britain. Its publication, known as *Magpie*, seeks to "provide pae-dophiles [sic] with their own journal and tries to further the understanding and acceptance of true love for children in today's society."[8] At one time PIE printed a limited edition publication entitled *Contact* which contained the letters of pedophiles from the *Magpie* subscription rolls. Although PIE has been hard-pressed by the British judicial system, its membership is unknown. Its principal goals, however, have been to lobby for revised child sex legislation and to coordinate its resources and efforts with other pedophile groups in western Europe.

The Diaper Pail Fraternity allegedly consists of a group of indeterminate size that advocates sexual relations with minors, particularly prepubertal children and infants. It reportedly pro-duced a publication, *Bedtime Stories*, which discussed such topics as the use of hypnosis to seduce minors and the variety of sexual activities possible with an adolescent.

Based in the Netherlands, Spartacus is a publishing firm that specializes in printed materials for homosexuals and pedophiles. It distributes materials for the pedophile market under the name Coltsfoot Press. *Paedo Alert News,* a glossy black and white magazine, is available through Coltsfoot Press; it contains international news, erotic fiction, and updates on the status of pedophiles. Coltsfoot Press sells a variety of books and collections emphasizing man-boy sexual relationships. None of these publications contains any graphic photographs of nude adolescent males.

Groupe de Recherche pour une Enfance Differente (GRED) is a French pedophile support group that began in 1979. In 1982, when it hosted its first national conference in Paris (with four representatives of PIE in attendance), the organization claimed an enrollment of 70 members. GRED is composed of five regional groups, overseen by an executive committee and assisted by technical commissions or work groups. Its publication is called *Le Petit Gredin.* GRED claims to serve as a lobby group whose purpose is to effect legislative and social changes for the sexual liberation of youths.

Reality and *Boy Love* are two underground, mimeographed newsletters printed in the United States. Because both are produced in the same city, it is likely they originate from the same individuals. *Reality* and *Boy Love* preach that existing legislation regarding age of consent is unfair to adults. Moreover, the writers of these amateurish newsletters argue through essays, poems, and biased documentation that "same-gender-oriented relationships" are natural and exist throughout the animal kingdom.

Signe de Piste is a publication that contributes peripherally to the pedophile life-style. Published in Canada, it is a collection of outdoor photographs of adolescent males in shorts and swimming suits, accompanied by articles on the activities of boys.

For a brief period of national media coverage, Tim O'Hara, spokesman for the Rene Guyon Society, advanced the belief that children—starting at infancy—desire and need sex with adults and other children in order to lead healthy and happy lives. The media's attention to the Guyon Society beliefs was due to the society's motto, "sex before eight or else it's too late." Although O'Hara's attempts to promote child-adult sex have proved to be highly transitory, his ability to capture national media coverage for his cause is noteworthy.

By publicizing their identities and philosophies, members of these organizations and editors of these publications have made themselves vulnerable to investigation. An underlying belief shared by such groups is that theirs is a persecuted cause that is not fairly represented in the laws or understood by society. By defining their conduct as "different" rather than immoral or harmful, they hope to achieve some measure of legitimacy in a sexually diverse society. The arguments they use to defend their position are intelligent and persuasive, but the facts often are adjusted to fit the circumstances of their activities. At odds with society's taboo against sexual relations with a minor, such groups struggle to survive on shoestring budgets, wavering memberships, and the constant scrutiny of law enforcement authorities.

Sex Rings

In the context of exploitation of children, a sex ring can be defined as a situation in which one or more adults conspire and organize for the purpose of promoting illicit sexual acts with and among minors. These acts include the production of pornography, prostitution, adult molestation of children, the sale and transportation of minors for sexual purposes, the use of juveniles to recruit other youths into the ring, and the use of blackmail, deception, threats, peer pressure, or force to coerce or intimidate children into sexual activity. (Some researchers have developed criteria to explain the dynamics of this phenomenon.[9]) The following elements seem common to all rings: (1) a high level of planning and cooperation among offenders, (2) multiplicity of victims, (3) longevity of the group, (4) victimization of minors by other children, (5) extensive range and sophistication of sexual activities, and (6) the potential to spill over into the public domain of exploitation, as in the sale of child pornography.

An adult acting alone or in collusion with others may exploit dozens of children for decades, thus spawning a new generation of future offenders. The following three cases illustrate, in varying proportions, many of the principal characteristics of sex rings. The first of these, "Lovers Part," describes a self-contained, exploitive group of adults who molested underage males exclusively for their own sexual gratification.[10]

LOVERS PART

A 13-year-old male had a lover's quarrel with his 45-year-old legal guardian. The child gave a friend over 75 pornographic photographs depicting numerous children having sex with other youths and adults. The friend turned the photographs over to the police, who began an investigation. Neither of the two officers assigned to the case had prior experience with sex ring offenses. The investigation lasted 36 days, with 555 manhours expended. No other officers were allocated to the case, which proceeded through the following steps:

- Stage 1: Physical evidence was collected, interviews were conducted, and search warrants were served at the offenders' homes.
- Stage 2: a total of 39 felony warrants and 41 misdemeanor warrants were delivered.
- Stage 3: Case preparation prior to prosecution lasted three months as the investigators attempted to follow multiple lines of inquiry.
- Stage 4: Five adults were convicted in one jurisdiction and three adults in another. One adult was not convicted. The average sentence was 4 to 10 months in the county jail.

This case was an investigation of the activities of six adults with three boys and three girls during a party that took place one weekend in July. As the police probe into the life-styles of the offenders became more meticulous, a host of unanticipated facts began to emerge.

As many as 100 or 200 juveniles may have been involved in the sex ring, which lasted about a decade. One of the adults, exhibited a pronounced sadomasochistic fetish. Behind a false wall in his closet he kept a complete stockpile of sadomasochistic equipment, and he had built a torture chamber in his bedroom, complete with electronic locks, shackles on the walls and ceilings, makeshift soundproofing, and sexual devices. The purpose of these elaborate measures was to permit the offender to engage in deviant acts such as whipping, genital torture, and beastiality with underage males. Besides recording his activities on film and cassette tape and through sketches, he also drafted an instructional manual complete with drawings and suggestions on the subject of sadomasochistic sex acts with minors. The following is an excerpt from his observations on bondage:

The victim should be nude and helpless, tied or chained by the arms, legs, cock and balls, sometimes by the neck. Tight ropes or chains should be used so that they sink into the flesh, causing pain. He should be spread-eagled, his arms and legs stretched until he feels as if he is going to split apart. No matter where the torture is to take place, it should be in a concealed and secluded spot where the slave's crys and screams cannot be heard. If in the home, the radio or TV can be turned up to drown out the noise.

The fundamental obstacles in this investigation were the difficulty of establishing rapport with the underage victims, hostility and lack of cooperation from their parents, and pressure from departmental authorities to close the case. Furthermore, due to the extreme nature of the sexual activities and ignorance as to how to present a case of this sort in open court, the prosecutor did not encourage the investigators to broaden the scope of their inquiries.

■   ■   ■

Dozens of underage males and females were recruited for this ring with the lure of alcohol, drugs, parties, and experimental sex. With conditioning and persistent seduction, these juveniles subsequently became recruiters themselves in what is known as the "spiraling effect" of sex rings. The more active a ring becomes, the broader-based are its membership and activities, extending outward and growing in size and sophistication. If the investigating officers had not successfully intercepted this particular conspiracy, there is every reason to suspect that it would still be in operation.

Another ring involved an official of the criminal justice system who misused his position of authority. He did so in order to achieve sexual satisfaction through the molestation of minors and the production of child pornography.[11]

THE SHERIFF'S VICTIMS

In a rural Midwest town, a sheriff had an unwritten policy among jail personnel that only he would supervise the showering of all new inmates, without the presence of other guards. Using the excuse of checking for lice, the sheriff ordered male prisoners, including juveniles, to apply soap to their genitalia until they experienced an erection. To those he liked, the young and frail, the sheriff made homosexual advances, promising in return an early release or a position as a trustee, which is associated with special privileges in the jail. These trustee privileges for victims included new clothes for school (paid for by the sheriff), placement in the work release program, trips with the sheriff outside the jail to pornographic movie theaters, extra visitation privileges, and unlimited access to a new color television provided by the sheriff.

All of these favors were bestowed on male juveniles (six of whom testified) in exchange for the following activities:

• Inmate 4 related that the sheriff had fondled him and had made Inmate 3 perform oral sex on him while the sheriff watched. Also, Inmate 4 was solicited by the sheriff to pose for pornographic pictures displaying various sexual acts.
• Inmate 6 stated that he was given a shower by the sheriff, who told him to play with himself until he had an erection. He claimed to have been masturbated on numerous occasions by the sheriff in addition to having to perform oral sex.
• Inmates 1 and 2 described frequent incidents wherein the sheriff engaged in oral sex and pornographic shooting sessions with them. Inmate 2 further stated that he participated in these various acts because the sheriff told him he was a personal friend of the judge and could therefore help or hurt the minor in court.

All six inmates claimed that the various sexual acts they committed were involuntary, performed because they felt something had to be done in order for them to survive in the jail. They considered their predicament the result of the position of power held by the sheriff, and they feared the consequences of noncompliance.

The type of crime committed or the past criminal record of the prisoner had little weight in the sheriff's decision regarding who would receive the desired status of trustee; body type was the determinant. According to the investigators, all of the victims were young, frail, and skinny. The sheriff offered protection for these underage inmates by placing them in a cell located in an isolated section of the jail, away from other prisoners.

Maintaining an outward appearance of respectability, the sheriff had the advantage of being a member of the local law enforcement community. A state supreme court of appeals appointed a judge to preside over the case outside the sheriff's jurisdiction. The assistant attorney general who was assigned to the case as prosecutor requested that the judges prohibit the sheriff from entering the jail during the investigation. The prosecutor wanted the sheriff suspended because he might impede the investigation by intimidating the young inmates (complainants) still incarcerated in the jail. To show proof of the extent of the sheriff's sexual involvement, over 100 pictures depicting pornographic poses of the inmates allegedly taken by the sheriff were presented to the judges. Both judges refused to examine the photographs, claiming they should not interfere with the office of the sheriff in the execution of his duties.

Charges against the sheriff could have resulted in a maximum prison sentence of 56 years and $115,000 in fines. Instead, the 39-year-old father of three children reached an agreement with the court. The sentence stipulated his immediate resignation, 10 years of probation, and the requirement that he refrain from any employment related to law enforcement and remove himself from any situation involving inmates, children, or incompetent individuals. A final condition of the sentencing agreement required the former sheriff to seek psychiatric treatment. This sentence was handed down approximately 6 months after the local court allowed him to continue at his post as sheriff and warden of the jail, during which time he had free and ready access to the victims as well as to other incoming prisoners.

■　　■　　■

The final sex ring case involves a mixture of profit and sexual pleasure motives associated with commercial trafficking. A child sex ring, whose operation spanned decades and involved over 20 victims, was uncovered through a 7-month investigation by Detective George Haralson of the Tulsa Police Department.[12]

A STING OPERATION

The key suspect, Gene Smith, was first identified through an undercover investigation in July 1984. Detective Haralson began corresponding with Smith through the mail; by September, they had progressed to telephone conversations. The suspect was unaware of Haralson's status as a police officer. The phone calls were placed to the detective from pay phones in the Houston, Texas area. The topics of conversation included Smith's sexual activities with young girls and photographs he had taken of children in various states of undress. Detective Haralson recorded each phone call and continued to build a case file on the suspect. Houston police detectives were kept abreast of the investigation.

In January 1985 Smith suggested that the two men meet on a weekend in Houston. Smith stated that he could arrange for the detective to meet a 12-year-old girl, known only as Jennifer. He described the girl as "money hungry" because he had to spend money on her each time they had sexual relations. With this thought in mind, he suggested that Haralson bring cash with him for this purpose, as well as a camera and "condoms and that good type of grease." A weekend date and location for the rendezvous was arranged.

Several weeks later Haralson checked into a Houston motel. Smith called to assure him that he would bring two young girls and a boy. Haralson waited for Smith while Houston detectives monitored the proceedings from a nearby room in the same motel. When Smith arrived at the motel room with a young boy, a 10-year-old girl, and a 12-year-old girl, he made it clear that both of the girls would be available for sexual purposes. The girls were instructed to bathe, and while they were doing so, Smith gave the detective explicit instructions regarding the sexual activities that would occur. At that point, Houston officers entered the room and placed Smith under arrest for promoting child prostitution, promoting child pornography, indecent liberties with a child, and sexual assault of a child.

From information gathered after Smith's arrest, Houston detectives pieced together the sordid story of a sex ring of adult males who photographed and sexually molested young victims, buying their silence with gifts of money or merchandise. Seven other child molesters were arrested in conjunction with Smith's sex ring. Over 20 victims were identified, some of whom had been sexually molested over an extended period. All of the girls, ranging in age from 8 to 13, came from a small, poor town outside Houston, where the residents commonly lived in campers, tents, and trailers. Prosecution of these offenders continued as this book went to press.

■   ■   ■

Offender Treatment

Can pedophilia be cured? It depends, in part, on the extent of the pedophile's involvement in exploitation. As a general rule the answer is no: Pedophilia in its extreme or persistent forms cannot be cured, only treated. To successfully cure a pedophile requires a fundamental restructuring of his or her sexual identity and the subsequent reordering of sexual desires and attitudes that are often resistant to change. Several basic treatment options are available, including the following: (1) psychotherapy (changed behavior through introspection); (2) behavior modification that seeks to remove desire through a variety of aversion therapies, including electric shocks, induced vomiting, sensory deprivation, and compulsory masturbation; (3) surgery (removal of the testes); (4) medication—for example, Depo-Provera, which reduces an adult's sex drive to that of an 11-or 12-year-old; (5) combinations of behavior modification and medication; and (6) incarceration, with periodic counseling.

None of these options can be considered a cure or provide permanent relief to a pedophile. They are merely stopgap measures intended to alleviate the symptoms. One treatment program that attempts to help an offender gain control over his or her behavior is known as "Together We Can."[13] In the following interview, the program director discussed many of the critical problems confronting pedophile therapy. This particular program is a variation of introspective therapy which measures success—however relative or transitory—in terms of the willingness of clients to radically reconstruct their sexual orientation.

TOGETHER WE CAN

Question: What is the general orientation or philosophy of your treatment program?

Answer: The basis of the entire program is that molestation is not a sexual dysfunction; rather it is a power dysfunction. And to mistake it for a sexually oriented dysfunction is wrong. What you often hear child molesters say is, "I prefer kids. I prefer the company of kids. I feel more comfortable with kids." What they really mean is that they have not gotten to the point where they feel equal to adults. When they're interacting with age mates, they feel powerless and generally inadequate. But with kids they clearly have the upper hand. What we call the erection and ejaculation part of the abuse is nothing more than icing on the cake. It is not their primary motivation, which is to feel powerful. We have people in this program who are attorneys, businessmen, and other people who seem in the day-to-day work world to have prestige, and who function well in positions of responsibility, yet they become child molesters. We have found a positive relationship between being a child molester and being the victim of molestation while growing up.

The basis of the problem is that most of our society's children are not taught to be in touch with how they feel. Let's take a molester who was victimized as a child. What happens is that the child turns to the molester out of loneliness and desperation. The molester can function as a very important person in the child's life. From the child's viewpoint, someone has taken the time to get to know him, to care for him, and, to listen to what he has to say.

Question: Can you describe the seduction process?

Answer: Usually the seduction, or setup, of the child takes place over a period of time so that the victim is drawn in and trusts completely and values the person's company above all others. When the abuse begins, the first feeling my clients have is one of total fear. Here's this trusted adult who is saying to the child that there's nothing to be afraid of; this is how people show they love one another. This is love, this is ours and no one will ruin it if we don't tell anybody. Typically it's not violent in nature, although as the relationship goes on and the kid begins to grow, remarks are made like, "It would kill your mother if she found out," or "If you tell anyone you will get into big trouble." Finally it may end with actual threats or acted out forms of violence. When a child molester says to his victim, "There's nothing to be afraid of," that's the beginning of a schism within that child. He ceases to be a total person and comes to be completely out of touch with feelings.

Question: Because of the trust that has been established by the molester?

Answer: Right. The sex offender wants to create the pleasant physical sensation. He does not want to scare or hurt the child, because that will interfere with further access to the victim. The child will become afraid, won't want to be around, and might tell. As times goes on, the child gets to the point which I call the moment of recognition of betrayal. Most of the victims I've worked with can pinpoint that moment. When they (victims) discover (usually between ages 10 to 13) that this doesn't happen to everyone, that it isn't okay, and that society has a nasty word for it, you would think the child might tell. But remember that tool number one was put into place a long time ago: pleasant physical sensation. A child who uncovers the betrayal also learns that people will not respond very favorably to disclosure. Also, after the initial shock of recognition that "I've been lied to by someone who has functioned as the most important person in my life" comes the acknowledgment that the experience felt good. That dilemma becomes a real source of guilt. He or she may go to the offender and say, "I don't want to do this anymore. I know it's wrong now." The molester will say, "Well, you liked it as much as I did." That fact creates a feeling of guilt in the victim. Consider, finally, what this experience has taught the child: If someone is bigger, smarter, and stronger, they can do to and with you whatever they choose.

Question: Is that the lesson a molester has learned?

Answer: Yes. Now you have a child who has grown up feeling powerless, used, and generally out of control of whatever happens to him or her. And of course all this leads to extremely low feelings of self-esteem. The most important thing to remember about a child molester is that, at the moment of confrontation when his power base is threatened by the victim who doesn't want to be touched anymore, he begins to realize what he has risked for this power.

Question: How does this relate to a feeling of power?

Answer: When his power is threatened, he becomes more abusive in an overt way, although I don't think there is anything more abusive than the subtle ties of sexual exploitation. A kid who is in touch with his feelings and who knows how to express his feelings makes a lousy victim. So the most important thing, from the molester's viewpoint, is to make sure the victim never gets a sense of autonomy or self-worth. By the time victims reach adulthood, they are completely split off from who they are. All they know is when they were little, they were totally powerless to change anything that happened to them. They go through life thinking they're less than other people, even though the offender has been out of their lives for years. The depth of destruction is incredible. It's interesting to match an offender's method of operation against that used by the person who molested him as a child. It's very likely going to be almost exactly the same.

Question: In other words, they are just repeating what happened to them?

Answer: Yes. In their minds, the time they felt most powerless was when someone molested them. They learned that by molesting, they can feel powerful. We realize now that the molester will search for a while, maybe resort to drink, use drugs, or push his wife around even though she's an adult and doesn't make a good victim. Yet nothing makes those powerless base feelings go away. How can you get more power than you can have over a child? Total manipulation, total dependence; it's an incredible high. You can make that child do anything you want, anything, if done subtly enough and in the name of love.

Also, the sexual acts are going to become more intense, particularly if the offender was himself victimized at an early age like 5 or 6. What this means is that the longer a sex offender remains at large, the more out of control or into obsessive compulsion that person is and the more intense or violent his acts are likely to become. One of the things that has drawn some of our clients into the program, without being court-ordered, was their recognition that they could kill their victim. That's the ultimate power trip. When I read in the paper where a father killed his whole family and turned the gun on himself, I believe that what happened was a child getting close to disclosure. Rather than have that occur, the father commits this ultimate power act and blows everybody away.

Question: So that principle of power forms the basis of your treatment?

Answer: Control in this program is a positive thing. I call control "self-worth." One thing I know is that no one who enters this program is in control.

Question: Of themselves, their behavior patterns, their everyday living?

Answer: Right. This is the first thing I tell people when they come here: "Feelings *are*. They are not right or wrong; they just are." But we all know there are feelings we're told we should not have. When hurt feelings intensify, they create a tension we call powerless base feelings. The molester will do anything to relieve the tension. Something has to be done inside. We make our clients look at how they set the whole thing up, going back 2 or 3 years before they actually lashed out.

One client felt really frustrated and powerless over a bad marriage. At his job he was very successful, made a lot of money, but he didn't think he deserved it. He hadn't gone to college. He was molested at age 6 by a man who lived on his street. Now, as an offender, he explained his method of operation. Kids were always at his home. He would play ball, wrestle with them, fix their bikes. He made his son's friends feel real comfortable at his home. His wife and son were out of town once while some neighborhood kids came by to play. One of the kids got wet and he sent the boy upstairs to dry off. He appeared in the room when the kid was naked. Apparently he started to set up the situation several years before the incident. By making friends with the boy's parents he made himself available. He knew this particular boy was lonely and that his home life was barren. By paying attention to and playing with the boy, at the time of the molesting act he knew he had total control or power over the victim.

Question: Where is the treatment in your program?

Answer: First of all we give our clients calendars on which they write and begin to identify their feelings. One feeling they can identify right from the start is anger—"I'm pissed off!"—a common feeling in the beginning. Many also can identify loneliness. Once we identify feelings we begin to learn how to get control over our reactions to them. If someone has a lifetime behind him of automatically blocking a feeling, it is going to take a long time to get to the point where he is aware of what he is feeling.

Question: How do you bring them to understand what they are feeling—through dialogue or group therapy?

Answer: Through group and individualized sessions, and we also give homework assignments. Like keeping a "feeling calendar." We ask them to write how they felt during any particular day and what occurred during the day that gave rise to that specific feeling and how they responded to it. That way we can break down all of it—feelings, thoughts, and actions.

We also require that everyone attend both individual and group therapy. During the individual sessions we concentrate on specific behavior, actions, and feelings. In group, I'll often have someone talk about an event which occurred when that person was clearly out of control. But keep in mind they are good con artists. Some of these guys have been committing sex offenses for 20 years or longer and never got caught.

During the beginning part of the program, we make every guy get up and do his line in detail. A line is how he set it up, what his method of operation is. That's a hard thing to do. We ask them to begin 2 to 5 years prior to the offense, where the buildup of powerless base feelings began. The interesting thing is that the longer the abuse, the more intricate the line becomes.

Question: What do you know to be common characteristics?

Answer: These are people who feel horrible about who they are. That's the most important thing people should know. And out of the need to feel more powerful, they subjugate the person who is the easiest to subjugate. If I feel small, weak, and stupid and I want to feel the opposite, the most logical choice is a child.

Question: Then what do you really do to change them?

Answer: We offer people alternatives. Life is not just being a victim or victimizer. And that's how it's perceived by our clients at first. They see it as a "they get me or I get them" situation. We provide them with a third alternative, control. We provide them with tools they can use in order to live a life of control. We tell these guys there is no cure for what you have; there's only control. It's up to you. You pick up these tools and decide whether or not to be in control.

Question: What is your method of teaching them control?

Answer: We try to hit people on as many levels as we can. Part of the healing process is the group work. I don't think you can do the necessary amount of therapy with a sex offender if you don't have that person in a group, because so many things happen in a group. Denials fall apart on a group level. You can look at other people and see that they are succeeding. You can look at other people and say, "This is really a nice guy and he molested a child, so maybe I'm not completely awful. Maybe I have a chance too."

Question: This is where some experts would disagree with you. They see it as sex drive, whereas you see it as a power-based problem.

Answer: Some people do. There are certainly different schools of thought. I have a guy who is 23 years old and was ordered by the court to Johns Hopkins for Depo-Provera treatment. He said it helped initially, but the level they went with him was not too deep. He learned some ways to interrupt fantasy. He was a compulsive masturbator and discovered ways to avoid situations that were potentially dangerous for him. But I don't think they got to the root of the problem, which is how lousy he feels about himself. Since he's been here, I've seen him change for the better. As he gets down in there and identifies the reasons for his feelings, it's clear his past behavior has always been in the driver's seat.

Question: What kind of success—which I realize is a very relative word—have you had in the seven years that you have been working with pedophiles?

Answer: Sex offenders should be monitored closely for at least three to five years after therapy. But to be honest, I don't know what they do after they leave our program. The people who leave here usually do so when their parole or probation is up. The really committed clients, those who know there is no cure and feel our program is a good support system, return even when their legal obligation is long past. These guys, I believe, make it.

Question: So you're basically a court-ordered program?

Answer: Yes, for the most part right now, although more people are coming in on their own.

Question: What kind of obstacles do you run into most often in dealing with this type of individual?

Answer: The obsession-compulsion behavior is really a very difficult thing to beat. The problem is that it takes time to rebuild self-esteem in my clients. Only with time does the program work.

■   ■   ■

Conclusion

The real-life situations presented in this chapter demonstrate the wide variety of pedophilic expression and how resistant pedophiles are to easy classification. These cases reveal a great deal about the pedophile's method of operation and value system. A committed child molester is not deterred by statutory prohibitions, cultural inhibitions, or broader ethical questions regarding victim rights.

Pedophilia is a sexual preference that, in its persistent state, cannot be completely cured without resorting to extreme measures such as massive sedation, hormone "adjustment" with Depo-Provera, or castration. These steps, moreover, simply eliminate the sex drive rather than supplant it with a more acceptable alternative. Wherever minors are found, so also are pedophiles. We have examined cases, for example, of molesters who victimized children at summer camps, gymnastic schools, beauty pageants (for minors), cheerleader and baton twirler camps and contests, church outings, hospitals, day care centers, Sunday school classes, marching band concerts, public beaches, swimming pools, children's theaters, juvenile correctional facilities, sporting events, and circuses. Not a complete list by any means, but an accurate sampling of the diversity of settings in which pedophiles have exploited minors.

Pedophilia is the bulwark of sexual trafficking in children, for without this consumer interest in gratification at a minor's expense there would be no child sex markets. By merely incarcerating some offenders or providing some type of treatment for them, we fail to address the fundamental question of why such behavior is so prevalent. Perhaps the most promising answer lies in the realization that most offenders were themselves once victims: With every exploitive act, a new generation of offenders is spawned. In that sense, pedophilia may be considered contagious.

Pedophilia is an issue of immense cultural significance, yet at the present level of public debate it is not likely to be seriously examined. Fostered by many factors in our unsettled and ambivalent social framework—especially in the area of differing sexual values—pedophilia continues to be an illegal, self-perpetuating activity that is frequently misunderstood, often overlooked, and invariably traumatic in its effects on the victims.

Endnotes

1. Source: Detectives Ron Lane and Larry Ross, Atlantic City Police Department, Atlantic City, New Jersey.
2. Source: Detective Sgt. George Haralson, Tulsa Police Department, Tulsa, Oklahoma.
3. For a comprehensive overview of the basic literature regarding the sexual pathology of pedophiles, see the selected readings section of this book.
4. Source: Detective John Cox, North Charleston, South Carolina.
5. Source: Lt. Thelma Milgrin, Wytheville County Sheriff's Department, Wytheville, Virginia.
6. Source: Detective Michael Keller, Missouri City Police Department, Missouri City, Texas.
7. *Wonderland*, newsletter of the Lewis Carroll Collectors Guild, Number 11 (Fall 1985), Chicago, Illinois.
8. *Magpie*, Journal of the Pedophile Information Exchange, volume 17 (Spring 1982).
9. One of the more complete reviews of sex ring types is provided by Ann W. Burgess and Marieanne L. Clark, eds., *Child Pornography and Sex Rings* (Lexington, Mass.: D.C. Heath, 1984).
10. Source: Detective John Cox, North Charleston, South Carolina.
11. Source: Detective's identity withheld by request.
12. Source: Detective Sgt. George Haralson, Tulsa Police Department, Tulsa, Oklahoma.
13. Source: Chris Corbett, senior counselor, "Together We Can," Pittsburgh, Pennsylvania.

Part Two

THE DIMENSIONS OF
SEXUAL TRAFFICKING

Part Two examines four aspects of sexual trafficking: hustling, pimping, child pornography, and the international child sex trade. The characteristics of these offenses are described in detail.

Chapter 3 discusses the fundamental dynamics of juvenile prostitution from the perspective of the underage male and female hustlers who work in various street and sheltered settings. The dysfunctional family is shown as providing the necessary raw material for the adult exploiter, who takes advantage of the minor's perception of life on the streets as a viable alternative to an undesirable home life. The hazards endured by the child prostitute are shown to range from outright violence to unending peonage.

Chapter 4 discusses the methods used by procurers of minors for the purpose of prostitution. Variations in the process of recruitment are examined through descriptions of the procurers: the "sweet mac" pimp, a chameleon-like individual who exploits the minors' vulnerabilities by capitalizing on the fragility of their self-image; the "gorilla" pimp, who uses force—including murder—to control his stable; the "business manager" pimp, a specialist who charges high rates and protects himself by exploiting his customers' fear of exposure and parents' avarice; and motorcycle clubs, which offer a sense of adventure and availability of drugs to attract potential teenage prostitutes. The difficulty of achieving successful prosecution of these exploiters concludes the chapter.

In Chapter 5, child pornography is defined and various uses of child pornography by exploiters are described. The multiple dimensions of child pornography are discussed in terms of quality of product and extent of distribution. Case studies illustrate the motives and methods commonly used by pornographers.

Chapter 6 examines aspects of the international child sex trade. Case studies from specific countries are presented as examples of the international trafficking in children for commercial sexual purposes, including torture, enslavement, rape, and even murder. International treaties and conventions which seek to suppress sexual trafficking are discussed in the context of the difficulty of implementing effective programs.

Chapter 3

HUSTLING

> *I first started to run away when I was 12; my stepdad wouldn't keep his hands off me. When I was 13, I met a 15-year-old girl in a group home. We became friends and told each other how we survived on the streets. A couple of months after we left the home she was found dead—murdered. I know it was because of prostitution. I started when I was 14, got involved with a pimp who sent me to different states. I really believed at the time that I would end up dead, like my friend, if I didn't do what he said.*
>
> BRENDA, A 15-YEAR-OLD PROSTITUTE

It is difficult to appreciate fully the predicament of underage females and males engaged in sex for money with adults. Otherwise known as "johns," "tricks," "squares," or "freaks," paying customers have made juvenile prostitution a lucrative enterprise. As an example of the money involved, an energetic girl can earn from $200 to $500 a night turning tricks. That rate translates into several thousand dollars a month and tens of thousands of untaxed dollars earned annually by a single juvenile hustler.

With that amount of money in mind, it is no surprise that juvenile hustlers, or "kiddie pros" as they are called, are considered valuable property by exploiters. The large amount of money to be made encourages the active recruitment of minors for prostitution. The criminal subculture of procurers, hustlers, and customers, however, is a far more intricate matter than the mere calculation of profit and loss. Juvenile prostitution is, in fact, one of the pivotal crimes of sexual trafficking. From it other forms of exploitation develop, such as involvement in pornography, apprenticeships, and recruitment.

In this chapter we shall examine the life-style of hustling from a variety of vantage points in order to illustrate the dynamics of this extraordinary problem. Teenagers tend to dominate the market, but the demand for pre-pubescent children is brisk. Adults are willing to pay up to $500 for an opportunity to have sex with a minor. Our findings, furthermore, suggest that a flourishing trade in underage male and female prostitutes exists throughout the nation—from Rockford, Illinois, to Des Moines, Iowa, to Honolulu, Hawaii. This traffic involves juveniles ranging in age from 10 to 17 who come from a wide variety of families and cultural settings, and it occurs in brothels, on the streets, within sex rings, and in a multitude of sheltered settings.

Types of Hustling: Street and Sheltered

Street and sheltered hustling are the two principal forms of prostitution for both adults and juveniles. Street hustling can be loosely defined as prostitutes engaged in soliciting customers in public view. Common locations are truck stops, public thoroughfares, rest areas on interstate highways, city recreation sites, and tourist districts. These areas are popular because they offer a visible, immediately accessible flow of customers. Street hustlers must proposition or solicit customers directly for business, although the sex act usually occurs at some less conspicuous location.

Table 3-1   Primary Settings of Juvenile Prostitutes

Street Hustling	*Sheltered Hustling*
Truck stops	Brothels and sex clubs
Public thoroughfares	Adult bookstores and peep shows
Interstate highway rest areas	Private houses and apartments
Central business districts	Boarding houses
Arcade game rooms	Massage parlors
Tourist locales	Hotels and motels
Red-light districts	Trailer parks
Bars	Sex rings
Convenience stores	Escort and out-call services
Lumber camps	Migrant labor camps
Pawn shops	Foster homes
Bus and train terminals	
City parks	

Table 3-2   Characteristics of Juvenile Prostitutes

Male	*Female*
Usually enjoys freelance status.	Often placed in brothels.
Turns fewer daily tricks than females.	Usually works for pimps.
Uses mechanical signs, body language, and verbal communication to solicit tricks.	Usually goes through apprenticeship period.
Earns less per trick than females.	Often initiated into circuit life.
Uses violence as tool of trade.	Receives sexual initiation at home.
Experiences peer pressure indoctrination.	Often involved in child pornography.
	Prefers truck stops as worksites.
Often has homosexual orientation and is bisexual.	Uses blackmail and violence as tools of trade.
Uses streets as primary worksite.	Often traded or sold by pimps to brothels or sex rings.
Considers customer as prey or masculine role model.	Speaks and dresses like an adult.
Usually dependent on drugs and alcohol.	

Sheltered hustling, as the term suggests, takes place behind closed doors and includes brothels, escort services, boarding houses, and massage parlors. Customers are referred to these places by pimps, by hustlers, and by other customers. In some cases, a middleman—for instance, a bartender, cabdriver, or hotel bellhop—receives a small fee or kickback for directing a customer to a juvenile hustler.

Sheltered prostitutes have the benefit of insulation. Their clients are brought to them, thus minimizing the risk of detection by police. The more attractive female hustlers do not have to compete on the streets, where the potential for violence and arrest is high. They are usually controlled or managed by an adult who is responsible for ensuring—to some degree—their safety and welfare—that is, he may protect them from violent or sadistic customers and act as their provider. Necessities of life such as food, clothing, and housing are normally made available, although by no means guaranteed, by the exploiter. The hustler is often treated as a piece of merchandise who is expected to make a consistent amount of money per trick on a daily basis.

Table 3-1 shows a breakdown of the two areas where juvenile prostitutes can be found. Some settings are contextual—for example, hustlers in the Northeast are less likely than those in the South to work in migrant labor camps. Other hustlers do not fit in

either category—for instance, cruise ship prostitutes. An underage
hustler may work several different types of locations, both street
and sheltered, in the course of his or her involvement with
prostitution. Table 3-2 compares the general characteristics of male
and female juvenile prostitutes within the context of both street
and sheltered hustling.

Boy Prostitutes

One of the more distinctive attitudes of juvenile male prostitutes,
or "chickens," is that many do not consider sex with an adult male
a homosexual activity. These same hustlers often describe customers as "fags" or "sissies" who stoop so low as to pay for their sexual
gratification. This attitude is typically expressed by hustlers who,
while preserving a heterosexual relationship with a girlfriend,
continue to sell themselves for money to men. Many of the
underage homosexual hustlers who prefer the company of adult
males, on the other hand, are immersed in the life-style of gay
hustling, whether on the streets, in bars, or in other locales. For
these individuals, prostitution is a way of combining business with
pleasure. The bisexual hustler, however, is ambivalent in outlook.
By viewing a half-hour of sex with a stranger as a business transaction, aside from the possible physical pleasure involved, they
attempt to keep separate their heterosexual preferences from the
homosexual act of prostitution.

Popular juvenile male hustlers have several traits in common:
youthful appearance, including smooth feminine features and lack
of muscle tone; exceptional sexual sophistication or skills; easy
rapport with customers; and a facade of naivete tempered with
street sense. More often than not, a hustler acts as a passive sexual
partner and is expected to have an orgasm; he is thus restricted in
the number of men he can accommodate in a typical day on the
streets. Some boys are willing to perform anal or oral sex in order
to make more money. Where the act transpires also influences the
cost: Hustlers working in peep show booths at adult sex clubs or
bookstores, for instance, earn less than their peers who travel to a
customer's home. According to our field interviews, the going rate
for half an hour of oral sex with a 13- or 14-year-old male is
between $5 and $20, a scale that is fairly standard regardless of
location.

Johns and hustlers rely on three basic forms of communication to establish contact and set prices: mechanical signals, verbal communication, and body signals. Some examples are as follow:

1. *Mechanical signals:* For example, a cruiser (john) flashes his car's headlights to indicate a desire for oral sex or blinks the tail lights for anal sex.
2. *Verbal communication:* A hustler approaches a customer directly to negotiate terms.
3. *Body signals:* The prostitute smiles at a cruising customer, holds up fingers to indicate price. Gay hustlers, whether adult or juvenile, solicit customers in some cities through a combination of body signals and colored wristbands or hankies that signify an interest in various sadomasochistic activities.

The price scale escalates if the potential trick is well-dressed, drives an expensive car, or requests out-of-the-ordinary sex. Also, rates increase if the customer wants to take a boy home, because, in the words of 15-year-old Kurt, "if you are going to get hurt, this is where it will happen." Any threats of harm perceived by the hustler can translate into higher fees.

The entire process of cruising by hustlers, making contact, quoting prices, and reaching final agreement happens within the space of a few minutes. It is, regardless of the type of communication or approach used, a fairly straightforward proposition, as explained by Thomas, a 16-year-old hustler from Indiana:

> You can tell if it's a cruiser by the way he's driving; the car will turn the wrong way or his lights will flash. He may wave you over, or he'll be playing with himself in the car. They just circle the block five or six times until you make contact with them. Like a parade.
>
> The first thing I ask them is if they're a cop, to avoid getting busted. Then I find out what they want. Different things, lots of them weird. I don't get in any car with some scaggy-looking fruit or a car with two guys.
>
> I don't do nothing for less than $20. My business is good; I got sugar daddies, guys who buy me things like clothes. In the summer you'll see maybe 25, 30 cars cruising the strip. So my friends and I don't have to fight over the first trick. Plenty to go around. The cops leave us alone most of the time. They're just used to seeing us out there I guess.

Last-minute haggling over acts or costs is negotiated inside the customer's car. After the sex is over, the john usually returns the

hustler to the original point of contact. A majority of these underage males are freelance hustlers or independents, who earn less
and turn fewer tricks than their female counterparts. Those who
do work for pimps, however, typically get to keep precious little,
if any, of their earnings.

Whether they are independent or under the aegis of a procurer,
the question remains: How do adolescent males become involved
in prostitution? Several explanations, none of them entirely satisfactory, offer some insight. The foremost of these focuses on peer
pressure as a prime motivator; the subtle influence of friends can
prod a novice to experiment with street hustling. In economically
depressed areas, prostitution is a relief valve for juveniles with few
practical skills and too much spare time. Their behavior reinforced
by associates, male hustlers use sex as a means to purchase drugs,
alcohol, and a modicum of financial status. Those without a home
may gradually depend on prostitution as a principal source of
income.

A second explanation is prior sexual abuse, either within the
family or by a stranger. The victim is socialized into hustling, or at
least comes to consider it as a practical alternative to molestation
and one that yields some gain. The process is gradual and insidi-
ous, but with experience comes familiarity, until what was once
inconceivable becomes routine. Rationalizations are used to justify
conduct and bolster a faltering sense of self-worth.

A third explanation involves a prior homosexual experience or
preference that encourages an adolescent male to experiment with
prostitution. According to this view, the hustler uses sex for money
as a facade in order to act out his own desires. Prostitution becomes
a convenient method for meeting other homosexuals, with the
added bonus that he receives payment for his services.[1]

One final explanation of why adolescents become juvenile prostitutes involves environmental factors. Lack of adequate parental
supervision, illiteracy, the absence of a structured set of values,
and the depreciation through abuse of the value of the human
body can cause an adolescent to experiment with hustling. Roger,
a 22-year-old street hustler, provides a not uncommon account of
his introduction to prostitution at age 15, which incorporates
several of the previous explanations:

> I started hanging out with some kids my age and older who
> roamed the streets—skipped school, that sort of stuff. They really

made an impression on me. No one was telling them what to do. They made their own decisions—you know, being free. I began sneaking away from home at night to be with these kids. For me to be accepted as part of the gang, I'd have to do things they were involved in.

This is when alcohol and drugs became part of my life. The combination of these two made our money grow small real quick. So we started doing small breakings and enterings to get the money we needed to keep us in our habit. This type of activity got too risky, and an older guy in the gang told me about a way of getting money easily and with less risk. At least it seemed so at the time. He called it hustling—selling ourselves to homosexuals for money, dope, booze. At first I was shy, really scared, but they shamed and embarrassed me into doing it anyways.

There were so many cruisers. They all had funny names. I remember one guy named Sweet Louise. He'd sometimes pick up two of us and take us to a dirty bookstore. We could make anywhere from $20 to $70 hustling in the bookstore. After we were drained, we'd call it a night.

It is easy to see how the cumulative effect of these intangible pressures and attractions could guide an individual like Roger from reluctant participation as a youth to routine hustling as an adult. The difficulty lies in identifying the precise stimuli, critical events, and stages that led to his involvement.

The world of adolescent male prostitutes is distinctive for their freelance status, passive roles in sex, lower earnings, bisexual behavior, and methods of customer-hustler communication. One other feature, however, deserves recognition: Violence is endemic to this life-style. The opportunities for bodily harm, either to them or to their customers, are rampant. Both customers and hustlers distrust each other, for each is using the other for self-serving purposes. The result can be an atmosphere of unspoken hostility. For 14-year-old hustlers like Bobby, violence is a practical tool of the trade:

Sometimes we go for the "quick hit" if a trick looks like he's got money. My friend talks to the guy, gets him talking, and I come in the other side or reach in through the window if it's open and smack him in the head with a stick—sometimes a tire iron. The guy's too dizzy to do anything so my partner takes his wallet and we scoot. Make some good money that way.

You got to look out for yourself, 'cause the tricks like to carry guns, knives, stuff like that. It don't pay to be empty-handed anymore.

Violence, moreover, invites retaliation in an equal or greater measure. Unable to request police assistance in the event of a mugging by hustlers, customers must resort to basic forms of self-protection, including concealed weapons. Since a police investigation might stir up unwanted, awkward questions about their sexual habits, both hustlers and customers are silent combatants in the realm of commercial sex.

One incident that accurately highlights the extremes to which this mutual mistrust can go concerns a 13-year-old hustler named Teddy from Virginia. Teddy was used as bait to attract a customer. He persuaded the adult to drive to a deserted locale in the country to have sex. After reaching a secluded spot in the woods, Teddy's friends arrived in two cars and blocked the customer's exit. Realizing he had been betrayed, the adult drew a revolver from the glove compartment and threatened to shoot Teddy. The other hustlers surrounded the car, removed the man, and proceeded to beat and rob him. They tied his hands to the bumper of one automobile, his feet to the other, and threatened to pull him apart. The hustlers ultimately left him naked in the middle of the woods, without his car or money, miles from the city.[2] In short, hustlers sometimes rob their clients in the quest for larger profits, and customers respond with similar brutality, each behaving simultaneously as exploiter-victim toward the other.

For a majority of adolescent male prostitutes, success is still measured in terms of rapid turnover, occasional tips, safe tricks, and ample pocket money. If there is a fortune to be made working on the streets, it has eluded these particular juveniles; nowhere will you find a wealthy male (or female) juvenile prostitute. Instead of prosperity, a hustler can expect to contract some type of venereal disease, from gonorrhea to AIDS, in addition to real or psychosomatic illnesses derived from the stressful nature of his activities. During the course of his initiation into the practicalities of hustling, he can expect to learn an enormous amount of practical information that will guide him through trouble spots and improve his prospects for making money. The facts of how to avoid the police, to steer clear of dangerous customers, to locate transient housing or profitable worksites, and to establish reliable contacts for purchasing drugs and alcohol are part of the "street curriculum" of hustling. This accumulated wisdom is, in turn, improved upon whenever possible and handed down to other hustlers to prepare them for the realities of street survival.

Girl Prostitutes

It is common knowledge among exploiters that the highest profits from prostitution are made with adolescent females. The demand for underage females, may, in fact, rival that for adult prostitutes. Pimps, brothels, pornography, and apprenticeships are components of this trade. Profit expectations are linked to several factors: the hustler's age and appearance (the younger, the more expensive), the type of sexual act, the location, the opportunity for blackmail, and the customer's willingness to pay exorbitant fees.

A majority of the female hustlers interviewed were the victims of prior sexual mistreatment at the hands of their father, stepfather, uncle, or mother's boyfriend. For them, prostitution was an exit from an intolerable home life and a practical option to the alternative of institutionalized care in foster homes or state juvenile facilities. One ironic side-effect of state intervention is that, in many instances, the offender is left untouched; his status as a wage earner is deemed more important than the needs of the victim. In response to the domestic trauma of an exploitive family, the adolescent victim often exhibits delinquent behavior and is likely to be labeled a delinquent offender and removed from the confines of her family.

Underage female hustlers are found in street and sheltered settings. They usually do not work the same location as males. A geographic boundary such as a store front or a thoroughfare may separate the male and female hustlers. This subtle division of prostitutes helps to reduce competition and minimize confusion for customers. Girl prostitutes use a direct, verbal approach to attract tricks. An interested customer pulls over to the curb, the hustler performs a cursory screening to make sure the customer is not a police officer, and a price is agreed upon. The girl enters the automobile, accepts payment, and the pair drive off to a designated spot to have sex.

This deceptively simple transaction tells us how, but not why, an underage female engages in prostitution. To understand this phenomenon, we must consider the following environmental, psychological, and economic influences:

1. Recruitment: A girl may be seduced, tricked, or blackmailed into hustling by a procurer. The techniques used by pimps are discussed in Chapter 4.

2. Peer Pressure: Like their male counterparts, potential female hustlers are particularly vulnerable to the persuasive power of peers. Prostitution is, in a sense, legitimized within the peer group, not through any formal process of admission, but by acknowledging it as acceptable behavior.

3. *Conditioning:* Living in an exploitive family where sexual mistreatment is practiced teaches the adolescent victim that the most effective way to communicate with adults is through sex. Such conditioning creates a distorted value system which can be encouraged by exploitive adults. The adolescent victim may view prostitution as a very realistic alternative to life at home because it enables her to interact on relatively equal terms with adults and to reinforce her sexual attitudes.

4. *Destructive Self-Image:* The victim, after extensive conditioning at home, feels she deserves to be a prostitute. Her self-worth is so diminished that her guilt is overwhelming. She assumes all or much of the blame for her predicament.

5. *Survival:* This is the most predictable explanation as to why minors engage in prostitution. Cities that do not provide sufficient resources to aid runaways or cast-off juveniles contribute to their delinquent status. The demands of survival—of seeking shelter, food, and clothing—limit the options of chronically unskilled, unemployed minors on the streets. A form of social Darwinism develops, which is to say that only the strong and resourceful succeed. Thus hustling offers a means of satisfying basic needs.

6. *Subcultural Drift:* Juveniles who are part of the subculture of sexual trafficking live outside the social mainstream. The transition from one form of exploitation, such as nude dancing, to hustling becomes a matter of degree. Lowered inhibitions, support by peers or exploiters, and conditioning encourages movement of the victim within the child sex markets.

Most girl prostitutes work at some point for a procurer, unless they are part-time or freelance hustlers. Freelance hustlers, or "outlaws" who work solely for themselves, must confront outright hostility from pimps and adult prostitutes who resent their independent status. Sheila, a 16-year-old, is an outlaw. Subjected to routine rape by her stepfather, beginning at age 10, she opted for prostitution, the lesser of two evils:

> *I started hitchhiking at 15—put my thumb out—and some old guy picked me up. I made $25 pulling a trick with him. This was the first time I ever sold myself and I was really scared. I told him to put the money in my pants pocket. I didn't want to touch it.*

> *My self-image sucked when it was all over, but I was going to be on my own and I had to support myself. It was the price I had to pay, but I can still remember it like it happened yesterday.*
>
> *A trucker later gave me a ride to Utah for a piece of ass. I knew I needed money for a motel and meals, so I would sell myself. Never have been arrested for prostitution. The cops in Utah knew I was a runaway, but they never turned me in. Hell, I had sex with them so they wouldn't bust me. Sometimes I even picked up tricks in front of the police station. Nobody cared.*
>
> *I carried a gun or knife most of the time to make sure I didn't get hurt by some trick. I met this black guy who taught me how to really survive on the streets. We stole checks, wrote them, all sorts of things. I'm at the point now where I'll kill anyone who tries to get over on me.*

Sheila's experiences are not unique. Freelance female hustlers must be capable of remarkable adaptation to new surroundings and situations in order to survive the hazards of aggressive procurers, vicious customers, and apprehension by the police. It is a precarious existence under the best of circumstances. They must learn a variety of skills, including how to dress, the language of commercial sex, posture and poise, ways to trigger a customer's orgasm with a minimum expenditure of effort and time, appropriate makeup in the case of veteran prostitutes, and—above all else—how to create the illusion of pleasure in a variety of unique settings.

Juvenile Prostitution and the Trucking Industry

A favorite locale for female juveniles wanting to turn a large number of tricks in a short time, relatively free from police interference, is a truck stop. Moving from cab to cab at $20 to $50 a trick, the hustlers enjoy a steady flow of clients. A nearby motel or restaurant is used as a place to relax, freshen up between customers, and socialize with other hustlers. An effective variation of this technique is to rent a room at a truck stop motel and use a citizen's band radio (supplied by a pimp or friendly truck driver) to help attract business by calling prospective customers directly. So prevalent is this practice, especially at some major interstate junctions, that the former owner of a massage parlor/brothel located adjacent to a truck stop complained:

They really hurt my business. Some nights I'd ride around the lot with my manager (madam) and count up to 25 to 30 girls jumping from truck to truck. Their pimps would be lined up in the back row, working the CB, lining up the johns. It was nothing to see nine or ten Lincoln Continentals lined up out there.

Truck drivers provide a second service to underage prostitutes. They are one of the principal conveyors of hustlers across state lines. Despite regulations to the contrary, some freight carriers transport hitchhiking juvenile prostitutes across the country. Hustlers are quick to appreciate that a ride with a truck driver offers security, free transportation, and rest. Exploitive drivers accept sex in exchange for a ride. Others simply wish to help the juvenile. In either case, the drivers become vulnerable to strong-arm or blackmail tactics by vicious hustlers like Toni and her friend Sugar:

The trucker gave us a ride down to Florida. We robbed him. It was a real dirty job because he was real nice to us, fed us good. We stole all of his bennies and then we ripped him off for about $200.

He said, "I got a family," shaking as he's taking his money out of his wallet. I'll never forget it. I was drunk and Sugar had a gun to his head.

We took his money and told him if he ever said a word, we knew where he was at, what his CB handle was, and what trucking line he drove for. Told him we were juveniles and he'd end up right in jail.

Toni and Sugar were two of several hustlers who professed an enthusiasm for the use of physical threats on truck driving customers. A few others described incidents where truck drivers would assist the hustlers in lining up tricks for sex or robbery. What little we have gleaned from male juvenile prostitutes, on the other hand, indicates that they are infrequently subjected to sexual intimidation by drivers in exchange for rides and rarely hustle at truck stops.

The trucking industry has done little to acknowledge or reduce its role in contributing to juvenile prostitution. By tighter enforcement of existing rules pertaining to cab passengers, the industry certainly could impede the mobility of hustlers, thus restricting their access to distant brothels and further exploitation in other cities and states. The cooperation of the trucking industry could make it more difficult for the runaway population to graduate into the life-style of prostitution.

The following case illustrates the dynamics of truck-stop hustling by both juvenile and adult prostitutes.[3] It describes a familiar scene at numerous truck stops across the nation where juvenile hustlers either ply their trade or look for a driver to transport them to a new working site. In "A Night on the Lot," Detective Thomas Horan recounts his experience when observing activity at several truck stops in Pennsylvania. Upon conclusion of his investigation, several individuals were prosecuted by local authorities.

A NIGHT ON THE LOT

Our agency had been receiving complaints from truckers, truckers' wives, local citizens, and others who stay up all night listening to the chatter on citizen band radios. The complaints were generally the same: that the prostitutes, or "commercial beavers" as they are known on the CB, are a public nuisance.

It was 7 P.M. when I first parked on the lot. On that hot summer night I listened to the CB chatter—with comments like, "Smiling Jack headed eastbound for St. Louis," and "Big Red coming in." Around 9 P.M. I heard a female voice, identified only as "Blondie," come over the CB, inquiring if any of those truckers were looking for some female company tonight. The response was deafening as truckers jammed the airwaves to make contact with "Blondie." The conversation was always short and to the point: She's selling her body and he's interested. There is, however, no mention of money over the airwaves. The girls knew their trucks and would ask, "Are you in a cabover or conventional rig, and what row or section are you in?"

Between 9:30 and 10:00 P.M., channel 19, the designated beaver channel, gets real busy. You begin to hear the voices of such characters as Hipshaker, Foxy, Little Lady, Short Cake, Little Devil, Angel, Snow, Good Luck, Suction Cups, and many others, all inquiring as to whether any truckers wanted female company. On a busy night you could hear 15 to 20 different girls soliciting sex. The pace on the lots I covered remained very quick until around 3 A.M., when most of the girls called it a night.

■　　　■　　　■

Our field investigations corroborated Detective Horan's major conclusions, which he reached after a two-month investigation of the truck stop sex trade. He observed that prostitutes work only the trucks and will not enter a car. The truckers act as lookouts for the girls and actually keep an eye on them. Demand for the services of these prostitutes is usually brisk and constant during the course of a night.

Most truckers will not engage in sex if the girl requires them to wear a condom, a fact often stated by truckers during their conversation with hustlers over the C.B. A number of drivers specifically request underage prostitutes. Generally white prostitutes outnumber black prostitutes five to one, and black prostitutes are subjected to considerable verbal abuse. Most prostitutes use some type of drugs.

Bordellos and the Circuit Life

An often overlooked aspect of juvenile prostitution is that girls ages 10 to 17 are sometimes placed in brothels or on a circuit. A circuit can be defined as a string or series of working sites scattered across a dozen or more states. Females in the circuit life are shipped off to different cities by a pimp or booking agent to work the streets, brothels, or out-call services. Alternatively, the victim may voluntarily decide to travel to commonly known locales or "strolls" that are part of an established circuit.

Through word of mouth and referral a hustler can stay actively working on the road for months on end. The more experienced hustlers scan the local newspapers upon arrival in a city to find the locations of adult clubs, bookstores, and massage parlors. A seasoned freelance or outlaw hustler may even book herself into a bordello for temporary employment. Barbara, also called Georgia Peaches, is well versed in the circuit life. She has spent much of her adolescence as a ward of various juvenile justice systems. After working two years as a full-time prostitute, beginning at age 15, Barbara estimated her gross earnings at about $20,000, all of which was given to her pimps or squandered.

BARBARA—ALIAS "GEORGIA PEACHES"

My pimp in Atlanta set me up to work in a prostitution house in Steubenville, Ohio, called Judy Jordans, a very, very popular place. He put me on a bus and someone was waiting at the depot for me at Steubenville. He was going to get money for sending me to the house.

I went up there with three pieces of clothing and stayed for a week and a half. I was supposed to be making $1,000 a week but made only $400 a week because the place was so cheap and rundown.

I left there and ended up in New Kensington, Pennsylvania. Met a man named Russell who wanted me to work for him on a 50/50 basis. I worked New Kensington for close to a month, turned about 150 tricks at $25 to $60 a head.

Later, I met a guy named Charles who was involved in a murder rap. He owned a bar in New Kensington and had an 18-year-old boy beat to death with a club. Anyways, he sent me to Barboursville, West Virginia, to work in a house. I caught a very rare kind of gonorrhea there, but didn't know I had it until much later.

Charles moved me to a city in New Jersey to work at Dolly's, another prostitution house. I was making about $1,000 a week. He had what he called "bookings" and kept moving me around. He had a big calendar and booked me in some place different every week. They say it is more proper, makes the prostitute look more professional.

The way it worked was Charles would call someone and tell them he had a girl, put you on a bus, someone would meet you, and take you to the house. This guy booked for three girls.

These people would pay me in cash. I split 50/50 with the madam. Plus I had to pay her $25 a day for board and extra for meals. I worked from 9 A.M. to 11 P.M. I could be with 25 guys in one night and make only $60 or so for myself.

Charles finally kicked me out because I had VD. I left with no clothes, food, or money. Then I got pregnant when I was back in Georgia.

■　　■　　■

The booking agent referred to by Barbara is someone who acts as a middleman between the hustler and bordello management. He works from a calendar, arranging working dates and transportation to a particular city in exchange for a commission or a percentage of the girl's earnings. An agent in Houston, for example, may book several underage prostitutes into out-of-state brothels over a six-month period. For each placement he is guaranteed a fee from the madam or pimp who has "leased" the hustler's services. If this same agent controls three or four hustlers, he can expect to make several thousand dollars a month with very little effort aside from the recordkeeping. To ensure that the hustler abides by the agreement and meets her work assignments, she is met at a bus depot or an airline terminal by someone from the brothel. In addition, she typically has little or no control over where, when, or for whom she works. A kiddie pro in these circumstances may be allowed either a 50/50 division of the profits or a percentage based on the number of tricks. The less fortunate are paid off in drugs or in pocket money. The average length of stay for a hustler is about two to three weeks.

Factors considered in determining a prostitute's length of a tour of duty at a particular brothel include the manager's observing the minor has contracted a venereal disease, her willingness to work long, hard hours, which means she must be able to sustain physical contact with a large number of tricks on a daily basis, and the possibility that local authorities will discover the minor's presence. The contract with the brothel, whether negotiated by the booking agent or by the prostitute, is usually of fixed duration and will account for matters such as the hustler's menstrual cycle.

From a pimp's or booking agent's point of view, the circuit approach to prostitution has distinct advantages. Brothels provide a buffer between the police and the pimp. The difficulties of building a case against a pimp are magnified in these situations, especially when the hustlers work out of state. Because investigations entail a substantial commitment of resources, time, and manpower, it is impractical for many police departments to pursue them. In addition, the circuit affords some degree of control over a hustler's movement.

A circuit is defined by profitable markets for prostitutes. A hustler may, for example, mostly work the eastern seaboard at familiar sites such as New York City, Washington, D.C., and Boston but also include on her agenda less likely cities such as Virginia Beach (Virginia), Springfield (Massachusetts), and Wilmington (North Carolina). For several reasons, including population growth, development of transporation networks, and increased tourist trade, each of these cities has become a thread in the intricate web of hustling circuits. Each generates wealth, as one pimp/booking agent so aptly explained, for the exploiter:

I could take a 14-year-old girl and live 10 years of luxury—I'm talking 10 new Cadillacs and 10 new wardrobes—by working her across the country in whorehouses.

I can place a $5 and $2 on a stroll ($5 for sex and $2 for the room) on up to servicing clients who frequent the best houses and who will pay $500 for a couple hours of sex with a 12-year-old. The houses I supplied were generally located in the upper-class neighborhoods. Better clientele aren't going to go into the slums where the riff-raff might rob them. So you find the houses located in the nicer residential areas where it's clean and people aren't afraid to go.

In a way, they are like a prison with bars and all. Not really bars, but gates and real pretty ironworks on the windows and doors. Cameras are in the rooms and outside, located where they can see who is coming up to the house. There are usually two or three housemen around whose job it is to keep things peaceful. All in all, a real nice place and they are located in places you wouldn't believe.

Life in a bordello for a juvenile is apparently little different than that experienced by adult prostitutes. The hierarchy of characters consists of the owner and the madam, service employees and bouncers, prostitutes and secondary actors such as customers and tipsters. An owner provides the financing, organization, and force to establish and maintain his investment in prostitution. The madam is second in command, exercising authority over such daily affairs as bookkeeping and keeping the house in order. Service employees attend to mundane tasks of cleaning, shopping, and preserving the peace. Lowest in the hierarchy are the prostitutes. Their movements and habits are closely regulated. A drug-dependent hustler, for instance, is an unreliable worker. Juveniles suffering from wanderlust or emotional problems are less likely to cooperate with the management; they require either constant attention or immediate dismissal (accompanied by a warning to keep silent about the bordello). Also, a close check must be kept over the flow of money from customer to hustler to madam. The most common channels are: the customer pays the madam directly; the hustler puts the money through a slot into a strongbox in the bedroom; or the money is fed through a pipe directly to a central receiving room and into a strongbox there.

A juvenile who works in a brothel quickly becomes a veteran hustler. Those who return time and again to work in bordellos develop an immunity system of sorts, a deadening of emotional nerve-ends. Parading semi-naked in front of customers, accepting

money, and proceeding directly to a bedroom for sex, followed by
a quick wash or adjustment in make-up before the next customer,
is a lot to expect from a 14-year-old girl, especially when she has
already gone through this process a dozen times during a working
shift. Even the "thoroughbreds," or experienced females of prostitution, have great difficulty adjusting to this degrading scenario.

Estimating how many bordellos employ minors or are connected
with the circuits is difficult. Several bordellos were brought to our
attention repeatedly by various pimps or hustlers in different
states. Certain brothels, whether disguised as massage parlors or
out-call agencies, have apparently been in existence for years, a
disturbing fact that implies collusion between the local police and
the proprietors. Furthermore, we believe that brothels which
employ minors continue to prosper because their clients are relatively discreet and because many police departments are naive
about the existence and number of such places. The facts are that
these places do exist, they do use adolescents, they have numerous
clients, and they often encourage parents to "rent out" their
children. One such place, identified by two pimps and a former
hustler, is described in the following excerpt by a convicted
exploiter:

> *This place is very expensive. The thing they specialize in is kids,
> but you can't have intercourse with these girls because a lot of
> them—well, they're pretty young. I'd say from 10 to 14 years old—
> 14 might even be high. The average is about 12. You have to be
> known. I can bring you in because I can vouch for you. If you try
> to get in on your own, they wouldn't let you in the front door. Once
> you're known, you can come there on your own. They never take no
> stranger off the street. Let me tell you about the customers they
> had. Attorneys, big shots like that, high-class people.*
>
> *It could cost around $500 for sex, depending on what you wanted
> the girls to do. But no intercourse. The people that run the house
> keep it all quiet because the mothers know. The girls are there
> almost seven days a week. They go to school during the day, you
> understand. This is with their parents' knowledge. In other words,
> the parents are selling their kids.*
>
> *They'd have, on the average, about six kids in the house, always
> changing. It's a nice-looking, ordinary house in a neighborhood.
> Customers come in through the alley. You park a block away and
> walk in. I don't know if they have a lot of business, but the business
> they do get is worth it because these people have money.*
>
> *The people that run the house are just ordinary. It's that kind of
> business. You come in through the back door, through the kitchen
> and into the living room. The kids come out and stand in front of*

you, just like a regular whorehouse, wearing panties. You make your choice, tell the madam what you want and pay up. Then you go to the bedroom.

Note this particular exploiter's lack of concern for the victims. His casual narration evokes the image of adults unashamedly using minors for profit and pleasure. Let us turn, therefore, to the perspective of the victim. Eve is a white, 16-year-old girl from a lower-class family steeped in physical and sexual abuse. Fleeing the threats of sexual violence by her stepfather, she has taken to the streets to escape. Eve is a veteran prostitute whose knowledge of the trade is remarkable. She is presently in a juvenile detention facility and will be released shortly back to the streets.

EVE

Don: Tell me, how does a 14-year-old girl learn to prostitute herself?

Eve: For me it came easily because, like my mom told me when I was younger, I have a nice face, a nice body, and men are attracted to me. Someone would see me on the street and just come over and start talking or drive by in a car and motion to me and I'd go over and find out what he wanted. Just get in the car and go.

Don: How did you know these guys weren't the police?

Eve: Usually you could tell by the car. If it didn't have whitewalls you didn't go, because it was usually an undercover car. [Government purchasing practices usually require police departments to use the lowest of three bids as an economy measure—i.e., blackwalls are less expensive than whitewalls.]

Don: Any other ways of spotting the police?

Eve: License plates. There was a certain amount of digits you'd have to look out for. Also, the way a person looks. If the guy was too overdressed or dressed too poorly, like a dirty teeshirt, it wasn't safe.

Don: Your first time on the streets. What was it like?

Eve: My pimp, a bartender, took me to Pittsburgh. I was on a corner in a pink skirt and he was in a cafe nearby. I was very scared, but I did it for the money.

Don: What kind of money are we talking about? Did he tell you how much to charge?

Eve: Ah, not in so many words. He told me the price ranges and it's really up to you how much you charge.

Don: How much did you cost in Pittsburgh?

Eve: Um, for certain things you'd never go for under $20. Or, in other cases, you'd never go under $50. There was always a certain rate for different things.

Don: Did you set the price by a guy's looks, his car, or by the sex act?

Eve: By the act. Prostitution made me feel real low but safe. Like I knew nothing would happen to me that I didn't want to happen. I made about $400 the first day.

Don: Moving from the streets, have you ever worked in a whorehouse?

Eve: Yeah.

Don: How did you end up there? Obviously you didn't just think up the idea.

Eve: A friend set it up for me because the police were cracking down on the street action.

Don: What was it like then for you, a 14-year-old, turning tricks in a whorehouse?

Eve: When I first got there an old lady—her name was Mary— sat me down at a table and she explained everything about the house.

Don: Did she ever ask you about your age? You certainly don't look 21.

Eve: No.

Don: She could tell. She had to know you were a kid.

Eve: I guess so. There were two other girls working. One girl was 13 and the other was 16. The old lady said we were supposed to lie about our age if the cops ever came. They never did.

Don: Tell me about the working routine.

Eve: You wear a body suit. When tricks come they ring a doorbell, the lady asks for identification, talks to them, finds out how many times they've been there before. Just procedures so nobody new ever gets in.

Don: They had to have new customers didn't they?

Eve: Yeah. Usually old customers bring new people. Anyways, we would stand in the lineup while the trick checked us out. If he picked me, we'd go upstairs, he'd pay me, and I would shove the money down a pipe to the downstairs money box. Then you check him for VD. You always worried about someone coming in that you knew.

Don: Okay, you're on the line, the doorbell rings. What are you thinking of when the guy opens the door and it's a trick?

Eve: What's next. What am I going to have to do when I go up those steps. The most fear is what is he going to want to do. Or if I get in that room and close the door, what could he do to me? He could stick a needle in my arm and kill me before anyone would know.

Don: What about prices?

Eve: Prices are exactly like those on the street, but at the house there are more tricks 'cause it's a lot easier.

Don: On a Friday or Saturday night, how many tricks would you have?

Eve: My first day, I'm pretty sure I had at least 30.

Don: Doesn't that get tiring?

Eve: Sure. It was a Saturday night. After the dog races are over, all the old men will come in, and sometimes the younger men.

Don: Did it bother you when the old men came in? I mean, how do you handle having sex with guys 30, 40 years older than you?

Eve: Scary. A guilty feeling in my mind. Every time an old man came in, I'd think of my grandfather. What if this guy were my grandfather? Sometimes I would just lay there and cry.

Don: Did you have to stay at the house?

Eve: No, you can go any time you want. It's not like a contract. I was scheduled to work there for two weeks, but couldn't stand it. They paid me my share and I left. I couldn't stand the paranoia.

Don: Paranoia?

Eve: Uh huh. Fear that someone would recognize me. Or maybe the place would get busted. The cops used to drive by and scream "Raid!" just for fun, just to see what would happen.

Don: So where are you headed when they release you from the center?

Eve: I dunno, probably back to the streets. I got somebody waiting for me.

■   ■   ■

Eve and Georgia Peaches are but two of several juveniles we interviewed who worked in bordellos and on the circuit. There is a consistency in their observations that holds true under close scrutiny. Other exploiters and victims, with slight variation, have independently acknowledged the bordello/circuit phenomenon. Whether the juveniles are supplied by parents, pimps, booking agents, or go voluntarily, brothel owners will continue to rent or lease the services of underage hustlers, provided the risk of arrest remains low. When the odds become too uncomfortable, the management may simply pack up, relocate to another state or distant city, and begin again. Considering that in many sections of the country law enforcement agencies do not share information, even with other departments in their own jurisdiction, these elusive bordellos are likely to maintain their unique status in the domain of juvenile prostitution.

Factors Affecting Detection of Prostitution

Underage hustlers are able to avoid detection or interception by the criminal justice system for several reasons. Foremost is the use of false identification papers for the "older-looking" kiddie pro. With a set of doctored papers, including a social security card, birth certificate, driver's license, and stolen credit cards, a pimp can manufacture an entirely new identity for a hustler. While these bogus credentials are not foolproof, they can easily pass a casual street examination by police officers. Alternatively, a hustler may carry no papers at all in order to complicate the task of identification for police.

A second reason is the arrest priorities of police organizations. Prostitution is a low-priority offense for many vice and street crime officers. Aside from periodic roundups, there is little incentive to arrest a hustler who may make bond and be back on the street before the arresting officer has completed the paperwork. This paradoxical situation is often reinforced by the absence of a clear community consensus regarding the enforcement of prostitution laws.

Third is the realization that neither the juvenile hustler nor customer is likely to file a complaint in the event either person is victimized (mugged or cheated out of money). The customer, in particular, has a great deal to lose by making his sexual preferences or contacts with a minor known to the police.

The "see no evil, hear no evil syndrome" represents a fourth reason. Juvenile prostitution is still an enigma to many police and social service agencies. Because these agencies do not know or wish to be taught how to recognize the presence of kiddie pros, they incorrectly assume that the problem does not exist in their jurisdiction.

A juvenile who can make herself look older than she actually is, even without supportive identification papers, will withstand a cursory examination by even alert police officers. With the correct posture, language, poise, adult dress, and air of confidence, a hustler can create the illusion of age.

A fifth reason that underage hustlers escape detection is the absence of effective curfew, truancy, and loitering laws or ordinances. Without them, juvenile hustlers cannot be held accountable for their presence on the streets. Unless they constitute a public nuisance because of their behavior, there is little that police departments can do to prevent them from gaining access to customers.

Escape from detection may also be the result of active cooperation by local authorities. Official corruption and collusion produces the worst of all possible situations: Kiddie pros cannot be intercepted because their official "guardians," such as the police or officials in the juvenile justice system, have joined the ranks of their exploiters.

A final reason for the success of hustlers in avoiding detection is their extraordinary mobility, which, when combined with their lack of accountability, makes them difficult to track. This unique problem is compounded by the failure of state protective agencies to exchange information or coordinate resources in the search for kiddie pros.

The cumulative effect of all of these circumstances is that many juvenile prostitutes, even those in plain view, become "invisible." Mobility, appearance, official negligence, bogus identification papers, misguided arrest priorities, and the lack of a complainant all favor the prostitute. Unless a concerted effort is made to identify and intercept minors engaged in prostitution, they are often overlooked. Complaints filed by private citizens and community action groups may result in a temporary cessation of hustling, but these measures do not endure. Given the demand for underage prostitutes, they merely shift the trade to new locations. Official crackdowns, in short, are an acknowledgment of the problem, but they do not provide a solution.

It is also possible, as demonstrated in the following case, for juvenile hustlers to be exploited while in protective state care by procurers who have successfully avoided detection or prosecution. Ms. Adams, the superintendent of a juvenile facility for girls located in the Southwest, explains how such a situation arose.

SHELTERED, BUT NOT SAFE

At the time of the incident I was an adult parole supervisor. I knew of a person, a black male, who along with several others was pimping about 15 adolescent females. Most of the girls were in the 12- to 14-year-old age range. The kids were being re-cruited out of a privately owned juvenile shelter. The director became aware of what was going on. Because the shelter was not a secure facility and the girls went to public schools, it was very difficult for him to maintain surveillance and deal with the problem. The situation became very bizarre.

Girls were taken to a clubhouse near the shelter. It was a fraternal organization clubhouse whose members were not in-volved in the exploitation. The pimps took the girls to the back room for their "initiation." They were involved in sex circuses with more than one girl and one male engaging in many forms of sex. Later the pimps drove the girls to a railroad trestle to pick up johns. The girls were never allowed to keep much of the money they made. The pimps usually paid them off with drugs for their troubles.

What made our investigation so difficult was getting the girls to talk about it. They feared for their own personal safety. Also, the girls had developed emotional attachments to the pimps, who gave them a little money, drugs,, excitement, and a good time. It was very hard for us to convince them that they were being used or to break the bonds set in their minds.

We found one female who agreed to be honest and point out the individuals who were involved and to give us the names of the kids and adults. She was willing to testify. You see the ringleader had been paroled for crimes not sexually related. He was very scheming, a real con artist. We could never charge him with any of the sexual charges. What we did was charge him

with technical violations of parole and failure to maintain a place
of employment and changing residence without prior approval.
He was difficult to catch because he was smart enough to play
the game.

The girl testified, but the three-man parole board decided
there was not enough evidence to revoke his parole. That was
exactly what the girls were afraid of, that if this guy got loose he
would come after them. They beat up the girl who talked to us
and the detectives. She refused to admit who beat her.

The case took six to eight months just to get it into a hearing.
It got to the point where even the staff at the shelter were being
threatened. I was followed home on numerous occasions by
people involved in the hearing. It's over now, but just imagine
the damage done to these girls.

Occupational Hazards of Juvenile Prostitution

Mastering the art of evasion does not, of course, make a minor
involved in prostitution immune to the gamut of occupational
hazards. To some extent, actual or perceived dangers to a juvenile's
body or state of mind overlap, triggering a cause-effect reaction, as
in the case of a pregnant hustler who decides to put her drug-
addicted infant up for adoption. The difficulty lies in deciphering
which hazard is the cause and which is the effect.

Consider the case of Suzanne, a 28-year-old social worker from
Arizona. Her experiences as a former juvenile prostitute are representative of many of the dangers associated with hustling.

SUZANNE

I took a bus as far as I could with the money at hand, which got
me to Oregon. When I got off the bus I met this guy. He seemed
real nice, like he cared about me. He wanted to know if I had
some place to stay and I said no, so he invited me to stay with
him. We went back to his house and talked for a few hours. I
told him I was a runaway and he promised not to turn me in.

Things were pretty good for about a week. There were other
girls my age in the same house, and it was fun to have someone
to talk to. Then this guy said he would show me something that
would help me make a lot of money real fast. He said I could

make about $200 for 30 minutes of work. That sounded good so he showed me how to dress and act and talk. Then he taught me the fine art of sex, as he called it. When we first had sex he was gentle, easy, and when it hurt he quit.

One day he said I needed to learn something else that would bring in even more money. I undressed and he said we were going to learn the art of anal sex. I told him no and began to dress. He got mad, took my clothes off, and tied my feet and arms to a small table. He left the room and came back with another guy (a pimp or john—I don't know which). I was scared. Both guys undressed and they joked a while about who would be first, until my pimp told the other guy to go ahead. When he was done, my pimp did the same thing, then told me to clean up and dress because he had some johns ready to pay big bucks to use me. He said if I was good, I could pay him off and leave.

Anyways, I was stuck with this pimp for about three years until he traded me to another guy who had a sex ring going. This new guy was into S&M (sadomasochism). At least with the other pimp I just worked a few hours a day. These new johns were into everything. They used every part of me, two, three, four at a time. You name it and they tried it. It finally got to the point where I couldn't live with myself, so I got some drugs from my pimp. At first I used them once in a while, and then I got hooked and had to turn more tricks to support my habit.

In 1971 I killed my pimp after he beat me. It was self-defense, but I spent the next two years in jail. The guards weren't any different. They used me sexually. For me it was one way to get what I wanted in jail. I got out and went back to the streets on my own, but was even more hooked on drugs and alcohol. A couple years later I had a baby and put him in a foster home before returning to the streets.

∎   ∎   ∎

Suzanne's experiences, starting at age 13, typify the harsh realities of juvenile prostitution. Table 3-3 presents a breakdown of the hazards of prostitution according to three simple criteria: (1) dangers directly affecting a hustler's physical state; (2) psychological pitfalls common to hustling; and (3) environmental or contextual obstacles that pose unique hazards to both the physical and psychological welfare of the prostitute.

Table 3-3:   Hazards of Juvenile Prostitution

Physical Hazards	Psychological Hazards	Environmental Hazards
Drug and alcohol abuse	Drug and alcohol abuse	Drug and alcohol abuse
Infertility	Delinquency stigma	Exploitive foster and
Sexually transmitted dis-	Sleep and eating disor-	group homes
eases	ders	Placement in brothels
Pregnancy	Hysteria	Adult criminals as com-
Cervical cancer	Homicidal rage	panions
Murder	Value replacement	Institutionalization
Genital disfigurement	Emotional abuse	Misguided agency care
Suicide and self-mutila-	Peer pressure	
tion	Gender-disturbed sexual	
Physical assault by ex-	identity	
ploiters		

Life Traits Common to Prostitution

As noted earlier, there are no consistent patterns or profiles that explain why minors are drawn into prostitution. Rather than pursue this line of inquiry, we sought to identify life experiences or traits shared by hustlers, in the hope that such background factors would help explain how and at what point in their development juveniles find themselves part of the hustling subculture.

The most frequent of all experiences is the dysfunctional family. Absent in these homes are nurturing relationships, positive child-rearing practices, and concern for the well-being or happiness of the children; physical and sexual mistreatment is often prevalent. Parents in dysfunctional families are indifferent to their children's development. They may be emotionally and psychologically crippled by their own personal problems; life is so complicated and difficult for them that they are unable to see beyond their own needs to those of their children. Neglect and a lack of supervision are the rule, and conflicts abound at every level as each member of the family seeks to establish status within the domestic hierarchy. For juveniles, who have the least amount of power in the family, freedom from this situation is seen to be in a life on the streets—the essential prerequisite of prostitution.

Incest or other intra-familial sexual abuse is common in the dysfunctional family. It may very well be the predominant life experience of female hustlers, both juvenile and adult. As a catalyst, incest prepares the victim for prostitution in three ways: (1) propels the victim from the family and into a makeshift existence; (2) lowers her self-esteem and inhibitions; and (3) serves as an initiation into a jaded view of sexual behavior. The effects of this traumatic experience endure as a psychological scar. Al, a brothel owner on the East Coast, gave his interpretation of the impact of incest on his hustlers:

> I spent a lot of time at the house talking to the girls. It's been my experience that if you take the 10 or 15 minutes to listen to a girl's problems, she works better. Anyways, I began to notice through our conversations that, for a lot of the girls—I would guess 75 to 80 percent—their first sexual experience was with their father or uncle or some other adult in the family. Also, the ages when it happened seemed to be low.
>
> Something they all had in common was a very low opinion of themselves, and this is why I believe they started in the business; they were there to degrade themselves. More than one told me how she hated her father or uncle or whoever it was who molested her. The hate and guilt these women felt definitely centered around sex, and here they were in a business catering to a man's sexual desires.

Al's observations are particularly germane, for the antipathy toward men expressed by many female hustlers as a result of prior abuse is a recurrent theme. It is as though they use their sexuality as a double-edged weapon; to humiliate themselves and at the same time to deceive male customers.

There is no way to adequately describe the traumatic effects of the incest experience on a child. The following is a poignant example of the deep psychological scars that remained with one young 16-year-old prostitute who suffered this tragic crime. At the age of 14, Kathy was stripping on table tops in bars and later worked for a pimp in Charleston, West Virginia, until her arrest and imprisonment.

KATHY

I never will forget it. I was 10 at the time. We lived in a two-story house, and one morning I was standing on the upstairs porch when I heard a scream. I looked down, and underneath the porch on the patio I saw my father tearing the clothes off my thirteen-year-old sister. I remember running down the stairs screaming—when I got there my father was on top of her yelling for me to leave.

Oh God! I remember the look on my sister's face as she held out her hand for me to help her—but my father was too strong.

When I was twelve, he raped me. God, I hate that man. No matter how many times I wash a day, I always feel dirty.

■   ■   ■

Male hustlers frequently exit a family lacking either a father figure or a positive role model. In these homes, the mother is the dominant parent and provider. This is not to suggest that a matriarchal family is more conducive to male prostitution, but rather that this is a common life experience for male hustlers. The need to reflect a masculine (father) image is a desire expressed by scores of male hustlers. To that end, juveniles seek the company of an attentive male to interact with them in a non-sexual context. Lenny, a 17-year-old prostitute, admits that hustling for him is a means for gaining the affection or attention of adult males:

> *My dad is dead, at least that's what my mother told me. I don't believe her, though. I haven't seen him since I was 4 or 5. When I get dressed up and stand on the corner, I get a lot of cruisers (customers driving around the block).*
>
> *I really like that. It makes me feel good. I have gotten to know a few of them and we ride around together and get high. A couple of times they took me out to dinner, in real nice places, too. I think of my dad. He would have talked to me like they do. They treat me like I'm someone special.*

Both male and female hustlers have a destructive or negative self-image of themselves. Prostitution, alcoholism, drug addiction, and suicide are all classic expressions of this sense of worthlessness and of a futile future. Kiddie pros typically speak with the conviction of worldly experience; having spent a portion of their lives as sexual victims, they project a cynical or indifferent attitude toward life. Beneath this carefully manufactured exterior is insecurity and self-hatred.

Some of these juvenile hustlers reach the stage where abuse, whatever its form, is welcomed or expected. Nancy, a former juvenile prostitute, describes the downward spiral of low self-esteem:

> *Looking back, I imagined myself to be this glamorous thing, having men lust after me. I got caught up in it. I really thought, I finally made it into the glamorous life. I've worked truck stops in North Carolina, South Carolina, Florida—hell I've worked my way out to the West Coast and back.*
>
> *The majority of girls are strung out on drugs. You can't avoid it; prostitution and drugs go hand-in-hand. My own habit slowly*

increased and I turned to more expensive, harder drugs. I didn't realize it then, but now I know the drugs deadened my conscience.

That's how you go on, and of course the more tricks I turned, the more drugs I needed. Most girls can't work the streets or houses and not take something that helps cover up or deaden the feelings prostitution brings out, like hatred and anger, the feeling that you're cheap and foul. People don't realize how expensive these drugs can be. Remember, I was feeding my pimp's habit too. I was booking $1,500 a week working the lot (truck stops), and with all that money, toward the peak of my drug use I was living in an $8-a-night flophouse above a gas station on the lot and owned two pairs of jeans and maybe two tops.

I finally reached a point where I was so empty and dead inside. Feeling pain let me know I was alive. I would go around with these bruises and broken bones (inflicted by her pimp) and people would say, "Oh you poor thing, look at you."

I know that doesn't make sense but the abuse kind of justified what I had been doing. It made it all okay because I was being punished. The whole time I was working all I wanted was to be loved; I just wanted somebody to take care of me because I couldn't take care of myself.

In the face of constant victimization, a juvenile hustler can succumb to self-destructive measures such as using drugs and inviting violence in the form of beatings or suicide.

The overwhelming majority of these juvenile hustlers are runaways. Runaways have two choices: learn how to survive on their own for extended periods of time, or submit to state supervision and institutionalization. Consider the following scenario. A 14-year-old female's stepfather is in the habit of making overt sexual advances. Her mother, rather than risk losing the family's "breadwinner," blames the daughter for provoking the stepfather. The girl knows that if she reports the incidents to the police, the already fragile family structure may disintegrate. In addition, the victim is aware that she may then be turned over to the welfare or social service department for placement in a state institution or a foster home to live with strangers. But she also realizes that some action must be taken promptly before the offender seeks her out again. For many juveniles in this no-win situation, running away and hustling becomes the only practical solution.

In addition to coming from a dysfunctional family, juvenile hustlers share other traits such as academic failure, disillusionment with and betrayal by parents or protective service agencies, narcissistic personalities, and learning disorders. All of these characteristics, however, derive from the effects of an exploitive family on the victim's frame of mind and cognitive development. These characteristics have no genetic imprint; they merely reflect the events or conditions that helped transform the minor into a prostitute. They also help explain how a juvenile's sense of self-worth can be diminished and the value of the human body depreciated through constant victimization. Given enough time, reinforcement, and repetitiveness, the dehumanizing environment of prostitution erodes a juvenile's confidence in his or her ability to make things happen or shape the future in a way that is not self-destructive. The irony is that hustling becomes a very logical, even reasonable, alternative to a greater evil, the exploitive family.

Conclusion

Hustling qualifies as the most dangerous occupation in the commercial child sex markets. That so many minors are trafficked for purposes of prostitution indicates that something is radically lacking in the response of society at large and the criminal justice system in particular. From the victim's perspective, this situation is sometimes aggravated by the laissez-faire attitudes of indifferent or unresponsive protective agencies.

The dynamics of juvenile hustling described in this chapter are common to kiddie pros throughout the world, from the street hustlers in Boise, Idaho, to the "Rent Boys" of London's meat rack district, to the prepubertal females working in Bangkok brothels. Underage hustlers are exposed to a host of extraordinary hazards and are susceptible to adult manipulation by exploiters such as pimps, madams, and customers.

Rehabilitating and retrieving juvenile hustlers from the life-style of prostitution requires a wide range of services and resources, including medical care, education, detoxification or drug rehabilitation, intensive therapy and counseling, and upgrading of job skills for placement in legitimate employment markets. A practical exit mechanism, including assistance in establishing a new residence, is required. Converting street values into acceptable behavior is an arduous process that entails rebuilding a hustler's self-worth. Most social service agencies have neither the resources nor statutory mandates to meet these needs. The best that can be hoped for currently is equitable, humane treatment in the distribution of limited services.[4]

Before hustlers can be helped, however, they must be found. A number of conventional and unorthodox sources of information regarding the whereabouts of these minors can be tapped. Physicians should be required to report all cases of sexually transmitted diseases to a central state agency, and such information should be shared with local social service agencies. Professionals in the human services whose positions place them in constant contact with juveniles should endeavor to identify children whose home life transmits the warning signs noted earlier, and an appropriate response should then be fashioned. Child care workers who operate shelters for runaways must do more than reunite families; as points of sanctuary, they deal daily with children who have either direct involvement in the sexual trafficking network or know of specific instances. Last, but least promising, adult bookstore employees can be encouraged to tell it like it is.

Inquiries should also be made to identify the number and location of part-time juvenile hustlers, in addition to the thousands of veteran underage prostitutes working in the United States. For the part-time hustler, prostitution is incidental—an immediate means to an end. Part-timers participate at their own discretion and basically on their own terms. Mobility, freelance status, and infrequent participation are the general trademarks of the part-time hustler.

Regardless of whether their involvement in prostitution is transitory or long-lasting, juvenile hustlers can be sure of finding enough customers. For the moment, the status of procurers, hustlers, and brothels is unchanged and has not been seriously challenged, although experimental diversion programs financed by the private sector and state agencies are gradually being implemented to stem the flow of juveniles participating in prostitution. A disturbing new development that must be dealt with is Acquired Immune Deficiency Syndrome (AIDS). This disease is a double-edged sword in that its spread will be fostered by the anonymity inherent in the victim-exploiter relationship, while at the same time it will drive up demand and price for sex with a "clean" minor.

Endnotes

1. For a more detailed analysis of the motivations and life-styles of gay adolescent hustlers, see *Adolescent Prostitution: A Study of Sexual Exploitation, Etiological Factors and Runaway Behavior, with a Focus on Adolescent Male Prostitutes* (San Francisco: Urban and Rural Systems Associates, 1982).
2. This particular incident was corroborated, in terms of basic facts, by several eyewitnesses but never reported to the police by the adult victim.
3. We are greatly indebted to detective Thomas D. Horan for his willingness to share information from his state study of sexual exploitation of children, in addition to the case titled, "A Night on the Lot."
4. A few of the community-based programs attempting to assist juvenile prostitutes include Children of the Night (California), Martin House (Illinois), Valley Youth House (Pennsylvania), and New Connections (West Virginia).

Chapter 4

PIMPS

> *How do I know these kids are worth money? 'Cause I been living off them for years, that's how. All kinds of people will buy them. You wouldn't believe it. What do I care if they want to throw away a couple of hundred dollars to screw some stupid 13-year-old? I could care less, so long as they give me their money.*
>
> PHIL, A 46-YEAR-OLD PIMP

A pimp is someone who makes prostitutes available for adult clients. In the case of minors, a pimp will actively seek out and recruit juveniles for the purpose of soliciting them either for customers or for placement in some type of sheltered setting. This type of pimp's success hinges on the susceptibility of his victims to manipulation and coercion.

The majority of men interviewed who specialize in procuring minors—most of them female and some as young as 11 years old—have never been investigated, successfully prosecuted, or convicted of pandering or of charges pertaining to sexual exploitation. Many obstacles impede investigation and prosecution. The difficulties of building a strong court case against a pimp are magnified by the unreliability of underage witnesses. Fearing—for excellent reasons—retribution at the hands of a procurer, a victim often prefers to endure ongoing exploitation rather than face the uncertain prospects of a witness stand or the distinct possibility that the accused will be acquitted. The lack of inter-agency cooperation in the sharing of leads and intelligence data benefits the procurer, who is usually low-profile, mobile, and street-wise. These problems stifle creative investigative efforts within police or social service departments that emphasize conformity to standard operating procedures.

In this chapter the methods, attitudes, and values of pimps, as

90

well as the effects of a procurer's activities on the victim, are examined. First, however, we must lay to rest the notion that adult procurers are exclusively male, hard-core offenders. To the contrary, our facts indicate that virtually all manner of adults solicit juveniles for prostitution. Parents rent out their daughters to brothels, minors recruit other juveniles into hustling, and legal guardians or caretakers devise sex rings for purposes of encouraging prostitution.[1]

Functions of a Procurer

Pimps are in the business of providing sexual services to a relatively discreet audience. Some pimps even sell themselves to make money, as in the case of those who cater to homosexual customers. Pimps must fulfill a variety of functions in order to be successful in the relatively competitive child sex markets. These functions or roles are logical extensions of their occupation.

A pimp who is committed to prostitution creates a fantasy environment for his potential victims. He showers affection and attention on the female minor, keeping an otherwise frightening world at bay and forming a family or mate bond with his victim. For a while the juvenile is made to feel important, secure, and at ease with her new surroundings. The most proficient procurers are psychological magicians who can preserve a fantasy of warmth and concern for their wards while they in fact victimize them. After months or years of familiarity, it is possible for the underage hustler to feel a deep affinity for her exploiter. This attachment helps a pimp deal with such occupational uncertainties as brutality and drug addiction, neither of which is conducive to a stable working relationship. For many hustlers, the illusion of being loved or wanted is better than having no binding human relationship at all or facing the prospect of being abandoned to the streets. Building a relatively structured relationship with a victim is, therefore, a prime objective of child procurers, for it is the means by which a juvenile's allegiance is transferred to her new caretaker.

A pimp's second function is to protect his prostitutes from violent customers and threatening situations such as arrest. For conniving pimps such as Brian, this function has a double edge to it, particularly when violence is part of a pimp's repertoire:

> *Sometimes I'd tell a trick to rough one up if I thought she was going to run. I'd be waiting outside the door, and when she screamed from this guy hitting her, I'd run in with my gun and shoot him (with blank bullets) in front of her. He'd stagger out of the room and disappear. I'd say, "See? I'll always be there to protect you, but now you're part of a murder."*

Should the pimp fail to be present at an assault, his hustler is likely to be brutally beaten or murdered by a sadistic customer. The loss of a hustler to violence, however, means nothing more to a pimp than diminished revenue and temporary inconvenience.

Many pimps provide false identification papers to minimize the risk of arrest and bond money to avoid income lost during incarceration. The function of creating "job security" for his hustlers is important to a pimp who manages several juveniles. Not all under-age prostitutes possess these papers and not all pimps know how to acquire them, but bogus documents are an asset to ambitious procurers. Posting bail for a hard-working hustler is one more way a pimp can make his prostitutes feel appreciated, although it has nothing to do with sentiment or compassion on his part. For a pimp, it is simply better for business to have his hustler on the streets.

Because few jurisdictions are likely to tolerate overt prostitution by minors, a procurer must function as liaison between a community's public morality and its private sexual appetite. To insulate his hustlers from official harassment, a pimp tries to pay off anyone who might cause trouble, such as the police or local gangsters, and to accurately gauge the possibility of arrest versus anticipated profits. To that end, a competent procurer may decide to survey the terrain before sending his prostitutes into a new area. This reconnaissance is intended to ferret out potential trouble from the local authorities and to determine the sort of reception his under-age hustlers will receive when working there.

A pimp also supplies the basic needs of his hustlers, such as food, clothing, transient shelter, drugs, and entertainment. Even these needs, however, are grudgingly conceded and provided in minimum quantities on the premise that without them a juvenile is incapable of working. Such fundamental needs also include medical treatment for venereal disease and hospitalization for abortions or pregnancies. In the latter case, a juvenile may be asked to put her baby up for adoption; in extreme situations, the infant may be taken from the mother and sold by the pimp.

One final role, described in detail in the following section, involves the period of training known as apprenticeship. It is during these days or weeks that a juvenile learns the realities of prostitution; a pimp must blend the fantasy relationship he created for his victim with the practicalities of making money.

Recruitment and Apprenticeship

"Recruitment" refers to the methods or techniques used to induct a minor into the game of prostitution. Depending, as we shall see, on a procurer's style, the methods can range from sexual seduction to physical force reinforced by drugs and blackmail. The type of recruiting techniques used illustrates a pimp's style or personality, and such behavior is persistent within the context of "turning out" juveniles—that is, making them into prostitutes.

Apprenticeship is the process by which a minor is taught how to be a proficient hustler. The transformation from naivete to sexual sophistication consists of the following elements:

1. *Sexual initiation:* The victim is introduced to an assortment of sexual activities as both participant and observer. Emphasis is placed on performance, satisfaction, prices, and the rapid turnover of customers.
2. *Appearance:* Language, dress, grooming, and demeanor are demonstrated and rehearsed in order to acclimate the juvenile to her new role.
3. *Conditioned attitudes:* To achieve the proper frame of mind for prostitution, the hustler must become dependent upon her procurer. The persuasive or forceful conditioning of a juvenile's attitudes and behavior may, in some instances, include tattooing, scarring, or the bestowal of a street name. These features help orient the victim's mind toward her commitment to prostitution.
4. *Tricks of the trade:* The juvenile is taught how to recognize undercover police, how to proposition customers, and how to victimize customers. The latter may be accomplished primarily through theft, armed robbery, or the use of blackmail.

Apprenticeships are also essential for some pimps, particularly those who place their hustlers in sheltered settings where on-the-job training occurs. Since recruitment is the mainspring of procuring, our attention shall focus on pimping styles. We have identified several basic types of pimps: "sweet mac" or "player," "gorilla," business manager, motorcycle gang, freelance procurer, parent, and another minor. Each has a fairly distinctive method of operation and each plays an important part in the ongoing sexual victimization of minors (see Table 4-1).

Sweet Mac, or Player

Willie, a 32-year-old pimp, exemplifies this type procurer:

> *Kids today are fascinated by the material things. Sitting on the hood of my ride and flashing, I'll have 30 girls who will talk to me while you in your Ford maybe will have one girl. Not only girls but boys will go out of their way to meet me. I don't need to be overbearing or use violence in copping anybody. It's hard to get young kids to get in your car to go for a ride but it's not hard to get them high, especially if it's free. By making this a habit, maybe three or four times a week, I can eventually have a heavy hand in directing their future.*
>
> *You'd be surprised what you can accomplish by getting a kid to drink liquor, smoke pot, or toot a little cocaine. Then start putting $20 in a 14- or 15-year-old's pocket. You'll find out how much influence I have. Man, I've pulled up in front of a house in my ride and the kid would jump off the porch running, and I'd hear their parents yelling, "You get in that car, don't ever come back!" Most of them don't.*

The sweet mac pimp is the archetypal procurer, the street equivalent of a child psychiatrist whose expertise lies in the study of human nature. Traditionally portrayed as a gentleman of leisure surrounded by the trappings of success, the sweet mac, or player, is a versatile manipulator of juveniles. The more successful players enjoy an extravagant life-style entirely out of proportion to their labors. Success and achievement are measured by possessions: an expensive wardrobe, a luxury car (ride), a jewelry collection, and an ample amount of discretionary income to be spent on entertainment, drugs, and similar diversions.

Sweet mac pimps may recruit both adult and juvenile hustlers. The dubious art of procuring is reflected in its jargon. Prostitution

Table 4-1 Pimp Profiles

	Sweet Mac/Player	Gorilla	Business Manager	Motorcycle Gangs	Parent Pimp	Juveniles
Clientele	Street trade	Street trade	Middle- and upper-class professionals	Street trade	Street trade	Street trade
Recruitment Methods	Glitter trap; seduction process	Purchase or trade; blackmail; kiddie pros as recruiters	Purchase from parents; lease or on-call agreement	Parties; drugs; intimidation	Prostitute their own children	Drugs, parties, and blackmail
Control Techniques	Withholding of affection; psychological intimidation	Direct supervision; blackmail; violence; fear	Threat of exposure; voluntary decision to hustle	Gang rapes; drugs; bounties; violence	Force; emotional coercion and deprivation	Blackmail with pornography
Training	Apprenticeship; initiation by a paid trick	Drugs; sexual assault; initiation by a pimp	On-the-job experience	Apprenticeship	On-the-job experience	Apprenticeship
Placement	Street; brothels (bookings)	Street; motel; apartment	Private homes; motels	Club-supported brothels; streets	Streets and brothels	Streets; apartments; motels; truck stops
Evasion Techniques	Bribes; relocation; low profile	Payoffs and bribes; false identification papers	Payoffs; lack of customer complaints; pimp's status in community	Transporting of hustlers out of state; false identification papers	Denial and relocation	Change of schools and false identification papers
Income Sources	Prostitution; pornography; drugs; legitimate investments	Prostitution; extortion; sale of kiddie pros; pornography; blackmail	Prostitution; pornography; fraud; legitimate investments	Prostitution; drugs and arms sales; extortion	Welfare; occasional temporary labor; prostitution	Prostitution; drug sales; theft; robbery

is the "game" or "life," recruitment is known as "catching or trapping," and one's ability to be a successful entrepreneur of hustlers depends on "flash," which is simply the facade of glamour presented to a potential victim. Cars, drugs, and excess pocket money are some of the ingredients of flash, but an inflated self-image is its foundation. Without resorting to outright violence, a sweet mac pimp can use flash and prior experience with other minors to move a victim gradually into a state of total dependency.

Such methodical planning is part of the "glitter trap"—the lure of excitement, possessions, companionship, and freedom. Offered in the name of friendship, the glitter trap can gradually wean a victim away from family and peers. Unable to recognize this subtle form of exploitation as an immediate threat to her well-being, the minor female may sever all ties with the past and accept the procurer as a surrogate parent or lover. A sweet mac with a chameleonlike personality can make the trap almost irresistible. As an excellent judge of character weaknesses in troubled youths, he offers them a path of least resistance from their problems. Consider Ben's tactics:

> Drugs and alcohol are exciting to a young kid. It offers a way for them to rebel not only against their parents but also society in general. I found in a lot of cases communication in the family was nonexistent, and of course the drugs allowed me to get the kid in a position to talk. Naturally, I get them to talk about their problems. Generally they were concerned about divorces or problems with their parents, remarriage and, of course, parents always telling them what to do. These type of kids, if you set it up right, will go at the drop of a hat. They are that easy to recruit.

In many ways the glitter trap is similar to the recruitment process of extreme religious cults. Alienation from society, un-questioned acceptance, and support and reinforcement of an alternative life-style characterize both processes. The victim is deceived into obedience by a self-serving entrepreneur who, in the case of the sweet mac, is quick to capitalize on the opportunity.

A sweet mac or player recruits and "turns out" (introduces to the trade) juveniles through three basic methods: seduction, acceptance of a "dowry," and psychological or physical force. During the seduction process the victim's sexual values are replaced by those of the pimp. As described in the following stages, the player carefully orchestrates the settings, emotions, and events that steer a victim toward prostitution.

The Seduction Process

Step 1: Entertain a girl with parties for several days. Make no demands on her, emphasize spontaneity and the freedom of being away from home, and encourage the victim to focus exclusively on self-pleasure. A favorite tactic is to take a prospective hustler to visit other cities or states.

Step 2: While on the road, the girl is bedazzled with spending money and what it can buy, such as drugs or new clothes. At some point in their travels, the pimp suggests they spend more time together.

Step 3: To make this possible, he moves the unsuspecting juvenile into an apartment on the premise that she can proceed to get her life in order. She may share the apartment with the pimp's "booster lady" or "wife-in-law."

Step 4: The booster lady, acting as a big sister, reassures the girl that she is among friends. At the same time she wears down the victim's fears of having sex with adults. This is accomplished, in part, through conversations, showing of pornography, and having the juvenile watch the older woman entertain tricks at the apartment.

Step 5: Several weeks pass. By now the girl is accustomed to the presence of customers and has witnessed a variety of sexual acts. Finally, she is introduced to her first customer. By prior arrangement with the pimp, a customer may be paid to be kind, loving, and gentle with the apprehensive female. At that point the initiation is over. The victim is now a member of the sweet mac's working stable (family of hustlers).

Variations of this tragic theme are common. In the following narrative, Taylor, a veteran player, explains his own version of the seduction process:

> *I've copped them out of the Y or places like Burger Chef. Listen, you walk into, let's say McDonald's, and tell the kid working, "Girl, don't you know you can get more than $3.25 an hour as cute as you are?" Then slip a hundred dollar bill down in her uniform, go out to the parking lot, let that sun roof back, turn the tape player on— just sit where she can see you. She'll be out of there and in the car in 15 minutes.*
>
> *I would sign up for swimming lessons at the YMCA. When I found what I was looking for, I'd tell her how pretty she was and what I thought of her body, and offer to take her out to dinner, all done with finesse. When she comes outside and sees that big*

Lincoln, you take her to the best steak house and pay the tab with a hundred dollar bill. After you do that four or five times you'll notice a change in her.

From there it's simple. All this time you've been expressing a desire for her and you show her by taking her to bed. When the time is right, you explain what all you can do for her and how you can take her to New York and put her in an apartment and buy her nice things. Most of all, you explain how you make this all come about. Four out of five you won't get, but the one that you do get makes it all worthwhile.

You explain to her how much fun that [sex] was, and didn't she know that if I was a john she could have made $200 for doing something fun and just that quick. Then you tell her how much we could have. You always say "we," by her doing something that simple three maybe four nights a week. All the time I was telling her how pretty she was and how much fun we could be having.

Payment of "Choose Money"

A second approach to recruitment of a prostitute is acceptance of a payment by the sweet mac. In this method, which is far more unusual than the seduction process, juveniles who wish to work for a specific player are expected to pay the procurer "choose money"—the rough equivalent of a dowry. This is a form of down payment required as proof that the hustler can indeed earn enough money to warrant a pimp's attention. It is also a way for a juvenile to buy her way out of an existing working relationship with a pimp. Unfortunately, because of market demand, players who would not otherwise waste time "babysitting" underage hustlers apparently are willing to accept choose money as a sign of good faith. That is, a sweet mac such as William is likely to invest his time and energies in underage prostitutes because the substantial profits tend to outweigh the somewhat predictable problems of manipulating or managing a stable of minors:

I was in an after-hours joint in Michigan, maybe eight or nine years ago, when I noticed this real young white girl walking around. At first I thought she was retarded or something, because she acted like she was in some kind of daze. She really looked out of place. Anyways, it turns out she had run from the pimp who had turned her out and she wanted to choose me. I told her to come up with $300 trap money and she did. Because of her age and constantly being flimflammed, she didn't have any concept of money. I would have to watch her all the time or else she would give a ton of it [sex] free, but she wasn't a bad investment. She bought me at least one

Cadillac. To get the most use out of her, we went shopping and I spent the trap money on clothes and a few wigs that really set her off.

She turned out to be a pretty normal kid. Every now and then I'd let her play with a friend's kid; they'd play dolls and things like that. The day after I accepted her trap money, I remember walking down the street and passing this drug store window. She had stopped and wanted me to buy her what was inside; it turned out to be a doll about her size. After about six months another pimp stole her or she ran off, I forget. Anyways, starting that young she's got to be dead or close to it by now.

There is no simple explanation of why a hustler would consent to pay choose money. A sweet mac's reputation, flash, personality, or managerial skills may account for part of the attraction. The idea that the juvenile is choosing the lesser of two evils by working for a well-known or popular procurer rather than alone on the streets without protection seems to be a more plausible hypothesis. Her exploiter is a passive recipient of a veritable gold mine in the realm of sexual exploitation. The hustler, in other words, volunteers her services in order to achieve a greater measure of security in a dangerous marketplace.

Coercive Procuring

Aggressive players will resort to psychological or physical coercion when seduction fails or choose money is not offered. Although they may not go to quite the extremes of brutality employed by other types of pimps, players tread a fine line between outright force and verbal persuasion. One sweet mac, for instance, after having spent several days entertaining a prospective juvenile who had run away from home, would rely on an implicit threat of blackmail:

I'd tell her we were broke and make it clear how she could get us home. Reminding her that she's already given it up for free gets her thinking. Of course I make it very clear that if she doesn't, I'll call her parents and tell them their daughter is a thousand miles from home and partying with a black man; that generally works with upper-class kids, but usually for only short periods of time.

The type of coercion used can be adjusted to fit the situation. Sometimes a reluctant victim who cares for her pimp but not the idea of prostitution may require an extra incentive to help make the transition to hustling. The threat of physical abuse or the withholding of affection by a player are two of the more common coercive techniques, even though neither may be exercised in reality. It is enough, in many instances, to simply plant the idea of immediate harm in the victim's mind:

> *Once I've spent all that money and time on a girl, taken care of her, she owes me. I tell her that what I'm asking isn't much. I tell her I'm going to put her on the stroll with one of my ladies and she had better come back with X amount of money or else. My lady tells her what "or else" means, and generally this works. If it doesn't, I might get physical, but if she leaves I let it go at that because she'll be nothing but trouble the whole time I have her.*

The income derived by a sweet mac's stable of kiddie pros may be diverted to outside investments such as a partnership in a nightclub, drug sales, or the purchase of a massage parlor. Known as "fall-back money," it enables a player to prepare for future hard times by recycling a portion of his wealth into such long-term activities or businesses. By rotating his hustlers to new worksites, with occasional bookings in brothels, a sweet mac can minimize risks and maximize profits. Much of this revenue, however, is quickly spent on personal possessions and entertainment.

The sweet mac procurer is an opportunist. His fortune and fame depend on a considerable amount of expertise as a seducer, attractor, or coercer of vulnerable juveniles. Success, in the words of a seasoned player, is oftentimes a matter of attitude:

> *Everything is devoted to the game (pandering), because if played right, it is beautiful. I see myself as a teacher. I'd find girls who wanted to be turned out but just didn't know it, or wouldn't admit it, so naturally I'd help them.*

Players armed with this sort of working philosophy can make an indelible impression on minors who are unable to recognize the subtleties of exploitation. A sweet mac's sophisticated approach to procuring, moreover, stands in marked contrast to the tactics used by other types of pimps.

Gorilla Pimps

Ramone, a 39-year-old pimp, is not atypical of his genre:

> *I remember this one 11-year-old girl I bought. God she hated me for what I did. She was truly beautiful. One night she was giving*

me some shit so I set her up in a room with six men. Jesus, did they
ever abuse her.

As evidenced by his street name and the above quote, the gorilla
pimp has a propensity to use force, fear, and coercion to recruit
and control hustlers. He acquires potential hustlers in the following
three ways:

1. *Direct purchase:* Moving temporarily into a slum district, the
pimp locates and befriends a drug-addicted or alcoholic parent. An
offer is made for the daughter. One soft-spoken procurer explained
that he had purchased an 11-year-old girl from a father in exchange
for a used car, and that he later acquired a second minor for $200.

2. *Parental pressure:* A gorilla pimp may prefer to use his wife
or the mother of a child for purposes of recruitment:

> *I worked on Helen first, the one I was legally married to. Told*
> *her how much money we could make with her kid. Finally she*
> *agreed and all I had to do was keep her (Helen) drunk. We started*
> *out with nude pictures when she was 11 and I turned her out*
> *[started her in prostitution] a year later. The other mother-daugh-*
> *ter act I met up north. I told her she could travel with me but she*
> *had to turn her kid out. She agreed and told her kid, "Do it or I'll*
> *knock your damn brains out!"*

3. *Seduction and blackmail:* This approach to procuring involves
either deceptive practices similar to those employed by the seductive player or outright blackmail. With an experienced nucleus of
underage hustlers at hand, a pimp can use them to act as recruiters:

> *After about a year and a half, these two kids really got good at*
> *recruiting. Influencing someone else to get into it (prostitution)*
> *tickled them to death. At first I'd have the girls bring their potentials*
> *to the apartment and I'd brainwash them or buy them clothes—*
> *even use fear to get them a few times. Later I found a better way.*

These underage procurers or recruiters serve essentially the same
functions as the sweet mac's booster lady. They indoctrinate other
juveniles into hustling and put them through an apprenticeship as
the need arises.

The "better way" mentioned above involves blackmail. A gorilla
pimp realizes that not every girl, no matter how badly she may
want clothes, money, or affection, will permit herself to be turned
out. Even the constant use of fear produces diminishing returns; a
juvenile's hatred for the pimp may prove stronger than her fear of

retaliation. Terry, a firm believer in the direct approach, briefly described one way he would force a victim, brought to his attention by other hustlers, into prostitution. After drugging the female at his apartment, he would allow a friend to abuse her sexually. In the meantime he either videotaped or photographed the event:

> *These young girls didn't depend on me. I depended on them, so I had to have a gimmick; mine was blackmail. I'd show the girl those pictures and say, "Do you want your mommy or daddy to see this?" or I'd tell her I was going to pass them out at school. If you don't have a gimmick like force or blackmail, you can't keep these kids. After I got them started, I'd put them on call for a couple of weeks. If her parents did find out, I was long gone. Before I left the area I'd take the pictures to some other pimp and ask for a couple thousand dollars.*

The gorilla pimp is violent, scheming, and capable of extensive planning and organization in order to avoid arrest. Terry, for example, traveled around the country with two families composed of two adult prostitutes and their 11- and 12-year-old daughters, who were later turned out. He was legally married to one prostitute and possessed a forged marriage license for the other. In addition, he periodically recruited juveniles for on-call, part-time work. Being on call means a minor is expected to be available, on very short notice, to hustle on weekends in other cities. The parents of these juveniles are invariably the last to learn of their daughter's behavior because they accept at face value her explanations, such as staying at a friend's house overnight.

Because of his particular methods of operation, a gorilla pimp must be extremely circumspect in matters of business. An astute procurer, consequently, will employ a set of standard operating procedures to minimize his risks when working a new location. These procedures can be loosely summarized as a series of decisions designed to ease the burden of making hustlers available for customers:

1. A careful reconnaissance of an unfamiliar city is performed, complete with referrals from inmates or street people as to the pitfalls and benefits of the local sex trade.
2. Assuming that the area appears safe to work, a procurer circulates news about his stable and introduces his adult prostitutes to a select group of people, such as bartenders. They, in turn, may receive a kickback or commission for

sending customers to him. If his adult hustlers do not experience any problems, the procurer may decide to promote his juvenile prostitutes. He may show nude or suggestive photos of these juveniles to entice prospective johns.

3. To ensure minimal interference, the procurer pays off the "right people" with a lump-sum payment or other gratuities, possibly including sex with one or more of the underage hustlers.

4. The adult prostitutes are placed on the street. Familiar with the routine of hustling, they know what is expected of them and require little supervision. Juveniles, however, are a different matter. More often than not, they will be put in a motel or brothel so that customers can be brought directly to them, or they may be dropped off to work at a truck stop.

5. After several weeks of shuttling and escorting the kiddie pros to and from different worksites, the gorilla pimp shuts down his operation and moves to a new city before the local vice or juvenile officers have enough time to build a case.

The gorilla pimp practices a violent form of procuring. His hatred and contempt for females is so complete and so ingrained that it permeates his life-style. The hustlers (adults and minors) who work for him have little hope for a better future and few expectations of being rescued by a protective state agency. Knowing that the gorilla pimp is willing to resort to murder or blackmail helps maintain a state of relative "harmony" within the stable of hustlers. The precarious existence of his hustlers is of no particular concern to the pimp. After all, as Marcus candidly admitted, the pimp is the person most responsible for their exploitive predicament:

> *I destroyed them. I know I destroyed them. I've tried to keep up to date on a few and I know they're dope addicts, alcoholics, or just common whores. Whatever their fantasy was about life, I destroyed it because whenever they get with someone they love, they say, "Look at what I was. Look what I've done."*

The following case is from a dialogue with a 55-year-old gorilla pimp. His statements are noteworthy for the insights they provide regarding the procurer's character, values, and motivations. Furthermore, they reveal an extraordinary callousness and indifference to the fate of juvenile hustlers. This particular gorilla pimp was expelled as a teenager from his home by an abusive stepfather and forced to survive on the streets. He has spent at least 15 years in various correctional facilities in several states. Some would argue that his harsh treatment of underage prostitutes is the result of a lifetime of personal trauma, beginning with an abusive family and continuing on into a career as an adult criminal.

A PIMP'S LIFE

I was working a couple of girls at one point and I went into a bar and grill. There was a woman in there with her daughter. She was loud, real loud, telling everybody she was from North Carolina and looking for a place to stay. I sent my old lady over to talk with her, and she invited her and the kid home with us.

Her daughter was fully developed. When I first saw her I told my old lady, "Hey, there's money." At that time my old lady had a 10-year-old daughter. I didn't use her for tricks then but did later on; when she was about 12 I got her started in the life.

This woman was an alcoholic, so I kept her drunk and worked on the kid, who was about 11 years old; I told her how she could benefit from prostitution. I broke her in myself. I'd use fear and feed her drugs. We'd tell her she could get money, get some new clothes; stuff her mother couldn't give her. Also, she'd be well protected.

In a few days she was ready. My old lady told her about sex. How to trick men, put on an act like she's enjoying it. If a broad is right she can have a john out in 10 minutes. I'd teach these 11- and 12-year-old kids how to go about it. Get 'em undressed, get 'em on the bed, get 'em off, then get them out of there. These johns are usually drunk or high, sometimes violent.

My girls loved me. I'd give them anything they wanted. Of course, they were afraid of me too. Scared to death. They had a right to be. I shot a couple of people in front of them. I shot a guy at a pot party, a sex party in Cleveland. A fight broke out, he grabbed a chair, and I shot him in the chest. These kids turned into real tough broads with all that violence.

The average whore is a tough broad. There's no game you can play on them. Start 'em at age 12 or 13 and in four, five years they go through a real change in attitude. I made my best money off the real young ones. Guys are always asking me, "Hey man, you got any young stuff?" Once these kids get the facts of life under their belt, that's it. After that you just take care of business.

■   ■   ■

The Business Manager

Richard, a 46-year-old pimp, exemplifies this type of procurer:

> *My customers are not going to tramp the streets looking for some sleezy pimp in a low-rider Cadillac with dingleberries hanging on the rearview mirror. They're not going to be caught dead on the street even associating with this type of person.*

The self-styled business manager is a memorable character. His type stands in marked contrast to the gorilla and sweet mac pimps. He is an entrepreneur, oftentimes the product of a middle-class or possibly upper-class background. Equipped with a college diploma and occupying a solid niche in the local business community, the business manager enjoys a reputation as an upstanding, well-bred citizen, as exemplified by Lee's background:

> *I am from an upper-middle-class family. My father graduated from Dartmouth, Phi Beta Kappa, and was an executive vice-president for a major corporation. Upper-class for me means making in excess of $75,000 a year. Of course, you can't belong to just any country club; it has to be the "right" club or church. My education included 14 years of private tutorial lessons in art. I've been to all the right prep schools and summer camps. I've attended five different colleges. In essence, I've had everything a young man needs to succeed in life.*

Violence, drugs, flashing, blackmail, or an elaborate seduction process are not the tactics of the business manager. This pimp caters to the desires of a wealthier clientele. Because these customers have their own reputations to protect, the business manager is insulated from the risk of exposure. His customers have too much to lose by turning him over to the police, including their social standing or jobs within the community. A business manager specializes in providing the following illicit sexual services: (1) prostitutes—adult and juvenile (primarily females); (2) adult and child pornography with models recruited from the local community; and (3) special requests—mother-daughter or group sex.

Exorbitant fees are charged for these services. For example, an evening of sex with a 13- or 14-year-old girl can cost up to $500, particularly if she is clean, free of disease, white, and attractive. If the customer wants a set of pornographic photographs of his encounter as a "souvenir," an additional $100 or $200 may be tacked onto the final bill. The wealthy few who are willing to pay the business manager's inflated prices do so for basically three reasons. First, the quality of a business manager's "merchandise" is usually superior to that available on the streets. His child prostitutes are not hard-core street hustlers but rather minors who are leased by their parents to the business manager for occasional tricks on a short-term basis. They are more likely to be sexually naive, free of venereal disease, and thus more attractive to customers. Second, a business manager is discrete; his high prices insure his confidentiality. As an agent, he negotiates prices and makes all of the necessary arrangements between the customer and the juvenile. And third, the sexual demand for juveniles is apparently so great that a business manager can set his own market prices. Well-to-do clients, in particular, are expected to pay more for their pleasures.

A business manager uses his legitimate investments and associations as a means for making contacts with new customers. The illicit revenue from pimping (or pornography) is laundered through legal investments with the aid of a cooperative accountant. For the more successful, the outcome of such diverse financial activities is, in the words of one middle-age business manager, "the best of both worlds: a solid credit line with the banks and a steady cash flow under the table. The more I succeed at one, the better off I am with the other. I'm locked into my community. I got a class nightclub, a laundromat, and corporate stocks. What else is there?"

Unlike the sweet mac and gorilla pimps, a business manager does not have to resort to trickery or force to recruit child hustlers, because some parents are willing to lease their daughters to him. One pimp explained that his friends in a local credit union referred him to financially strapped parents who might be interested in his sexual proposition. Richard, another pimp, has his own method for persuading part-time female hustlers to turn out their daughters:

> I'd tell them, "Let's have lunch." We'd meet and I'd say, "Listen, if you and your daughter want to turn tricks, we can go from $100 for you to $500 for you and the kid." If she agreed, she'd ask the kid, not me. The parents made the proposition.

> *I would meet the kid, though, to make sure she was willing and the mother wasn't lying. I'd point blank put it to the kid what is to be expected. I'd tell her, "Now honey, this is the way it is. I've got a businessman who likes young girls. He'll want to go to bed with you. He'll want you to take all of your clothes off. He'll want to put his hands on you, but you know you can handle that. And your mom will be there and the guy will do the same to her. It's up to you. Do you want to go along with it?"*

Greed and the desire to maintain a certain standard of living are the two principal reasons why parents allow men like Richard to persuade them to solicit their own children. Richard knows this, too:

> *The tightness of the economy brings people's morals down to a dealable level. I can deal with these people because they need money. Who the hell wants to see the tax man pull up to their home in a van and start carrying their furniture out or some repossession man coming with a wrecker and sneaking their old Cadillac out of the front yard? All this in front of the neighbors.*
>
> *Parents do this [turn out their children] to save their reputations, their homes. I'd also deal with divorcees that have lived in style for ten years and their old man dumps them. Now they're in some damn housing project telling their kids, it's okay, it's going to be okay.*

To protect his many investments, the business manager pimp retains an attorney, an accountant, and incriminating evidence as insurance against a parent or customer who threatens to press charges against him. Business managers do not like to be labeled as pimps or procurers. Nevertheless, they are essentially no different from the sweet mac or gorilla in terms of sexual exploitation. Their profits are some child's loss. Cut from the same fabric as other pimps, business managers offer a higher quality of service to discriminating customers who are often involved in the legal, financial, religious, and moral affairs of a community.

Motorcycle Gangs

Paul is a 29-year-old motorcycle gang member:

> *I'm still very surprised how easy it is to pick up girls to belong to the club. Drugs were the main thing, like speed, PCP, that stuff. Usually the girls wouldn't be attracted to the club unless they were pretty bored at home. We offered them a different life-style.*

Four major motorcycle gangs are involved in juvenile prostitution: the Pagans on the East Coast, the Bandidos in the Southwest, the Outlaws in the South, and Hell's Angels on the West Coast. (Not included are ultra-violent, right-wing groups that specialize in racist brutality.[2]) Each of the four major motorcycle gangs operates and exercises control within a broad geographic region, although they all maintain chapters scattered around the nation.

A newly initiated member to a club is sometimes rewarded with a female whose primary function is to make money for him. In the case of underage females, this can include hustling, stripping, selling drugs, and related criminal activities. A portion of the juvenile's income goes into the club's treasury. Female juveniles, some of them from middle- or upper-class families, are lured into the club life for a variety of reasons. As one male club member explained:

> *The attraction was the drugs and the free life. These girls would do anything to stay with the club. They like to party, get high, travel. We travel all over the country. The girls lose their self-respect in the end. I'd say 50 percent of them stay for 6 or 7 years.*
>
> *The girls that worked for me were basically looking for a daddy. They couldn't take care of themselves. One girl I had, a 14-year-old, liked to party. She used to cry a lot. She needed to be loved. Others liked to get whipped and beaten. Anyways, it was basically the excitement of the club that drew them.*

The hustlers are typically placed in some type of sheltered setting, such as a massage parlor or club-owned bordello. When necessary, a club provides false identification papers so that an underage female can move freely from state to state. This is especially important if the girl's parents or the police are looking for her.

Because the juvenile is often treated like communal property, she can be sold, bought, and traded because the club's interests are paramount. One club member succinctly described a juvenile's situation:

> *If their old man tells them to hustle, then they better do it. No one forced them to join up with our club. We got rules about joining and leaving and trying to get back in. You can't do that kind of shit; we don't run that type of club. If they got a complaint, too bad. Nobody wants to listen to some dumbass 14-year-old whine because she's got to screw for money. Nobody wants to hear her noise. Why should they?*

A juvenile who wishes to leave a club may decide to run away, in which case a bounty of $100 or $200 may be offered for her return. The club usually alerts other club chapters near her home town and along the principal access routes to it. This loosely knit network of interception points can be effective, especially if the girl's former owner or boyfriend offers a bonus for her capture. For those unfortunate enough to be caught, the outlook is grim. They face the prospect of gang rapes, beatings, intimidation, and, in extreme cases, murder. The brutal treatment of a captured runaway is used as an example to others who might be considering flight from the club, as in this incident described by a club member:

> *This one girl who tried to run away was about 16 or 17. She ran away because her old man had beat her up real bad a couple times. She was terrified of him; he was pretty vicious to everybody. Loved to fight and hurt people. Crazy. They found her in the lower part of the state, working in a restaurant. They brought her back, held her at a chapter house, and then she was taken to a party where she pulled a train with 20 or 30 guys. Some guys were pretty brutal with her. Most of the other girls were made to watch all of this, to learn a lesson. All this time the girl was crying and begging for help. No one did. We left her on the ground when it was over, naked and bleeding.*

When we first learned of these and similar incidents, we were skeptical. Through sheer frequency of reports and the corroboration of witnesses, our doubts turned to conviction. We are certain that incidents of young females being raped by 20 or 30 gang members, of beatings resulting in internal bleeding and hospitalization, and of juveniles being locked in "trains" (vans with cages for transporting passengers) and shipped to club fortresses are true. A former gang member provided his impression of a clubhouse located in the Northeast:

> *One of these places is a regular compound with a security system, block walls around it, a swimming pool, garage, three houses, game room. The walls are about 15 feet high, concrete block. This place is out in the country and the girls there are real young, maybe 13 or 14. Visitors weren't allowed to talk with them. A real fortress. The police know about it, busted it a couple times, but it's still there. So are the girls.*

It should be noted that not all of these females are reluctant or compelled to hustle for a living. Some, out of affection for their "old man," are willing to prostitute or hire out as an exotic dancer. Others train in anticipation of a career as a petty criminal, including shoplifting, writing bad checks, and selling drugs. In time they acquire the gang's attitudes and values toward commercial sex as simply a convenient avenue for profiteering. For them, prostitution eventually becomes less of a novelty and more of a commonplace practice, reinforced by the attitude of other juveniles in the same predicament. Their welfare, however, is of marginal concern to the gang. Although many club members would not agree with this statement, the treatment of juvenile hustlers by club members is tantamount to slavery.

Despite the attempts of some gangs to capitalize on the image of motorcycle clubs as reflected in newsstand magazines aimed at bike enthusiasts, they remain, as a group, an ensemble of exploiters with regard to the welfare of juvenile runaways turned prostitutes. Individual members may treat these young girls with a modicum of affection, but, collectively speaking, motorcycle gangs victimize these females in the form of kidnapping, coerced hustling, placement in brothels or on streets, and in the use of terror and drugs to maintain control. An unknown number of the more disenchanted juveniles may manage to escape or are voluntarily discharged or released each year from motorcycle gangs, but no accurate estimate of turnover and replacement rates is available.

The Difficulty of Successful Prosecution

The stakes involved in procuring minors are high. In the interest of self-preservation, some pimps take drastic measures to protect themselves from possible arrest and prosecution. A juvenile hustler who cooperates with the police is—in the words of Robin, a pimp—courting disaster:

> *Pandering can be a very serious charge, especially when children are concerned. Christ, they can throw away the key on that one. If a situation comes down where the kid is going to talk (provide evidence for the state), you have people out there that you know. People that you can say, "Well man, take this $500 or $1,000 and shut that whore's mouth," and it will get done. You're better off trying to fight one beef (conspiracy to commit murder) than 20 (charges relating to procuring a minor).*
>
> *Death in the streets is nothing. You lay someone in an alley with a needle in their arm. There's no investigation. The police say, "Ah,*

she was nothing but a goddamn junkie whore," and write it up as a suicide or overdose. You can off [kill] a person real quick—anybody.

Robin's observations may seem callous or overstated. Our interviews with vice and homicide detectives, however, indicate that "death in the streets" is a common occurrence for renegade hustlers. Pimps, as one veteran investigator explained, can be ruthless in their methods:

> *When we found her, she was dead. All we had was a young girl's dead body found lying along a secondary road; dead for about four hours from several stab wounds. And, of course, no identification. I got called to view and photograph the body and to try to find out her identity. From my observations of the body on the road and at the autopsy—real short mini-skirt, no underpants or bra, and real heavy makeup—I knew she was a hooker. By just looking at her, you knew she was real young. It turned out she was arrested just two nights prior to her death for prostitution. Looking back, if she had not been arrested in this area, I doubt if I would have identified her.*
>
> *After spending several weeks interviewing street people, especially hookers, pretty soon I began to find out a little bit about her. Like how she was really pretty, new to the area, only around about six months or less, and the name she used on the streets. One of the girls put me onto her pimp. It turned out she had just been sold to this pimp called "Lemonade."*
>
> *The parents came to identify her body. The mother said that her daughter was only 16 years old. She told me that the kid started to run away from home when she was 13 and by 14 she was leaving for four or five months at a time. After I got her name and identification from her parents, I ran some checks and found out she was arrested in another state at age 14 for prostitution. She was processed through the system as an adult and apparently released within the same day.*

There are two primary methods for achieving a successful prosecution for soliciting charges. The first is to have a member of the pimp's stable present testimony against him. The second is a collateral approach whereby law enforcement officers gather and present evidence in support of charges relating to procuring. Neither method, however, is free of problems. Prostitution is a dangerous life-style. Given the prospect of violence and retaliation by a pimp, few juveniles are willing to step forward in an open court to provide incriminating statements.

Without the hustler to testify, the police are forced to make the connection between the prostitute and pimp. The process is long and drawn out. First, the police must be solicited or have direct knowledge of solicitation before they can establish the association between hustler and pimp. Proof of the connection must be ironclad and show beyond a reasonable doubt that the pimp is reaping a financial benefit from prostitution. Tangible proof of this nature is extremely difficult to acquire; at the very least a team of three or four officers is needed to perform a surveillance of the pimp's and hustler's movements, as well as a thorough investigation of such pertinent records as welfare, employment, and credit status in order to prove that the procurer has no other means of financial support. Assuming both the investigation and subsequent prosecution are successful, a suspended sentence and probation are frequently given. Pandering, in a majority of states, is a misdemeanor where adults are concerned.

Herein lies one of the most pronounced shortcomings in the manner in which law enforcement agencies respond to juvenile prostitutes: All too often, underage hustlers, upon arrest for prostitution, are treated as adults by police. This allows the arresting officer to avoid processing the hustler through the system as a juvenile, a procedure that involves a substantial expenditure of time and paperwork compared with a quick release (accompanied by a fine) for an adult prostitute. The result has been an enormous gap in the protective safety net for juveniles at risk on the streets. It is not that law enforcement agencies are completely indifferent to their plight, but few apparently realize the true hazards of releasing a 14- or 15-year-old hustler back onto the streets and into the custody of a pimp.

John Driscoll, district attorney of Westmoreland County, Pennsylvania, offered the following insights regarding the attitudes displayed by local criminal authorities toward the investigation and prosecution of juvenile prostitution:[3]

> *What we see most directly and close up through our own investigations are cases of prostitution that originated in areas other than within our county. For example, we have had investigations of young girls from Chicago, Buffalo, New York, and Akron, Ohio. Several of these investigations were for the murder of girls. Generally, though, we don't have a major public nuisance in terms of volume of cases.*
>
> *Most of the pimping operations we have had trouble with are in*

the truck stop areas on Interstate 70. From our experience, we find that pimps use fear tactics on their girls. This makes it very difficult to get a conviction. The criminal intelligence we receive from prostitutes is given because they can do so anonymously or trust the detective. They are a good source of information, but there is the fear that we will learn something about their pimps. These hustlers have little or no defense against their pimps. The criminal justice system does not offer a prostitute much in the way of a support system. She is very much alone—particularly the young ones we run across. The characters of these girls are such that their only real crutch is, ironically, the pimp. As a result, the meager protection and support he gives becomes extremely important to the prostitute. Law enforcement, in general, cannot match that; we can't reach them.

The problems we have in prosecution are to overcome the reticent attitude of those involved in the street and inertia by the criminal justice system toward these types of cases. Lack of familiarity and investigative techniques are also a problem. Perhaps the biggest obstacle is the absence of a continuing program of investigation in this area. At present we need to put our resources and efforts in other directions. Keep in mind that most prostitutes plead guilty; few pimps intend to finance a million-dollar defense just to protect the reputation of his prostitute. He is more interested in expediency and having the hustler back on the streets. Because prostitution can become quite complex as an investigation that involves a lot of field work and interviews, it becomes the type of effort we put forth on major crimes. Incarceration for the prostitute is far more the exception than the rule. Judges want normal judicial results and are reluctant to bring a hammer down on a young hustler because prostitution is somewhat akin to the pollution of a stream: A little bit is something you can tolerate. Only if it becomes a public outcry or nuisance will it draw genuine judicial attention as a matter of policy and sentencing.

Frankly, sanctions against prostitution aren't present in the system. A judicial response will never be as effective as cultural or family-oriented controls. The remedies available in the criminal justice system are too structured, too expensive, and they involve a risk which may endanger the life of a prostitute of any age.

In the presence of the current official attitude and the shortage of practical resources within the system to protect juvenile witnesses in cases involving procurers, it may often be safer to forego prosecution in order to keep the victim alive. This dilemma—in effect, the lesser of two evils—is the outcome of judicial inequities and the interrelated problems of case building and prosecution.

Conclusion

This chapter has focused on several basic types of procuring styles, particularly those involving a high degree of organization and planning. A freelance pimp, on the other hand, is someone who turns his girlfriend or wife to prostitution. There is nothing unique about this type of pimp or his method of operation: He sells his hustler, at bargain prices, to anyone. The freelance pimp is a minor character in the hierarchy of commercial sex. Exploitive parents fall in this category because they have only their children to sell and do not usually seek to involve other minors in prostitution. They simply hope to benefit, in some fashion, from assisting in the procurement process. Juveniles who procure do so for a variety of reasons, including the following: (1) they derive satisfaction from participating as an exploiter; (2) pimping provides a temporary respite from the pressures of prostitution; and (3) their pimp demands cooperation in seeking out additional hustlers. They are incapable of drawing any sort of moral distinction between hustling and procuring that might inhibit them from recruiting more victims.

Identifying and tracking any type of procurer, whether a sweet mac or a parent, is, as noted earlier, a formidable undertaking. By ignoring the presence of procurers who specialize in minors, the criminal justice system is announcing, in effect, that these victims have no specific status under the law.[4] It is not a case of police departments not wanting to do anything about pimps or juvenile hustlers; what is lacking is the requisite training and a consensus as to how to proceed. Perhaps Dawson, a gorilla pimp active on the East Coast, best summarized the situation:

> *Where are these kids going to go? They can't run to some shelter; they have to come out sooner or later. What else is there? The courts will stick their ass in a foster home or center. No kid in his right mind wants that shit, believe me. They'd rather hang out with me, party, hustle, you know, live a little, and not get stuck in some rut with a bunch of square dudes.*

Endnotes

1. With the exception of Dr. Frank Sacco's analysis in Chapter 8, the role and significance of exploitive parents in the promotion of prostitution of their children is an untapped subject of scholarly debate and research.

2. At the time of this writing, no reliable estimate was available of the approximate number of female minors engaged in prostitution because of their involvement with motorcycle gangs.
3. District Attorney John Driscoll's remarks are particularly applicable given the extraordinarily low rate of prosecutions for juvenile prostitution in the state of Pennsylvania.
4. What at first glance may appear to be a rather cynical remark regarding police enthusiasm and expertise in the area of procuring investigations is founded on our first-hand knowledge of numerous cases across the country that involve endangered juveniles and pimps. With very few exceptions, these investigations were stillborn and rarely moved beyond the stage of preliminary inquiry.

Chapter 5

CHILD PORNOGRAPHY

The nicest thing about the business is that the prices never go down; if anything, they will go up if the heat is on. I've been at it about five, six years and can set my own prices most of the time. Give me a pretty, cooperative 14-, 15-year-old girl and I'll be sitting pretty with the money I make off her for a long time. Longer than you can imagine. Unless the kid's a screw-up and tries to run to the law, my chances of getting busted are pretty low. Keeping on the move helps, so does paying off the parents when I need to. And the nicest thing of all is I always got lots of customers.

CHARLIE, A 39-YEAR-OLD PORNOGRAPHER

Child pornography, one of the most distinctive crimes of sexual trafficking, can be defined as the use of underage persons as subjects or models in the production of sexually suggestive, provocative, or explicit materials. The finished products can include photographs, films, magazines, slides, drawings, and videotapes. Such materials vary widely in content and production quality, from a single black-and-white photograph of an adolescent female undressing to a choreographed videotape of sexual acts between adults and minors, complete with sound, a staged setting, props, costumes, and animals. There is also demand for visual depictions of minors considered "soft core" in content. Such materials can be described as sexually suggestive or provocative but they often do not involve any form of nudity or overt sexual expression.

Passing judgment on specific visual depictions involving minors can be difficult. It may seem relatively easy, for instance, to distinguish between a situation in which a pornographer photographs a 10-year-old female in various nude poses and that in which a father takes a picture of his 2-year-old daughter in a

116

bathtub. In the former scenario, there are legal prohibitions banning such behavior that consider (1) the victim's age, (2) the absence of informed consent, (3) the offender's age, (4) the immorality of the sexual act, and (5) physical harm to the victim.[1] But what of the latter case? The photograph is not obscene to the father, but if a pedophile with an interest in prepubertal females sees a photo, it may serve to trigger sexual arousal. Or, if the father's photograph of his daughter is transferred to a family album, it may later be viewed by someone who believes that any nude depiction of the human body is obscene. We now have a situation where, according to the use, context, and sexual orientation of the owner or viewer, a photograph involving a minor can be considered asexual (by the father), erotic (by a pedophile), or obscene (by a third party).

The question of what constitutes child pornography is extremely complex because the standards applied are highly subjective and contingent upon a host of cultural, sexual, moral, and religious beliefs that do not readily translate into law. For instance, an artist who sketches nude minors may be considered to be creating erotica or merely aesthetically pleasing images. Members of nudist camps who photograph children may be thought to be doing what most parents do or creating pornography. The sculptural renderings of nude children available in the Caribbean area are considered art in some countries and classified as obscene according to the cultural standards of other nations. These examples raise more questions than they answer about the nature and parameters of child pornography.

Discussion of pornography in this chapter will avoid these subtleties of definition and instead focus on the use of minors in pornography as a form of sexual exploitation. It is our position that there is no value in or acceptable reason for the production or ownership of photographs, films, or similar materials that show minors engaged in sexual activities with adults, other children, or animals. Our criteria for defining child pornography are consistent with statutory definitions and community standards.

The Uses of Child Pornography

There are a number of uses associated with child pornography—or "kiddie porn," as it is popularly known—including the following:

1. *Blackmail:* Pimps view child pornography as a working tool by which they can acquire new hustlers or extort money from customers through blackmail.[2] A pedophile may use photographs or films of his underage victims to blackmail them into silence. Pornographers also keep negatives and copies of their materials to guarantee the cooperation of exploitive parents.

2. *Profit:* Many who participate in child pornography do so because it generates wealth. These exploiters may personally have no sexual interest in or enthusiasm for minors.

3. *Instructional Aids:* An exploitive adult often uses adult and child pornography as an instructional aid to indoctrinate victims into various sexual practices.[3] The exploitive adult also uses the pictures to demonstrate that such behavior is permissible: "If other adults and other children do this sort of thing, then it must be alright."

4. *Self-Gratification:* Child pornography either sparks or contributes to a heightened state of arousal preparatory to masturbation.

5. *Conditioning:* The exploitive adult uses kiddie porn to lower a minor's inhibitions and resistance to sex. With proper reinforcement, the victim can be conditioned into a state of acceptance of his or her exploitive situation.

6. *Advertising:* A procurer often uses pornographic or suggestive pictures of his hustlers to entice customers (see Chapter 4).

7. *Collections:* Most hard-core pedophiles possess an extensive collection of adult and child pornography. The value of such merchandise is relative to and depends upon the collector's particular sexual tastes (see Chapter 2).

8. *Sexual Record:* Some exploiters use pornographic photographs or films of victims to record their sexual encounters. Visual evidence of sexual accomplishments serves a variety of secondary functions, including blackmail, masturbation, profit, and instructional aid.

9. *Access:* The mere possession of child pornography is frequently sufficient to provide an exploiter with access to other offenders and markets. These materials are helpful in terms of profit-making, ordering additional pornography through an exchange, and as a sign of good intentions with fellow exploiters. Simply put, child pornography is the currency of exchange and, in many instances, is the medium of communication among exploiters in the private and public child sex markets.

Essential Elements of Child Pornography

The child pornography industry has four operating levels: production, distribution, sales, and consumption. Our findings indicate four major market areas for kiddie porn: international, national, regional, and local. Each of these market areas overlaps to some extent with another. A photograph of a nude adolescent male sold locally in Arizona, for instance, could also appear in an international child pornography magazine produced in the Netherlands. Table 5-1 summarizes the essential elements of child pornography. Each of the four market areas is further discussed in the following sections.

The International Dimension

It is often assumed in the United States that child pornography is a foreign phenomenon and that the bulk of pornographic material available on the world market is produced in and disseminated from destinations outside the United States by such groups as COQ International and the Liberation Press. Unfortunately, child pornography is not exclusively a foreign phenomenon. To begin with, the volume of material produced by child pornographers and pedophiles on a routine basis within the United States is enormous. Second, the evidence confiscated from sex rings and convicted pedophiles indicates that many offenders produce child pornography for their own consumption in sufficient quantities to warrant elaborate classification and index schemes. Third is the fact that soft-core child pornography is much in demand and expensive. Usually consisting of suggestive pictures of minors either naked or partially dressed, these materials originate in a variety of settings. Pictures of children taken at nudist camps, for instance, qualify as soft-core pornography. Such materials can be produced in the United States at minimal cost and risk to the photographer. Finally, no federal enforcement agency has sought to comprehensively monitor or identify the volume and distribution of child pornography manufactured within the United States.

The international market tends to specialize in the manufacture of medium- to high-quality child pornography that often involves the use of sophisticated reproduction techniques such as offset lithography and can result in full-color publications. The production process is designed for mass reproduction. A case in point is

Table 5-1 Child Pornography Points of Production

	International	National	Regional	Local
Production Format	State-of-art technology in audiovisual equipment, development, and mass reproduction processes.	Essentially the same as international.	Private developing studios and labs; lower quality of material.	Lowest quality of all the markets; relies on retail level technology (instant cameras, photostats).
Distribution Methods	Mail, courier, direct sale.	Adult bookstores, mail (commercial and Postal Service), direct sale.	Mail (commercial, U.S.), direct purchase or exchange, adult bookstores.	Direct purchase or exchange, mail.
Producers	Syndicated sex rings, entrepreneurs, and freelance photographers.	Organized crime and freelance pornographers.	Primarily freelance pornographers, with some work hired out on contractual basis by local pimps or pedophiles.	Community or neighborhood pedophiles, sex rings, and pimps.
Evasion Techniques	Mobile production and development sites, false identities, multiple disguised mailings of merchandise.	Use of middlemen to arrange routine purchases, parental release form, and mobile production and development sites.	Transient identities and locations of pornographers, rapid turnover in children used as models, and parental release forms.	Victims coerced or blackmailed into silence; offender's mobility and good reputation often insulate him from suspicion.
Status	Still available, with emphasis on use of Third World youths as models; periodic inroads into traffic by foreign police and U.S. federal law enforcement agencies; reactive nature of police investigations precludes permanent abolition of production and distribution.	Extremely resilient, despite harsh federal laws occasional disruption of the flow of merchandise. Resold in neighboring countries and exported to Asia, Europe, and Africa.	Extremely difficult to intercept on proactive basis. Pimps and pornographers use juvenile hustlers and molested children as subjects. May later emerge in foreign publications. Parental consent binds guilty parties to secrecy; increasing emphasis on suggestive materials.	Pornography made at the local level is the mainstay of the pedophilic subculture; typically discovered during police search or accidentally via postal investigations.

the 8½-by-11-inch magazine titled *Adam Junior*, which is published by Gerd Berendt Verlag in Europe. This magazine is directed at pedophiles with an interest in adolescent males. The glossy photographs (black and white, with a few in color) show nude underage males alone or with other youths in different outdoor settings. The cover is unremarkable except for the title; the interior includes a title page of nude or abstract drawings, followed by a series of photographs. This particular editorial and production format is used by the same publisher in similar magazines, such as *Braune Jungs und blauer Himmel*. The only essential difference between these various magazines is their titles. A standardized format enables the publisher to manufacture and reproduce a large number of professionally packaged pornographic magazines. Some of the predominant characteristics of this market include the following:

- The use of couriers and the mails for distribution.
- An apparent trend toward using Third World children as subjects for magazines and films.
- High-quality merchandise that employs state-of-the-art technology, such as video tapes.
- Multiple "covers" used by a producer to disguise his identity and point of production, including constant relocation, the creation of "shadow" or bogus companies, and sending materials abroad from countries where the likelihood of detection by customs officials is less due to the sheer volume of outgoing mail.
- Extremely high markup on quality merchandise, especially films or magazines involving scenarios, staged settings, and more than one child.
- Marketing to both homosexual and heterosexual exploiters with an interest in child pornography.
- Production of more explicit materials than soft-core or suggestive publications.
- Constantly changing titles of merchandise to stimulate interest in a wider range of publications.

The National Dimension

The national dimension in child pornography consists of materials made entirely within the United States, using child subjects from

Canada, Mexico, and Central America as well as from this country. The finished product is sold primarily inside the United States through the distribution channels provided by organized crime and regional entrepreneurs with business ties to syndicated adult bookstores. (Organized crime has expressed an interest in adult pornography, but evidence of its direct involvement in child pornography is not conclusive. To the extent that extensive distribution networks exist, they appear to be *ad hoc* arrangements.)

As in the international market, the quality of kiddie porn produced in the United States is fairly high. To achieve this quality, distributors depend on reliable printers and developers who are willing to risk arrest for a lucrative financial gain.

Several basic characteristics describe the national dimensions of child pornography. Professional printing and graphic techniques enable pornographers to maintain a high profit margin. An organized distribution system involving the United States Postal Service, private carrier services, adult bookstores, and prior contacts enables pornographers to advance their merchandise to the point of consumption efficiently. Law enforcement officials and exploitive parents can sometimes be paid to tolerate the pornographer's activities and to minimize legal interference. Parents receive payment when they consent to the photographing of their children. A nationwide clientele is relied upon to purchase books, magazines, and films depicting child sex acts. Additionally, many pornographers use nudist camps as a primary source of many of their underage models. We were also able to ascertain that materials, once circulated in the country of origin, may receive secondary distribution in the international market or may be bartered for equivalent foreign merchandise.

Stewart, a 43-year-old child pornographer, has been involved in the national markets for more than a decade. Stewart was identified by a United States postal inspector in 1987 as "one of the kingpins in child pornography on the East Coast." Recently convicted in United States District Court for the Northern District of West Virginia after a multi-count indictment involving the distribution and commercial sale of child pornography, he is currently confined to a federal penitentiary.

While he was incarcerated in a state penal facility, prison officials intercepted and kept three photo albums sent to Stewart. All of the approximately 100 photographs were of females ranging in age from 11 to 14. Although the females were posed in what might be considered provocative or revealing ways, none of the photographs displayed nudity. Stewart contended that he had a legal right to receive those materials while imprisoned, regardless of his prior criminal record.

Stewart is a freelance pornographer with market ties to national buyers and organized crime. What is especially intriguing about him is his (1) method of operation, (2) his distinctions between nudity and pornography, and (3) his grasp of the profit potential of this trade, as displayed in the following case. His observations about the dynamics of the national market in child pornography coincide almost precisely with those provided by other pornographers interviewed. Stewart's involvement in child pornography centered almost exclusively on the production, as opposed to distribution, of such materials.

STEWART

Child pornography is a very big business. It wouldn't be hard for you to start if you knew where to sell them. That's the key. Somebody has to put in a good word for you to sell them. You might have some pictures to show, about ten sets. If you had ten sets, you'd make a phone call to either Pittsburgh or New York. They'll come down here and look at 'em. If they like what you got, they'll buy them right on the spot. Nothing is ever guaranteed, but chances are you'll get up to $25,000 if the girl was cooperative and pretty. She has to pose as you want her to, pose for about 250 pictures or so. Some of them can be real gross, with a dog for example.

The parents are always there when the pictures are taken. Every time I did this I made real sure the parents signed a release. But let me tell you this: I was never involved in no pornography; I was just involved in taking nude photographs. The release form was a legal document drawn up by an attorney. Mostly it was to keep me from getting blackmailed. If I photographed some hop head's daughter and she blew her money on drugs and came to me saying she wanted more, this form saved me. I had a note from you saying I could bring your kid to my cabin. I tried to cover myself pretty good but still got stopped quite a few times by the police just for harassment.

I would take the pictures, give them to the parents, and they would sell them. I never sold any of these pictures directly to customers, just to buyers who resold them to customers. If the kid is exceptionally good looking, you can use her two or three times. She puts on a little wig, a change of clothes, maybe some makeup. Let me tell you something else about kids. I have found more cases where their uncles, or especially their dads or brothers, have had sex with them. These are most of the people I've known or had personal experiences with. I don't believe what the books say about incest. I think their percentages are way off base—way too low.

You'd be surprised how many girls between sixth and eighth grade go for older guys. I don't know why. I have never threatened a girl, forced a girl into anything. A camera is a big part of the attraction. You can go to strange places—like I used to hit the beaches up in New Jersey a lot. I'd have a radio, camera, and see a couple of nice young girls laying there on the beach, so I'd say, "Excuse me miss, but would you watch my camera while I take a swim?" Later I'd come back with two ice creams for them. It's as simple as that. You start asking to take their pictures. If you ask for some cleavage they'll show you the whole breast. My conquests sometimes happened like this, I'd meet one young girl, do something to her she'd like, and she would involve another girl who would get another girl, and so on. I'd get five for the one I met. It usually led to pictures, but I always had their parents' permission.

I knew these pictures were being sold by the parents. They'd give me a percentage. What you do with them is your business. If you got $15,000 or $25,000 for them, then I think you should be very generous with me. Give me $5,000 or $8,000 in return after you sell the pictures. I've never been cheated. They all treat me fair and come back for more pictures. The parents came from all kinds of backgrounds; clerks, steelworkers, plumbers. You signed the release form before I'd even talk to you to show I didn't solicit you. So, no matter what you say in court, I got the form you signed drawn up by my attorney. You can probably use your kid three times in pornography. Sell the pictures in the states, Canada, and once overseas. If the girl is local, the pictures are sold on the West Coast or, chances are, in Canada. I kept a lot of the pictures I took of girls in my cabin for my use. My studio was on a farm where I could develop my own films and photos.

I would take about 250 pictures. That's a set. There's 100

pictures in a book, and the parents would pick out the best ones. There was a limit as to how far I went. Nothing but the legs spread. I never let sex interfere with my business. I've been in the business of photographing nude girls for about 25 years. I've had thousands of girls as models for my books. The reason I got so popular was because I didn't do nothing to the girls. They really trusted me. I've even photographed mothers and daughters in the nude.

With a camera, it's so easy to get a young girl. You don't have to hold out a sucker or offer $5. I've had people look me up and ask me to photograph their kids. You can make a damn good living doing this. I made a lot of bucks on what the parents gave me for a percentage. If I had been involved in pornography all the way through from taking pictures to selling them, I'd be a very, very rich man. I never had sex with kids under 12. I do believe in taking anything I can get. I don't believe in God, only in what I can see and touch. I don't believe what I do is that wrong as long as I don't force anybody or blackmail them. I never had that many guy friends because the guys I knew were assholes. Guys look for trouble, so I'm a loner—don't drink or hang around bars.

I consider my photos to be art. Did I tell you that I sold a picture to Hallmark Cards? I sent them a profile of a little girl with the words, "I love you daddy." I've also had some of my pictures displayed at fairs. Pornography isn't my bag. You're talking about a lot of time if you get caught. Plus there's other things involved. I don't want no little girl coming up to me in five years and calling me a dirty old man. I just took pictures of girls masturbating, that sort of stuff.

If you brought your kid to me, asked me to photograph her, and agreed to put it in writing, then I'd pose her the way I think the pictures would sell. But I wouldn't pose her with another guy. She would just masturbate or use something on herself. Most of these girls are very young, undeveloped, don't forget. Is this pornographic? It might be suggestive, I don't know if that's pornographic. It might be. I really don't know, never gave it a thought. Nudism is one thing. Pornography is another. Anything that shows a sex act is pornographic. The best thing you can have is two girls together. If you can get twins, you're in the money. I've photographed twins. They sold real well.

The people that buy these pictures don't travel just to look at one set of pictures. They won't cross the state line unless you have 10 or 20 sets. Organized crime from New York will send someone down to look at the pictures. They make offers for the pictures right then and there. I don't ask no questions. It's too damn dangerous. These guys, I think they get all the profit 'cause they're paying for the pictures. Whoever publishes the books, they might even control that, does a good job. It's a nice technicolor book, no name on it. The pages are glossy. It's a well-made book and would cost you about $50. A new book comes out all the time. They're numbered so you can get the whole series. You couldn't go into a book store and buy one— not unless you're known. They have everything under the counter, if you know where to go. Anything you want, tapes, 8mm films, kids with dogs.

Parents will fix you up with other kids. The word gets around about what I'm doing. Once the kid has been photographed a few times, that's it. The parents have to go out and find new talent. It's a very touchy thing when you're dealing with a kid. I never photograph any kid right after I meet her. I have to get to know her first. I'd take her into another room and talk with her. I'd tell her to use a bad word and if she would come back to her parents and tell them the word, I wouldn't touch her, wouldn't photograph her, 'cause that means she'll tell the people next door. If she didn't tell, I would explain how far up the ladder I wanted to go, how far I wanted the pictures to go, and how far I wanted her to undress. I never exceeded these steps. There were many girls who would say no and I'd drop it at that point. The parents were always there. Nothing was ever forced on the girl.

Parents would invite me to their house. I'd get to know the girl and see how she acted. They had to have a certain look on their face. That's really important. They couldn't show fear or doubt in the pictures. They had to show happiness or love, take my word for it. To get that look, I'd give them something, from tricycles to stereos. It depended on what they wanted. You have to be able to express excitement in the pictures. Props help a lot, like mirrors and stuffed animals. If I took pictures of your girl, the chances are I did it at your house because she knows daddy is right next door. She knows she's safe, not alone. If she hollers, she knows daddy will come and help her. When I took pictures, it was only her and me in the room but the door was never locked because some kids get embarrassed.

A lot of my clients came from nudist camps. Nudist camps are the biggest part of it. You can go to a nudist camp, take the mother and daughter at the same time. Mothers and daughters posing at the same time is the biggest money maker in pornography. Say if a mother has two daughters. Get the mother in bed with the two daughters. That's the biggest moneymaker. You're talking big bucks—as much as $50,000.

Mothers are a bunch of assholes—most of them—because they sell their daughters. A mother is the greediest son of a bitch in the world. There's some good ones, like the ones that try to get their daughters into commercials with my pictures. The others are dogs. They don't care how far you want to go. I've had mothers ask me to bring in dogs to lick their daughters because that kind of picture pays more. They wanted pornography. It don't matter to them just so the girl isn't hurt.

It's a business. People buy it. Who's to say it's wrong? Like I said, I've been involved in nudist camps. I'll photograph anything or anyone in the privacy of my home from 6 months to 96 years old. I don't give a goddamn who knows it or how many pictures I take. I'll fight it in court if I have to. Pornography with little kids, five or six years old, is a no-no. I've taken nude pictures and am not ashamed of it. I would mind if you took pictures of my daughter 'cause you're not in the family.

These cops, they think they know where to go, what to do about pornography. They don't know nothing about this stuff.

■   ■   ■

Regional Markets

Our findings indicate the existence of several transient regional markets in child pornography that operate roughly along the same guidelines as the national markets. A regional market is composed of producers who use minors from a broad geographic vicinity—such as the South Atlantic coast—as models. The materials are made and distributed within the region first and later recirculated outside the area if enough buyers can be located. Such merchandise is typically of a lower grade than that available in the international or national markets, with the emphasis being on volume rather than quality. Also, the pornography is more likely to be produced in less-staged surroundings such as a bordello, motel, or private studio in someone's home. Not as much attention is paid to the use of sophisticated audiovisual equipment, elaborate scenarios or seduction scenes, and a child's physical attractiveness.

Six traits are common to the production of child pornography within a geographic region. (1) Regional producers generally do not provide the same high production quality as pornographers whose merchandise is intended for national or international distribution. (2) A sexually exploitive relationship often develops between the victim and the pornographer before the photographs are taken. (3) The freelance pornographers who provide the bulk of the merchandise in regional markets usually lack the coordinated efforts exerted at more sophisticated national and international levels. (4) Photographers use "bogus" kiddie porn models to attract customers; such models possess a youthful appearance and present the appearance of juvenility. (5) The lower production standards usually result in a lower profit margin. And (6) there is rapid turnover relevant to the number of subjects needed to supply demand.

One example of a regional child pornographer is Robert, whose activities include the sexual molestation of minors. At age 32 he has completed five years of a sentence of fifteen years in a state penitentiary. A former steelworker, his charges included statutory rape, aggravated assault, simple assault on children, and the production and distribution of child pornography. Divorced and with two daughters (ages 6 and 12), Robert has been sexually involved since age 17 with child pornography. Although his production facilities and operations were designed for local distribution, he occasionally sold or swapped child pornography to fellow collectors from other states. Until his arrest by postal inspectors, his behavior went virtually unnoticed and unreported, for approximately fifteen years. Robert was unable to provide a reasonable estimate as to the amount of profit he derived over the years from the sale of child pornography.

ROBERT

Question: Did you ever have occasion to photograph children?
Answer: Yes, I had a personal collection of over 300 different pictures of children, all girls between the ages of 9 and 12. I

kept them from my wife and daughters by hiding them in a partition-like wall I built in my basement.

Question: How tough was it to get kids in that age group to let you photograph them?

Answer: My parents own and operate a real estate company with a lot of apartments and rental houses in different neighborhoods. So I'd get to meet kids who lived in different areas of the city or I'd go to arcades, schoolyards, even hospitals, and offer kids money to take their picture in the nude. Any place where there are children I can usually find a willing one. Like I told you, I don't bother with anything over 12 years old.

It's not that hard to persuade a kid to come with me for a photo session; I never forced a child to take photos. I'd pay them anywhere from $5 to $20. If they said no, that was it, I'd let them alone. But most of the kids I asked needed the money, wanted the money. They knew they could always depend on me for money, and I could depend on them for photos. If I asked one hundred kids, I'd get anywhere from 35 percent to 50 percent to come with me.

Question: Did you ever have any contacts or hassles with parents?

Answer: No, I never had any contacts with parents. I've heard of parents entering into deals involving their kids, but I never did. Police really underestimate the amount of people and the kinds of people involved in child pornography. I personally know of a lot of professionals—you know, doctor or lawyer types who wanted pictures.

Question: What did you do with your photos?

Answer: I sold most of them. I'd take 8 by 10 photographs, sold them for $30 apiece. I'd also exchange them with other pedophiles and pornographers. We'd exchange them hand to hand or through the mail, which is how I got caught.

Question: How did you meet other pedophiles?

Answer: Through magazines and circulation newspapers, underground stuff like NAMBLA, PIE. There's so many. Although now you have a problem with the postal inspectors.

Question: Is that how you got busted?

Answer: You got it! I kept a list of about 200 names of people living throughout the United States for the purpose of selling and swapping child pornography. It takes a lot of time to develop a list of that size. Nowadays everybody is real cautious. Anyways,

I'd just start writing to people, pedophiles I'd met or who listed an address in a magazine. Once I got their trust, we'd start selling or swapping pictures and names of other pedophiles we knew.

A pedophile is always afraid that the postal inspectors will get their mail. These guys, when they raid a home which deals in child pornography, will take the master list if they find it and start writing to the names on the list. That's how the authorities first became aware of me. I was on somebody's list who got busted. They (postal inspectors) started writing to me under a different name and sending me photos for which I'd send them money. We went back and forth a couple of times. They kept records of it. When they arrested me, they had the evidence right there.

Question: Did you ever pay a child to have sex with you?

Answer: Sometimes I'd have to pay, but I also would just meet little girls and talk them into it. I would have maybe 50 sexual relationships with girls 12 and under in say a year's time. It's tough to get kids that young. I'd mostly get their parents' confidence so they would leave their kids with me. You know, like a babysitter.

Question: Where would you find the younger kids you paid for?

Answer: Usually in the arcades around the city, in the streets, or in the neighborhood. It's the same as pornography; if I can get a kid to pose nude for money, she will usually do the other things for money too. I can always get the kids because in a way I love kids and they would do me favors and these favors kept me out of jail. It's like this. I could take their photos and send them to people and make money while also having access to my sexual preference and the kids would never tell. This went on and on for years until I got caught.

Question: Are you talking about actual sexual intercourse with a child as part of your relationship with young girls?

Answer: Yes, both sexual intercourse and oral sex; me on the child and the child on me.

Question: Are you receiving any treatment in this prison?

Answer: Yes, a little. There are about 65 inmates in here doing time for child abuse offenses like mine. Not all of them are receiving treatment; it's a voluntary thing. I am going to try my best to get the help I need. It's the only way I'll be able to stay out of this place once I do my time.

■   ■   ■

Local Markets

The volume of kiddie porn at the local level may surpass that of all the other markets. A local market consists of pornography produced by community or neighborhood exploiters. The models are often minors known to the offenders as a result of an ongoing relationship. Pornography in these instances is often a derivative of a persistent exploitive environment wherein the victim progresses from sexual misuse to posing for the offender. With few exceptions, virtually every pedophile is likely to produce, collect, sell, and trade child pornography. Jeannie, a 14-year-old prostitute, had from time to time been paid to pose for pornography. Her street savvy in setting up blackmail schemes with her pimps demonstrates the possibilities available to an exploiter with an interest in child pornography:

> We'd get a guy, some rich-looking dude, to a motel, and while I was screwing him, my pimp would arrange it so somebody, maybe him or another girl, would take some photos of us. Then we'd tell the guy that he better pay up for the pictures or it'd be his ass. It worked pretty good most of the time.
>
> I never let nobody take pictures of my face. I guess I really didn't like doing that stuff, but the extra money was nice. Sometimes we'd switch off and I'd take the pictures while another girl turned the trick. He (the pimp) used to hold some of 'em back from the trick, just as protection I guess. I saw him sell some of them to some guys once.

Not all models in a local porn market are prostitutes or runaways. Many are children involved in a sex ring or caught in an exploitive situation. Given exploiters' predilection for preserving their sexual experiences, it is conceivable that many sexually victimized minors have had their pictures taken at some point and thereby unwittingly contributed to the local kiddie porn trade.

Child pornography made at the local level is particularly difficult to intercept, for it is produced in very controlled settings. Frequently, the offender is skilled at photography and maintains a modest but efficient developing laboratory or studio at home. Over the year, an offender is likely to build an extensive collection of "home-grown" hard- and soft-core child pornography. The content of local child pornography can range from sexually explicit photographs to innocuous pictures taken of adolescents in bathing suits or gym clothes. Even the latter have value to collectors in the local market, for nonsexual representations of children are often erotic to those already predisposed toward minors.

The local markets in child pornography differ from the other markets as follows:

- The materials produced are intended primarily for personal consumption rather than for commercial sale or distribution.
- Films and photographs are of lower quality than what is available in the other markets, although technological advances, especially in camera and videotape equipment, are closing the gap.
- Production originates with the activities of pimps, pedophiles, and sex rings rather than from commercial pornographers, whose principal motivation is financial profit.
- Materials are distributed through the mail and by direct exchange, as opposed to distribution through syndicated bookstores and courier-buyers.

The Economics of Child Pornography

The traffic in child pornography is carried on by an assortment of entrepreneurs, from the independent producer who works with criminal syndicates to a neighborhood pedophile with an aptitude for photography. It is a sale, trade, and barter market, with the greatest profits reserved for those manufacturers of high-quality pornography who possess extensive mailing lists or ample sales outlets. Trade activities, such as the swapping of photographs, do not necessarily yield income. Bartering involves an exchange of services and merchandise and can produce profit through the acquisition of services. A pimp, for example, may use pornographic pictures of a minor to blackmail her into prostitution; in return for the pimp not distributing the photographs, the juvenile agrees to hustle. In this situation, the procurer has profited financially from the possession rather than the sale of pornography.

The amount of income generated from the sale of child pornography is a matter of widespread speculation because of the absence of reliable data. Not known is the amount of new child pornography available for sale annually, at all four trade levels, or what percentage of the more dated material is recirculated and resold.

The profitability of pornography, however, is not in doubt, because of the high ratio of income to expense. Expense consists of those costs accrued as a result of producing, manufacturing, and distributing the materials, as well as overhead, operating expenses such as supplies and equipment, and payoffs to suppliers of juveniles or occasionally to the juvenile victims themselves for their participation. The aggregate of these expenses leaves ample room for high profits. As in any market, volume is beneficial. The pornographer who has a large clientele or a steady buyer at the wholesale level is assured of enough profit to offset the risk of detection, arrest, and confiscation of his goods. The question of what constitutes enough profit in child pornography is answered partially in the following interview with a local operative. Given ample financial incentive, some parents will exploit their children for the production of pornography. In this case, the photographs consisted exclusively of seminude and nude children (primarily females) in suggestive poses.

PORNOGRAPHY AS A BUSINESS

Question: Is pornography profitable today?

Answer: Even today, the most money is made in child pornography because it's hard to get and willing children are hard to come by. First of all, young boys are not that much of a money maker; they're pretty much out as far as good money is concerned. The ones that make money are those who are professional. They look at it like a business.

Question: Do the kids make money?

Answer: Ah, most of the time the kid is brought in by a parent. The parent is propositioned with money.

Question: What kind of money are we talking about?

Answer: Well, it goes anywhere from nickels and dimes to big money: $5,000, $10,000, $20,000 a spread. A spread, you're talking 500 to 1,000 photographs shot at different times in different settings. Outdoor, mockup playground settings, this type of thing. Girls, say between the ages of 8 and 13, are the very salable objects. Twins, identical twins, are the prime pictures, the most salable.

Question: Why is that?

Answer: It's in demand. Identical twins are an unusual setup; specifically young girls without overdevelopment and preferably with little or no pubic hair on their body, etc. A good spread, done well from a professional standpoint with lights and back-drop and producing artistically "good photographs," is worth twenty grand—$20,000 for 1,000 pictures.

Question: So I would bring in a girl—my daughter. Would I bring her to you?

Answer: I would act as a middleman. I'd deal with you and with the photographers. I'd set the price with you.

Question: And how would you do that? What are your criteria?

Answer: The criteria would be, first of all, they'd have to be nice-looking girls. Clean, couldn't look like urchins or trash. They had to look like the girl next door. Pigtails, the whole nine yards. You'd come to me and we'd negotiate a price.

Question: How would I know to go to you?

Answer: Most of the time you'll find that some people come into my bar and start talking about pornography. From their comments you'd figure out they weren't against it. Somebody would ask something about this, that, or the other.

Question: Somebody would ask about what?

Answer: Well, for instance, do you know where I can get some photographs of a woman and a donkey or a dog or young kids. You'll find it's the upper-middle class that has the money to spend on these pictures. The lower class doesn't have the money.

Question: So if I wanted to buy some pictures of twins, how much would it cost me as the consumer?

Answer: For 500 of the best, you'd have to spend $2,000.

Question: Now these would be pictures I don't buy in a book?

Answer: No, no, no. These might even be people you know, their kids.

Question: They're my personal set?

Answer: Right.

Question: And they won't be duplicated in other places?

Answer: That arrangement can be made, and if it is, of course, the price goes even higher.

Question: Sort of like an art collection?

Answer: Yes it is. If I arrange with you to take these pictures of your daughters, I'd give you $5,000 for the session. You bring the girls in, make sure they've done their hair, taken a bath, and have a change of clothes. We'd want a cheerleader's uniform complete with boots, nightgowns, different underwear, school dresses, bluejeans, bathing suits. They bring their own attire most of the time. I take the pictures, give you $5,000 after the session is over with. Generally the girls are rewarded with their own little color television or maybe a bicycle.

Question: Would you agree with the parents on all that?

Answer: You agree with the parents on the money. Then you tell them, "Listen, first of all you will sign a waiver, a legal waiver that says we have your permission to take these pictures of your girls." That's a prerequisite. That's the only businesslike way to do this and it keeps your can out of prison. Secondly, I want to talk to the girls. The prerequisites there are that the parents will be at the location but they won't be in the same room because the kids feel safer with them in the immediate vicinity but they don't want them in the same room while they're being photographed.

Question: Do you photograph boys?

Answer: Very rarely. There just isn't any money in it.

Question: Okay, let's go back to the session. How would you get these kids to cooperate? Are we talking about perverse things like sexual intercourse?

Answer: No. The first thing you do is assure the girl that there's not going to be any physical contact between her and the photographer or with anybody else. This is strictly a photography session. If you lay it on the line, most kids believe you. They're harder to con than adults. After they are assured you're on the level, they could care less.

Question: What happens then?

Answer: You tell the girls beforehand, "Listen, honey, you know I made a financial arrangement with your parents. We also plan to reward you." They get the reward, like a television, when they are through. If you treat that business as a business, you have very few problems. There are people in the business that want to sexually abuse the kids, try to get in animal acts, perverse things in front of the camera. This type of thing is no good. It doesn't sell and brings a lot of heat down on everybody. There's no sense in it.

Question: So you're talking about first-class photos of children in various poses of nudity?

Answer: Right.

Question: Okay, so if I rent my children to you for an afternoon. Is that against the law?

Answer: I'm sure they'd find a law to match the act. Somewhere I suppose it's against the law. But a good businessman takes every precaution.

Question: Would you research me if I said I had a couple of kids to photograph?

Answer: Certainly. You'd give me your name and phone number. After finding your address in the phone index I'd call the telephone company and credit union to see if you paid your bills. Find out where you work. Somewhere along the line I'll meet someone you know and I'll find out what kind of person you are.

Question: Would you ask me for references?

Answer: In an oblique way, yes, but most of the time you wouldn't know what I was asking.

Question: What happens when the session is over?

Answer: You go to people that are in the book publishing business that you've known for several years. Tell them you have got some very nice pictures—for example, of two cute blond-haired girls and you need $20,000. It's just that simple. I had to give up maybe $10,000 for the pictures so I have to make a little. They come, look, and usually take around 500 of the best. Half are just discarded. This includes the negatives.

Question: And the negatives?

Answer: Yes. They don't want any competition from anyone for the same product. They're not stupid, not when they pay that kind of money.

Question: Who are "they"? Don't name them, but can you describe them?

Answer: They are businessmen who own publishing companies. They are connected with organized crime. Obviously, since it's a contraband article, not available on the newsstands, you're going to have to pay $25 or $30 for one of these magazines. There'd be about 15 or 20 color photographs and an equal number of black and white.

Question: And these magazines generally do not deal with sex acts, just nudity?

Answer: Right. You're dealing with voyeurs, not perverts as such. You are talking about a local businessman who wants to look at a young girl. Your local insurance agent. They are the ones who can spend the money on these photographs.

Question: Were you part of the distribution?

Answer: No, all I did was sell the negatives and photographs.

Question: You are a businessman. When you get paid $20,000, how much have you made in profit?

Answer: Counting basic overhead, about $10,000 or so.

Question: Did you have to pay a photographer?

Answer: I paid a photographer because it's cheaper than buying $7,000 or $8,000 worth of photography equipment.

Question: That's pretty profitable after overhead.

Answer: Yes it is. Most of the photographers in that line are homosexuals, so you don't have to worry about them fooling with the girls.

Question: Were you there at the sessions?

Answer: Absolutely. It's my neck, my butt, and my money that's riding on the line. Damn right. I'd usually be out of sight but nearby with the parents.

Question: What would you talk about with them while their kid is being photographed?

Answer: Oh, talk about business. If the guy is in the insurance business, I might try to work a discount on a policy. You try to get the parent's mind off of what is really going on. They don't really want to do this, so you have to direct their heads somewhere else.

Question: Did the parents know what you were going to do with the photographs?

Answer: Sure. This was plainly stipulated in the legal instrument that they signed.

Question: Did a lawyer draw up this contract?

Answer: Yes.

Question: And he knew what he was drafting?

Answer: Sure he did. There are perverted lawyers just like there are perverted doctors, salesmen, anything.

Question: Did you ever have problems getting people?

Answer: No. It's just word of mouth. There's no real problem finding parents who are interested. None at all.

Question: Did you ever have more business than you could handle?

Answer: You have more people wanting that easy money than their kids are worth. Some of these young girls are ugly. How do you tell a parent, "I can't take pornographic pictures of your kid because she's ugly?" A touchy thing.

Question: Did it bother you to be involved in this sort of activity?

Answer: Didn't bother me because I figured, in all likelihood, that the kid has been abused a lot more than I'll ever abuse it. At that age, girls are a lot smarter than men give them credit for. They know what's going on. I have no respect for the parents, but it's a business. They come to me. I don't go looking for them.

When you explain to the kid, "Your mom or dad needs the money and that's the only reason you're here," most will accept that because they know basically what's going on at home. The worst psychological damage occurs in the parent-child relationship. I don't think I am that damaging to the child because I'm honest about what the whole thing is about. For me it's money. For the kid, it's taking care of their parents. For the parents, it's the money.

Question: Would you use the same kid again and again?

Answer: Normally no, because twice around is about all the circulation the pictures can stand. You've saturated the market at that point with that face and body.

Question: Who was easier to work with, mothers or fathers?

Answer: Mothers. Much easier with mothers. Daddies cherish their little girls. Mothers are hard core. They're in business to make money.

Question: Was there ever any anguish shown by these parents?

Answer: Yeah. There was this one woman who had a real sweet girl who said, "Lord I hope this stops here." I said, "It's up to you whether your kid becomes a prostitute or a junky. You need the money so you sold your kid." That's what it boils down to. Sometimes cases like that make a parent think really hard what their kid is all about. Maybe they're better off. Who knows?

■   ■   ■

Conclusion

Child pornography, a medium by which the victim is reduced to an object or animal state, satisfies both the pleasure and profit expectations of exploiters. Kiddie porn has a multiplicity of functions, and how such materials are used depends on the exploiter's purpose and interests. In any event, it can certainly be said that these interests never coincide with a minor's welfare.

Nowhere is the need for victim advocacy more dramatically illustrated than in child pornography. This traffic in sexual depictions is subsidized by adults in sufficient numbers to encourage both national and international production, sales, and distribution. Each market level is independent of the other, but all depend on illicit consumer demand for success.

This chapter has not dealt with federal or state apprehension of child pornographers, because current arrest figures are irrelevant in light of the fact that this offense is a multilevel, complex, and sophisticated phenomenon that often goes undetected. The rapid growth of communications technology, moreover, is making it easier and safer for pornographers to operate outside the limits of the law. Computers, portable developing studios, video cameras, instant processing film, and photostatic copiers have eased the burdens of production for pornographers and, in so doing, further complicated the task of law enforcement.

Whatever definition one accepts for child pornography, the dissemination of these materials is contradictory to international law (see Chapter 6) and national and state statutes. The recent creation of a child pornography analysis unit within the Department of U.S. Customs is an attempt to centralize and synthesize data that can help identify or intercept active pornographers. At least one enforcement branch of the federal government has thereby acknowledged that the abolition of child pornography requires a long-term commitment of resources.

Endnotes

1. In addition to these circumstances, most state legislation in the area of sexual trafficking considers such factors as repetitiveness of offender's behavior, prior criminal record, extent of involvement, and age difference between victim and offender.
2. See the section entitled "Gorilla Pimp" in Chapter 4.
3. See the section entitled "Sex Rings" in Chapter 2.

Chapter 6

INTERNATIONAL CHILD SEX TRADE

by Kenneth J. Herrmann, Jr., and Michael Jupp

The sexual exploitation of minors is by no means restricted to the United States. Like loosely spun threads, the crimes of sexual trafficking interlace throughout the world. A nude photograph of an underage prostitute taken in Canada, for instance, may find its way into the hands of a South African collector of child pornography. Whether in Argentina, China, Australia, Switzerland, Thailand, Mexico, the Soviet Union, or the United States, sexually exploited juveniles have much in common. They are all politically powerless victims of exploitation in a criminal subculture that transcends national borders.

These exploiters promote trafficking through a combination of illicit and quasi-legal methods. In the illicit category fall such familiar activities as the marketing of child pornography, prostitution, nude dancing, procuring, sex rings, and outright molestation. These crimes are prohibited by laws that vary within nations according to the severity of statutory penalties, definitions, elements of the offense, and age of majority. Quasi-legal activities, however, escape detection under various national statutory enactments. They include exploitive adoption schemes, a sex tourism industry for pedophiles, indenturing, and the publication of magazines or newsletters that advocate sexual relationships between adults and minors.

This tragic state of affairs, wherein a child is subjected to multiple levels of victimization, is compounded by a lack of cooperation among nations in abolishing the trade. Over the years, one agency that has successfully accumulated evidence and information regarding the international trafficking of minors is Defense for Children International (DCI). DCI is one of the very few international agencies that actively monitors, seeks out, and investigates allegations and facts pertaining to the exploitation of children. Michael Jupp, DCI's executive director, offers the following exploratory findings and field observations regarding the global child sex trade.

Transnational Incidents

Geographic borders pose a minimal obstacle to those who would sexually exploit children, as shown in the following case. In this example, an American citizen sodomized a Mexican minor. Investigation of the incident revealed that the exploiter had on earlier occasions invited other juveniles from Mexico and the Dominican Republic for illicit sexual purposes. In this instance all criminal charges against the sodomizer were dropped.

AN IMPORTER IN NEW YORK

On August 1, 1984, an older white male was arrested by police officers of New York City's 7th Precinct for sodomizing a 9-year-old Mexican boy. The child, José, had been registered two or three days earlier at a summer day camp on New York's lower east side by the same man.

An observant youth worker noticed that José was depressed, crying and walking as though in pain. She took him aside and asked what was wrong. The story, as told to investigators from Defense for Children International–USA, was that José was born in Acapulco, Mexico. The father of his large and very poor family was approached three weeks before by a visiting Anglo who offered to take the boy to New York, provide him with an education, teach him English, and eventually find him a job. An unknown amount of money changed hands and José was brought to the United States, without proper documentation, past immigration officials. The effect on José of such a change in environment, from sunny Acapulco to the lower east side of New York, was doubtless traumatic. He had been separated from family, friends, school, his entire way of life, only to become a victim of sexual assault by an Anglo.

The youth worker called the New York State hotline for child abuse at 11 A.M. for advice. Nothing happened. Further calls were made and still nothing happened. By 3 P.M. the day camp staff were worried, since the man was due to pick up the child at 3:30 P.M. and no social worker had arrived to investigate. DCI was notified and, as a result of advice given, José was taken to the local precinct station. At 5:30 P.M. the man was arrested and informed that he would be charged with sodomy.

Additional inquiries by DCI members in the neighborhood uncovered evidence that the Anglo had, on at least two prior occasions, brought back other young boys from Mexico and the Dominican Republic. Background details about these boys were available from the local school system, and the information was passed on to the police. It was also discovered that the man advertised regularly in a local paper as an "experienced babysitter." His occupation was listed as school teacher. Medical evidence regarding the abuse suffered by José was considered inconclusive by authorities. The child was eventually returned by New York City officials to his parents in Mexico, and the case against the school teacher was dropped.

THE NYKANEN–COLLINS REPORT (JULY 1985)

Leads from DCI enticed Mark Nykanen and Charles Collins, correspondents employed by the National Broadcasting Company (NBC) in Chicago, to investigate three aspects of the child exploitation market: child pornography in Europe, sex tourism in Thailand, and multi-country adoption practices. These investigations into trafficking in children required interviews in England, the Netherlands, Germany, Thailand, the Philippines, the Dominican Republic, and the United States. In January 1986, NBC broadcast the results of their investigation.

The reporters began by contacting sources used in prior reports on child pornography. At one point they were offered wholesale quantities of child pornography by one Helga S., whom the reporters found to be free and living in Holland. They found that despite police intervention, adult bookstores in Amsterdam contain a readily accessible supply of child pornography. Law enforcement officials expressed the opinion that producers of child pornography are active in Holland, but that they circumvent inspection by United States Customs agents by sending their merchandise to other European countries for shipment to the United States.

Purveyors of child sex tours to Thailand were found to offer their wares through at least two European travel agencies, one based in West Germany and the other in London in the office of a multinational travel organization. According to his report, Nykanen purchased a child sex tour from a London travel agent. When he arrived in Thailand at his destination, a pimp whom he met through the Bangkok branch of the multinational travel agency delivered a 13-year-old girl to his hotel room.

With regard to adoption schemes, United States Naval Intelligence agents stationed in the Philippines who were interviewed by Nykanen and Collins confessed growing concern over the adoption of children for immoral purposes by some American servicemen. A travel agency in Manila admitted to having routinely worked with subscribers to pedophile magazines.

The Nykanen-Collins study concluded by showing the ease with which children can be adopted abroad and then brought to the United States to be sexually abused. The conviction of two men, Laurence Jacobson, a Florida resident who purchased children from the Dominican Republic, and Donald Stevenson, who had brought children from Vietnam, illustrates the bogus adoption schemes. Perfectly humane motives underlying the adoption process can be subverted in the transnational context to serve the exploiter's interests. Economic difficulties in Third World nations, especially countries along the Pacific basin, provide a multitude of minors who serve to advance illegitimate goals, according to this NBC report.

A PROMOTER OF RAPE IN BANGKOK

In July 1985, Manit Thamaree, a small-time Bangkok entrepreneur, was arrested by Thai police. His crimes included (1) the production and distribution of child pornography that showed children being raped by Western adults and (2) the organization of packaged sex tours that arranged for Western males to have sexual intercourse with young Thai children. For these offenses Manit Thamaree received a 12-month prison sentence.

Thamaree's case, unfortunately, is far from unique. He was a producer of what is euphemistically referred to by law enforcement officers as "good class" child pornography in the form of professionally reproduced, glossy magazines. According to customs officials, these magazines were being produced in Bangkok and offered to customers in America. His distribution list for the United States amounted to more than 200 customers. The magazines depicted scenes of children, ranging in age from 7 to 13, engaged in sexual activities with adults. According to investigators, Thamaree offered correspondents in the United States the opportunity to visit Thailand and rape children.

Following his arrest, Thamaree was found in possession of thousands of negatives and prints of white males raping children. All of the photographs and slides appeared to have been taken in Thailand. Many of the pictures had notations on the reverse side that identified the perpetrators as "Americans," "Australians," or men from different European countries. Two facts are unusual about this incident. The first is that Thamaree was arrested. The second is that his arrest was the result of international cooperation between local law enforcement agencies in Michigan, the U.S. Customs Service, and the Bangkok Police.

■   ■   ■

A Global View of the Child Sex Markets

The international trafficking in children for commercial sexual exploitation involves torture, the purchase and sale of children, unlawful incarceration of children so that others may profit, the premeditated rape and mutilation of minors, and, not infrequently, the death of the underage victims. In almost all of these offenses against minors, whether the acts involve prostitution, pornography, or the sex tourism industry, four parties are involved in the transaction: the perpetrator, the vendor, the facilitator, and the child. Perpetrators are usually male and subscribe to a variety of rationalizations to defend their conduct. In some countries perpetrators rationalize their sexual involvement with children in religious terms, as exemplified by the young temple prostitutes of India.[1] Or, as in the case of Chinese subcultural beliefs in East Asia, some perpetrators become involved with minors on the erroneous assumption that intercourse with a child leads to male longevity.[2] A third rationale is the dubious conviction that sex with a minor is beneficial to the victim, a philosophy espoused by the North American Man-Boy Love Association, Lewis Carroll Collector's Guild, and the Paedo Alert News.

Vendors (procurers, pimps) extend the services, capital, and resources that make sexual trafficking both possible and profitable. Profits are frequently maximized by keeping children under the most atrocious living conditions and by denying them a fair share of the income generated by their labors. When children attempt to sell their bodies directly to customers, independent of a vendor, they risk physical harm by adult entrepreneurs and are often forcibly introduced into a structured system.

Facilitators (recruiters, landlords, film laboratory technicians, financiers, and parents) expedite the process by which children are victimized and, in many cases, benefit financially from the activity. The larger the profits, the greater the probability that officials and elected representatives are amenable to bribes. Whole sections of the tourist industries of certain countries, such as Thailand, have developed around an existing commercial sex infrastructure. The detrimental effects of this trade, both to the victims and a country's reputation, are ignored in favor of the perceived immediate need for foreign exchange.

The essential party, finally, to an exploitive act is the child. But there is a problem in defining the word *child* for this discussion, because it can refer also to the age of majority or to the age of consent, which can vary from 14 to 21. The generally accepted international definition of a child is someone under the age of 18, but a clear and uniform yardstick is lacking.

Arguably, minors sometimes have the right to exercise an element of choice in their sexual encounters, although the degree of freedom available is dependent on many social, cultural, and economic factors. This element of freedom, however, is illusory when the only alternative to starvation and homelessness is prostitution. Many victims of the sex trade are sold by their parents to child labor brokers, who often divert the victims from more legitimate forms of employment such as factory work into prostitution on the streets or in brothels.

If and when police decide to take action against the child sex trade, it is frequently the victim who is treated as a criminal and incarcerated rather than the adult perpetrator, vendor, or facilitator. While there are a few isolated programs that attempt to "rehabilitate" children caught in the commercial sex markets, most victims are left to fend for themselves. In the Philippines, for example, government and private agencies deal with less than 1 percent of the children in need of services.[3] The Aquino government, faced with years of neglect by the Marcos regime, is attempting to cope with the child beggars, bar girls, shoeshine boys, and other children who ply their trades on the streets. By working with UNICEF and introducing new programs, the current government is attempting to reduce the levels of victimization for its country's unwanted children.

Most Third World service programs designed to aid victims of sexual trafficking, however, are paternalistic and ineffective. They often lack a comprehensive social policy analysis, are not multidisciplinary in nature, and seldom offer viable economic alternatives for the victims.

The Child Sex Trade in Human Terms

The actual number of children involved worldwide in commercial sexual exploitation is not known. The very nature of the trade makes quantitative studies extremely difficult. Official statistics tend to underestimate the numbers, and reform groups lean toward overestimation. Only occasionally, as a result of a tragedy or an infrequent arrest, do we receive a fleeting glimpse of the potential number of victims involved. The following incidents, documented by reports and newspaper clippings in the *International Children's Rights Monitor* (a journal published by DCI), suggest that countless minors are involved in the child sex trade.

Item: A fire in Phuket, Thailand, left five young prostitutes dead. One of the girls who died had been bought for a $33 advance on her wages. One who was injured was purchased for $43; she was 15 years old and required to service up to 10 customers in a 12-hour working period. She received five cents for each customer, and was told that the "redemption clause" in her indenture contract was $109, or 2,180 customers. Some of the child prostitutes were handcuffed to their beds, a fact that may account for the high mortality rate from the fire. Many had numbers tattooed on their bodies and were sold in advance through special catalogues.

Item: In Dhaka, India, an 11-year-old girl was sold by her 14-year-old friend to the madam of a brothel for 2,000 takka, or $65.

When the girl attempted to resist the men who were forced upon her, she was tortured and eventually died.[4]

Item: In Iquitos, Peru, the demand for 12- to 16-year-olds is reported as "very high among migrant workers," who themselves live an unnatural existence in company-owned camps and enclaves. The companies allegedly supply the young prostitutes and even offer young virgins as gambling prizes.[5]

Item: In the boom towns of South America, reports allege that over 50,000 children and young people struggle to survive in situations of extreme deprivation or as street prostitutes.[6]

UNICEF estimates that between 70 and 80 million street children live in the world's urban centers.[7] *Parade* magazine estimated in 1987 that 1.3 million runaways live in the United States.[8] The U.S. Department of Health and Human Services estimates that about 50 percent of the runaway population are victims of some sort of commercial sexual exploitation. Similarly, in the Philippines, the Ministry of Social Services and Development concluded that child prostitution rivals begging as the major occupation of the 50,000 to 75,000 street children who roam metropolitan Manila.[9]

In Bangkok, Thai social workers estimate that underage prostitutes number in the tens of thousands.[10] One of the two U.S. customs agents who visited Thailand while investigating the Thamaree case told of being taken on a tour of child brothels by a Bangkok police colonel. At one bordello, the prostitutes were reading comic books and looked no older than 12 or 13. The Thai police officer seemed to share the frustrations of many law enforcement officers throughout the world: minimal sentencing by the courts; insufficient police personnel; corruption among underpaid, lower-ranking officials; inadequate social service programs to provide for the victims; and a general lack of political resolve to end the problem.

Whether there are, as claimed, 8,000 underage prostitutes in Paris (a city of 2,317,000), or 150,000 in the United States (out of an estimated total of 62,000,000 minors in 1985), or 50,000 minors involved in prostitution in Thailand (where 38 percent of the population is under fourteen) is debatable. What is beyond dispute is the fact that enormous profits are extracted from this market and from the peripheral offenses such as child pornography and sex tourism.[11]

Given the absence of verifiable figures or records of victimization, there can be no doubt that such activity warrants intervention and rehabilitative efforts by the world's governments. The Canadian Government Commission on Sexual Offences Against Children acknowledged the sheer complexity of the issue of juvenile victimization regarding prostitution in this statement:[12]

> *Publicly, there is widespread indignation and condemnation concerning the plight of these youths. Their visible presence on the downtown street corners of many large Canadian cities is seen in some quarters as a failure of existing public services, social, enforcement and legal, to deal adequately with the problem. A sharp disparity exists between what is said should be done and what is actually done. While in the rhetoric of public debate the needs of these youths are allegedly recognized, the services available to them are either limited in scope or, in some instances, have been curtailed. . . .*

On September 14, 1984, the Italian daily newspaper *La Repubblica* printed a full-page article on child pornography in Amsterdam. The publication of this report was prompted by the death of a 6-year-old girl, Thea, from a cocaine overdose. Thea had been systematically drugged and forced into prostitution. She was also used in the production of pornographic videotapes. As part of the investigation, police seized several videotapes showing sexual relations between adults of both sexes and children, between children and children, and between animals and children. All of the children were under 6 years of age.

Child pornography must be recognized as hard evidence of the sexual exploitation of minors. One international exploiter, a commercial school photographer, was arrested in Manhattan on February 16, 1985 and charged with sodomy and abuse of two 11-year-old boys. He was found to own about 1,000 pictures of underage males engaged in sex acts.[13] In another case, a 70-year-old Canadian retired public employee was arrested in Manila and held on three counts of inducing lascivious acts. He was charged with paying underage females small fees for allowing him to photograph them in erotic poses.

The above scenarios are continuing events within the international child sex trade. They constitute a routine form of trafficking that often is ignored by developing nations and is supported by wealthier countries. A concerted effort by each nation could help curtail such expressions of the child sex trade as indenturing, sex tourism, and foreign adoption for illicit purposes.

The Complicity of National Governments

Many nations allow the exploitation of children—or even promote it. Let us consider this lack of governmental responsibility in the context of adoption schemes, indenturing, and sex tourism.

Adoption Schemes

Obtaining children from Third World countries and bringing them into the United States is relatively easy. According to Bill Pierce of the National Committee for Adoption, at any given time as many as 2 million couples are hoping to adopt a child, while only 50,000 children are available for adoption. One effect of this imbalance is a thriving intercountry adoption trade that in 1984 involved approximately 8,327 children.[14] With few exceptions, the export/import of children is meant to be mutually beneficial to the minor and the adoptive couple. Legal adoption, however, is a complicated, time-consuming, and expensive business costing about $15,000. Because potentially large profits can be made, unscrupulous individuals seek ways to circumvent official channels. A lawyer in Bogota, for example, was charged with buying children for $600 each and then selling each child for considerably more.[15]

Such illegal adoption schemes are not, however, restricted to purchase with parental consent. The international press has reported incidents in which black market rings have stolen children in Taiwan, El Salvador, Sri Lanka, Peru, and Mexico for resale in the United States, Germany, Italy, Switzerland, Sweden, and other Western bloc countries. The U.S. Consulate in El Salvador, under pressure from the Catholic Church to stop the stealing and "farming" out of children, now requires the mother of any child being made available for adoption by U.S. citizens, to come to the consulate in person to sign the relevant papers, rather than going to a local notary—a more stringent standard.[16]

Even though the evidence points to a growing U.S. black market in children from abroad, the motives of most adopting adults are honorable. Sometimes, however, these children are brought to the United States for immoral and abusive purposes, such as molestation, prostitution, and pornography.

Indenturing

Indenturing is the employment of children from poverty-stricken families as house servants for rich families. Commonplace in many parts of the world, including Central and South America, Africa, and Asia, it is a practice that dates back hundreds of years. Indenturing is viewed by the parties involved as an equitable exchange of goods and services: A family that cannot afford to keep all of its children accepts a cash payment, and the wealthy family gains a servant. The minors receive training and perhaps an education. There is always the possibility that the child may enter into a good marriage or have a successful career and thus move up the social ladder.

Unfortunately, indenturing often leads to exploitation and abuse of children. The seduction or rape of the parlor maid by the master of the house was the subject of many a nineteenth century novel. The woman was frequently blamed and cast out either pregnant or with a young child. A long way from home, unable to return to her family because of shame or the financial burden resulting from the penalty clause in her indenture contract, she turned to prostitution as the only means of survival.

The realities of contemporary indenturing are just as harsh. Children as young as 8 in Thailand, the Philippines, and other countries are sold by impoverished parents to agents from Bangkok and Manila. Instead of being placed with rich families, the minors are diverted to brothels in distant cities. A 15-year-old prostitute whom we interviewed had traveled from Santo Domingo to St. Maarten and told a story almost identical to the Victorian melodrama just mentioned. She went to work as a maid in the house of a radio personality at the age of 12. He seduced or raped her, and she was pregnant by the age of 13. After the infant was born, the baby was taken from her, and the offender applied to the courts for custody on the grounds that the mother was immoral. She was expelled from the house and resorted to prostitution.

Sex Tourism

In Japan and Western bloc countries such as the Netherlands, Australia, and England, exploiters have developed a tourist industry that specializes in sex tours of the Far East and other undeveloped parts of the world. The potential profits in this market have not escaped the attention of certain senior politicians. For example, as part of a major bid for a share of the international tourist trade, the Deputy Prime Minister of Thailand is quoted as asking provincial governors:[17] "to consider the natural scenery in your provinces together with some forms of entertainment you might consider disgusting or shameful, because they are forms of sexual entertainment that attract tourists. We have to consider the jobs that will be created." With this type of official encouragement, it is not surprising that fines in Thailand for prostitution offenses are remarkably low—$16 for a recruiter and $22 for a brothel owner or operator—or that bribery and police protection rackets are common.[18] During a raid on a brothel in Thailand, for instance, 29 prostitutes under the age of 19 were released from prisonlike conditions. These girls had also been shipped once a month to Malaysia to entertain customers. Another report speaks of child traffickers taking 11-year-old girls from the hill tribes of Burma, bribing border officials, and smuggling them into Bangkok.[19]

The two industrialized nations that have probably been the most prolific in their exploitation of juveniles are Japan and the United States. Reports indicate that a separate subsection of the Japanese travel industry is devoted to transporting its customers to foreign countries where female prostitutes are made available. DCI estimated that in South Korea there are 5,000 "Kinsaeng Houses," a type of restaurant catering to Japanese male tourists and to which formally trained prostitutes are attached.[20]

During the Vietnam War, the U.S. military developed "recreation and rest centers," a type of government-subsidized tourist trade, provided for U.S. servicemen in various parts of East Asia. These R&R centers were invariably associated with brothels and prostitutes. Apparently little was done by military authorities to monitor the age of the male and female hustlers. Even now, returning community-development workers from the Philippines have reported to DCI that child prostitution seems higher in the vicinity of U.S. military bases. It has been alleged that military personnel figure at a disproportionately high rate in the pedophile exchange lists confiscated by some police departments. Similarly, the establishment of the new U.S. military bases in Honduras appears to have given rise to an increase in the incidence of child prostitution in that country. Newspaper reports from the Hondurans have been so vehement in their complaints about the conduct of some off-duty servicemen that the U.S. ambassador was obliged to go on local television in an attempt to placate the populace.

At least two travel organizations are known to exploit foreign children. One, a West German agency, caters to heterosexuals who wish to have sexual experiences as part of their tour package. Both agencies offer guides to help the tourist negotiate the prices of child prostitutes and give advice on such matters as what hotels to use, how to circumvent local laws, and how to deal with local officials.

International Law: Cooperation and Enforcement

The instances of abuse enumerated above are contrary to the provisions of many international conventions. The following multilateral conventions and their amending protocols provide at least theoretical coverage for the sexually exploited juvenile. Even if the nation fails to subscribe to the convention, violation of principles dating from the turn of the century holds the government in power up to reproach among the community of nations.

Beginning in 1904, the conventions listed below gradually expanded the coverage of human rights and raised the expectation of eventual equality under all civilized governments:

1. International Convention for the Suppression of the White Slave Traffic of May 18, 1904 (Females)
2. Agreement for the Suppression of the Circulation of Obscene Publications, May 4, 1910
3. International Convention for the Suppression of Traffic in Women and Children of September 30, 1921
4. Slavery Convention of September 25, 1926 (Male and Female)
5. Convention for the Suppression of Traffic in Persons and of the Exploitation or the Prostitution of Others, 1949
6. Supplementary Convention on the Abolition of Slavery, the Slave Trade, and Institutions and Practices Similar to Slavery, September 7, 1956
7. Convention Concerning Forced or Compulsory Labor of June 25, 1957

A UN Declaration of the Rights of the Child, which was adopted unanimously by the UN General Assembly on November 20, 1959, states in Principle 9, "The child shall be protected against all forms of neglect, cruelty, and exploitation. He shall not be the subject of traffic, in any form . . .." The issues of child prostitution and sexual exploitation are also included in the proposed UN Convention on the Rights of the Child, which is currently working its way through the UN committee process and should be completed by 1988.

The sexual exploitation of children probably has more international ramifications than any crime except the traffic in illicit drugs. As with the trade in drugs, there have been solemn international treaties dealing with the various aspects of the child sex trade since the turn of the century. Yet, like domestic child protection legislation, such international treaties are often unenforced, and few countries—including the United States—meet their international obligations.

There is no official international body directly responsible for overseeing, investigating, or monitoring the condition of children engaged in commercial sexual exploitation. The two groups that come closest to dealing with this issue are UNICEF, through its mandate to protect children generally, and the International Labor Organization, with its responsibility for ensuring adequate protection in the workplace for employees. Neither of these agencies has an enforcement function, and both rely on the goodwill of sovereign governments to pursue their work on behalf of children. These agencies can advise governments when they believe that a certain condition exists, but in the final analysis they can only perform work requested by the sovereign government.

Organizations that have spearheaded attacks on violations of the rights of children have been international non-governmental organizations. These are private, voluntary organizations such as the Anti-Slavery Society of Great Britain and the Minority Rights Group and Defense for Children International. These organizations and others like them, in conjunction with churches and local grassroots groups, have brought to the world's attention many of the critical conditions affecting children. In Southeast Asia, for example, women's groups, trade unions, and churches have campaigned against the sexual exploitation of children. Private volunteer groups have provided the press and the UN Center for Human Rights a forum for the discussion of these issues. Two major reports were submitted to the Economic and Social Council of the United

Nations on the subject of trafficking in persons (1983) and slavery
(1985).[21]   Whereas organizations help identify the scope of the
problem, international laws are the mechanisms, in theory, for
enforcement and regulation of the child sex trade. In reality,
however, countries that do not enforce domestic legislation regarding the human rights of minors are unlikely to be effective advocates of international statutes. Political priorities, of course, influence the level of national and international enforcement. For
instance, the participants in a February 1986 LAWASIA conference
on Child Labor and Prostitution in Kuala Lumpur, while divided
on the best tactics to adopt regarding child labor, were unanimous
in their condemnation of child prostitution and the need for stricter
enforcement of existing laws and international agreements, as
indicated in their declaration of purpose.

DECLARATION ON CHILD PROSTITUTION
LAWASIA CONFERENCE: KUALA LUMPUR, FEBRUARY 1986

WITH REGARD TO CHILD PROSTITUTION:
This conference, together with the LAWASIA Human Rights Standing
Committee, having shared their expertise and having considered the
papers presented at this meeting:

- recognizes the immense problem of child prostitution existing in all
  countries of the region, is shocked and outraged at the enormity of
  the problem that has been allowed to continue unabated;
- recognizes that the dimension of the problem is such that immediate
  remedial action is both necessary and possible; and

CALLS ON GOVERNMENTS IN THE REGION

- to take all necessary steps to totally eliminate child prostitution from
  the region;
- to immediately take steps to ratify the UN Declaration on the Rights
  of the Child, the Convention for Suppression of Traffic of Women
  and Children in 1921, the Convention for Suppression of the Traffic
  in Persons and the Exploitation of Prostitution of Others 1950, and
  the Convention for the Suppression of the Circulation of and Traffic
  in Obscene Publications, 1923, if such UN instruments have not
  already been drafted;
- to study cultural patterns that endorse and foster the practice of
  child prostitution;
- to revise all relevant legislation, much of which is derived from
  outdated colonial legislation that is no longer relevant to the current
  manifestations of the problem, and in particular to impose stiffer
  penalties as a deterrent measure and reform any legislation that
  views the child as an offender rather than a victim;

- to provide rehabilitation programs for children who have been victims of child prostitution;
- to take steps to introduce and enforce regulatory controls to prevent exploitation of children in tourism, in particular to ensure that all tourist literature and immigration documents contain a statement on severe penalties for sexual exploitation of children;
- to increase awareness of the social implications of the problem and the legal controls at all levels, in particular amongst those involved in the administration of justice;
- to take all necessary and effective measures to ensure the protection of the rights and interests of refugee children so that they are prevented from being lured into prostitution;
- to promote an international prohibition on advertising of child prostitution; and

ENCOURAGES NON-GOVERNMENT ORGANIZATIONS IN THE REGION

- to conduct campaigns to pressure governments in the region to take the above-mentioned steps to eliminate the practice of prostitution;
- to draw attention to the UN instruments pertinent to child prostitution and to encourage and monitor progress being made in regard to ratification of such instruments;
- to lobby at national and international conferences on tourism against the practice of child prostitution;
- to promote an international prohibition on advertising of child prostitution;
- to foster greater international cooperation on this issue and to pursue their activities when appropriate on the regional and international level through existing organizations such as the Child Workers in Asia Support Group and Defence for Children International;
- to encourage UNICEF to take account of these conclusions and recommendations in devising their programs for the region.

THIS CONFERENCE RECOMMENDS THAT LAWASIA

- sends the Conclusions and Recommendations of this Conference to all governments in the region and seeks a response to the issues which they raise;
- seeks funds to publish and disseminate and does publish and widely disseminate the materials for this Conference;
- includes in its Human Rights Bulletin for dissemination throughout the LAWASIA region information on the human rights of the children, and conducts, subject to availability of funds, further workshops, seminars and conferences to promote further public awareness of the plight of exploited children;
- encourages practicing lawyers in the region to promote the rights of these children through the courts, to establish their rights and

dignity as human beings, and to foster further public awareness of the problem.

The Politics of Sexual Trafficking

One of the frustrations of trying to combat the commercial sexual exploitation of children is the inconsistency of governments' actions.[22] It is one thing to take a stand against the crime of exploitation, but quite another to mobilize a society's resources to implement an effective program. National and international politics, therefore, are important variables that affect the role of governments in preserving the rights of children.

Governmental interest in the issue of child sexual trafficking peaks and wanes and official policies constantly change. The following are a few examples of this inconsistency:

- In the Philippines, the Marcos regime noted that no problem existed because sexual exploitation is illegal.
- In Thailand, the crimes of sexual exploitation are denied, on the one hand, yet encouraged, on the other, for the sake of gaining foreign currency.
- In Denmark, such illegal activities are considered to be rare occurrences.

On the basis of these official attitudes, which deny rather than confront the problem of sexual trafficking, efforts to abolish the child sex trade within and between countries have been no more successful than those intended to end the trafficking in drugs. This failure is particularly true in regard to sexual exploitation because (1) the victims usually cannot escape their predicament, (2) offenders avoid public exposure, and (3) politicians are understandably anxious to report success and conceal failure. Inevitably, if official indifference and complacency continue at the international level, more and more children will be victimized. The resources of numerous governments are not used on behalf of exploited minors for the following reasons:

1. Children have very limited economic power. Because they are in the marketplace only at subsistence wages, and in small number, they have no financial influence on government policies.

2. For a government to admit its inability to cope adequately with a social problem can be politically self-defeating and embarrassing. A convenient way to rationalize the lack of action is to claim that (1) the problem does not exist, (2) the size and scope of the problem are insignificant, or (3) efforts to deal with the problem are effective.

3. Corruption and complicity by government officials, particularly in underdeveloped nations seeking foreign exchange, may prevent potential advocates from mobilizing resources on behalf of victimized children.

Nonetheless, the commitment of governments is necessary if international sexual trafficking is to be eradicated. The first step in any country is to seek public recognition of the problem and public support for the use of the needed resources for dealing with it. In this vein, several nations have begun to assist minors who were sexually abused by parents or others legally responsible for their care. Laws have been passed (see Chapter 7) and reporting procedures established. Unfortunately, to date, international condemnation of sexual exploitation of children remains primarily a matter of political rhetoric without a substantive base in enforcement.

Endnotes

1. "Report of the Working Group on Slavery in its Eleventh Session," United Nations Economic and Social Council, Commission on Human Rights, Sub-Commission on Prevention of Discrimination and Protection of Minorities (August 21, 1985), E/CN.4/Sub.2/1985/25.
2. "Prostitution in Thailand," *Center for Women Policy Studies*, Vol. 8, No. 2 (Spring 1985).
3. "Program for Kids Launched" *Manila Bulletin* (April 14, 1986).
4. ABC Radio News, Human Rights Bulletin, LAWASIA, Vol. 4, No. 2 (July 25, 1985).
5. "Children in Especially Difficult Circumstances: The Sexual Exploitation of Children, Prostitution and Pornography," report for UNICEF prepared by The Anti-Slavery Society for the Protection of Human Rights (1984).
6. "Report of Mr. Jean Fernand-Laurent, Special Rapporteur on the Suppression of the Traffic in Persons and the Exploitation of the Prostitution of Others," United Nations Economic and Social Council (March 17, 1983), E/1983/7.
7. *Japan Times* (May 1985).
8. "It Can Happen Anywhere, Kids for Sale," *Parade Magazine* (July 20, 1986).
9. "Child Prostitution Now a Major Problem," *Philippines Daily Express* (May 28, 1984). See also "Suffer Children," *The News Herald* (Manila) (April 16, 1986).

10. Siamrath, Human Rights Bulletin, LAWASIA, Vol. 4, No. 2 (July 25, 1985). See also endnote 5.
11. Daniel S. Campagna, "Sexual Exploitation of Children" (Wheeling, W. Va.: West Virginia Criminal Justice Institute, 1985), pp. 6–26.
12. Report, "Sexual Offences Against Children," Canadian Government Commission on Sexual Offences Against Children (Ottawa: Canadian Government Publishing Centre, August 1984), v.1, catalog nos. J-2-50/1984E.
13. "Nab Photog on Child-Sex Rap," *New York Daily News* (February 17, 1985).
14. "Adoption Factbook," (National Committee for Adoption: Washington, D.C., November 1985).
15. See endnote 6.
16. "Abductions in Salvador Fill a Demand: Adoption," *New York Times* (December 17, 1985).
17. "Prostitution Tourism," in Perpignan, Sr., *Women in a Changing World* (World Council of Churches, No. 11, December 1981).
18. See endnote 5.
19. "Thai Report Highlights Child Slavery Problem," *International Children's Rights Monitor*, Vol. 2, No. 1 (1985).
20. It should be noted that there is no official documentation to substantiate the existence of 5,000 Kinsaeng Houses in South Korea.
21. See endnotes 1 and 6.
22. Dr. Kenneth Herrmann, Jr., Dept. of Social Work, SUNY at Brockport, N.Y.

Part Three

ADDRESSING THE PROBLEM

Previous chapters have discussed the composition and dynamics of the various child sex markets. In Part Three we search for ways to deal with the sexual exploitation of minors. Chapter 7 weighs the prospects of reform through state and federal intervention in the form of statutes and judicial advocacy. Alternative sentencing options are discussed as a possible method for breaking the cycle of sexual victimization.

Chapter 8 examines the victimization cycle. Different types of exploitive parents are discussed, and particular attention is paid to the role of dysfunctional families in the creation of sexually victimized offspring.

Chapter 9 looks at the issue of victim advocacy. Four practical approaches currently in operation are reviewed: treatment for the victim, federal child sexual exploitation task forces, police-social worker teams, and case preparation. Each represents a grassroots approach to the problems of sexual trafficking and child victimization.

Chapter 10 presents strategies for change, including a host of alternative measures designed to help agency practitioners improve the quality of their services. In addition, a broad range of low-cost, resource-effective options are recommended for immediate implementation in the criminal justice, social, human, and youth service systems.

Chapter 7

SEXUAL TRAFFICKING AND THE JUDICIAL RESPONSE

State and federal laws prohibit most forms of child sexual exploitation, including prostitution, molestation, procuring, sex rings, pornography, and the transportation of minors for sexual purposes. The extent to which these laws actually restrict the child sex markets by acting as statutory barriers between victim and exploiter, however, is debatable. In this chapter we examine the official reaction to the issue of sexual exploitation, as well as appropriate punitive responses to the crimes of sexual trafficking.

The Legislative Response: Statutory Intervention

An economic link between victim and offender is often forged when minors are excluded from legitimate employment opportunities. Indeed, a number of federal and state laws prohibit minors from acquiring any gainful employment. When legitimate opportunities do not exist,[1] survival for children who lack the support of their family may depend upon entry into a commercial sex market. State legislators have long recognized the relationship between exploitation and the profit motive, as one legislative resolution of the Arizona legislature states:[2]

> *The production and sale of such child pornographic materials results in millions of dollars of profit . . . and the abundance of these materials in Arizona indicates that this state contributes substantially to that figure.*

161

The state legislature of New York has acknowledged the unhealthy relationship between exploitation and profit as a reflection of statutory failure to provide for juveniles at risk. Furthermore, it declared that the state has an obligation to break the bonds of economic exploitation associated with the sexual victimization of minors:[3] "The legislature finds that there has been a proliferation of exploitation of children as subjects in sexual performances. The care of children is a sacred trust and should not be abused by those who seek to profit through a commercial network based upon the exploitation of children."

While many legislators clearly understand the need for action, not all legislation effectively addresses the problems of sexual trafficking. Vague language and overly broad coverage in state and federal laws have led critics to question whether such statutes are consistent with the provisions of state constitutions and the federal Constitution. Most challenges are based on alleged violations of the First, Sixth, and Fourteenth Amendments, which guarantee, among other rights, freedom of speech, freedom of the press, the right to a speedy and public trial by an impartial jury, the right to be informed of an accusation, the right to confront witnesses, the right to assistance of counsel and compulsory process, and the right to equal protection under the law. As a general rule, nevertheless, a state's interest in insuring the welfare and safety of children is deemed to take precedence over the possible infringement of an offender's constitutional guarantees.

Judicial responses to constitutional challenges are based on past experiences with economic and social welfare legislation and on prior decisions in cases in the areas of child neglect, incest, sexual assault, and obscenity. These laws permit a state to intervene in a minor's life. A juvenile runaway, for instance, can be involuntarily placed under state supervision in an institutional setting. Although actions of this kind often raise the question of whose best interest is being served, they translate a child's entitlement to protection into concrete action. Like child abuse laws, however, sexual exploitation statutes are often viewed as an unreasonable assault on familial integrity and individual freedom.[4] Substantive due process minimally requires, therefore, that intervention be reasonably related to the promotion of a valid state interest: in this case, the protection of a human resource.[5] Advocates of intervention by the state in matters of sexual exploitation argue that such steps are justified because, in the words of Justice Herbert A. Pickford of the Supreme Court of Virginia, "(t)he state has a compelling interest, one central to its right to survive, in protecting children from treatment it determines is physically or psychologically injurious to youth."[6]

Defending the state's interest in this matter can be properly traced back to the development of child neglect legislation, the percursor of sexual exploitation statutes. Child neglect laws developed from the belief that the welfare of the child is of paramount importance and that the legal rights of the parent should be respected if the welfare of the child is not endangered.[7] Similar concerns were expressed at the national level in *Prince v. Commonwealth of Massachusetts* (321 U.S. 158, 64 S. Ct. 438, 88 L.Ed. 645, rehearing denied 321 U.S. 804, 64 S.Ct. 784, 88 L.Ed. 1090 [1943]). Justice Rutledge recognized that the state has an ongoing interest in protecting children against such abuse as might prevent their "growth into free, independent, well-developed men and citizens."[8] The *Prince* decision held that the state may constitutionally intervene in the parent-child relationship for the purpose of enforcing its child labor laws.

Child neglect statutes have been criticized as overly broad when they focused on criteria other than a minor's condition—for example, parental conduct or character. Even then, as the U.S. Supreme Court observed in *Ginsberg v. New York* (390 U.S. 629, 88 S. Ct. 1274, 20 L.Ed.2d 195, rehearing denied 391 U.S. 971, 88 S. Ct. 2029, 20 L.Ed.2d 887 [1968]), the state has a more compelling interest in the protection of children than in the control of adults (parents). Because child welfare legislation is often based on intuitive and emotional assumptions, it is reasonable to suppose, in the words of *Columbia Law Review* editor Robert Buckholz, that "the narrowest possible means by which the state could fully implement its interest in child protection would be a statutory formulation focusing on the child's condition and requiring a determination that the proposed state assistance would in fact benefit the child."[9]

Unfortunately, criteria deemed suitable for child neglect cases often fail to accurately encompass child exploitation situations. In this regard, laws meant to eliminate child prostitution and pornography, for example, have come under increased congressional scrutiny since the *Ferber* decision,[10] in which the U.S. Supreme Court upheld the constitutionality of a New York criminal statute prohibiting the knowing promotion of sexual performances by children under 16 by the distribution of materials depicting such performances. Frequently, laws that govern sexual trafficking are inadequate in their protection of children. As stated by the federal judge for the Western District of Oklahoma in 1986:

> *Such statutes are supplemental to other statutes readily applicable to activities associated with child pornography such as rape, incest, sodomy, child abuse and neglect, contributing to the delinquency of a minor, indecent exposure, and obscenity. These other statutes are somewhat limited because some impose liability upon parents and guardians only, have relatively weak penalty provisions, outlaw physical abuse only, and are not only difficult to prosecute but are also low on the priority status of prosecutions in general. (Hon. Lee R. West)*[11]

This observation brings the central problem into focus. Legislators must make suitable legislation a higher priority. For, in the words of David Shouvlin, "without the incentive of probable conviction, prosecutors are unwilling to prosecute, police are dissuaded from making arrests, and pedophiles (and others) are left to sexually exploit children without fear of reprisal."[12]

Congress chartered the National Child Labor Committee in 1907 to "promote the welfare of America's working children, investigate conditions in various industries, and spearhead the push for state legislation."[13] On June 24, 1924 Congress proposed an amendment to the United States Constitution banning child labor, which 28 state legislatures had ratified by 1937. In 1938 the Fair Standards Act was passed, prohibiting the labor of children under the age of 16 in most jobs and barring persons under 18 from dangerous occupations.[14]

Although it was intended to prohibit the economic exploitation of minors, the Fair Labor Standards Act inadvertently provided a variety of opportunities for adults seeking to profit from the financially disadvantageous situations of minors. Directed exclusively at the abuses of child labor in manufacturing, the act left significant gaps in the protection of minors in non-manufacturing activities which were subsequently exploited by sexual traffickers.

Since 1937 the bulk of federal legislation in the area of child protection has focused on child abuse and neglect, primarily within the family. In 1981 the U.S. Supreme Court granted a petition for certiorari in the *Ferber* case which raised this question: To prevent the abuse of children who are made to engage in sexual conduct for commercial purposes, could the New York State Legislature (or any legislature) prohibit the dissemination of material which shows children engaged in sexual conduct, regardless of whether such material is obscene?[15] The Court responded affirmatively to the question, stating that "child pornography, like obscenity, is unprotected by the First Amendment if it involves scienter (a defendant's guilty knowledge) and a visual depiction of sexual conduct by children without serious literary, artistic, political, or scientific value."[16]

Before the *Ferber* decision, 47 states and Congress had legislation specifically addressing child pornography. In the wake of the *Ferber* decision, Congress amended the Protection of Children Against Sexual Exploitation Act of 1977, passage of which was necessary because existing laws provided inadequate protection against the use of children as prostitutes or as the subjects of pornographic materials.[17] The amendments produced four changes in prevailing federal law: (1) the age of majority was raised from 16 to 18; (2) pecuniary penalties were raised to $200,000 for persons and $250,000 for organizations; (3) the commercial purpose requirement was deleted; and (4) the obscenity requirement was deleted. The legislative committee concluded that "since the harm to the child exists whether or not those who initiate or carry out the schemes are motivated by profit, the subcommittee found a need to expand the coverage of the Act."[18] The U.S. Court of Appeals for the Eleventh Circuit in 1985 found that the amended version, known as the Child Protection Act of 1984, did not violate the defendant's constitutional right to privacy.[19] In 1986 Congress passed the Child Abuse Victims Act of 1986, which increased the minimum term of imprisonment to five years for an individual guilty of the sexual exploitation of minors.

In 1984 Congress enacted the Missing Children and Assistance Act, which established a national clearinghouse and resource center to "provide state and local governments, public and private non-profit agencies, and individuals with technical assistance in locating and recovering missing children."[20] As a result, the National Center on Missing and Exploited Children was created. Funded by the Office of Juvenile Justice and Delinquency Prevention, the Center was directed to extend, among other services, "assistance to state law enforcement agencies in investigating and prosecuting cases of missing and exploited children."[21] The center is also responsible for maintaining a nationwide, toll-free hotline, and has orchestrated a variety of media campaigns designed to publicize the plight of missing children. One of the center's principal functions is to collect and disseminate data on the problem of sexual exploitation to state agencies.

At the federal level, sexual trafficking has been addressed by legislative remedies which provide penalties but meager financing for state and private agencies. Sexually exploitive acts prohibited by federal statutes include child pornography, sexual abuse, and child prostitution. The Child Abuse Prevention and Treatment Act (42 U.S.C. § 5102 *et. seq.*) sets a broad federal standard to which state laws can be compared. This act, which has been amended several times since its inception in 1974, makes it unlawful for any person to employ, use, persuade, induce, entice, or coerce any child to engage in, or have a child assist any other person in the production of, sexually explicit or simulated conduct. This prohibition holds true for anyone, including a parent, legal guardian, or custodial adult who allows or knowingly permits a minor to enter into such a situation.

Punishment for Sexual Trafficking

Debate continues over what constitutes appropriate punishment for child exploiters. Do fines and prison sentences reduce the level of trafficking? Is there a cause-effect relationship between severe punishment and reduction in the number of sexually victimized minors? There is not—at least presently—a sufficiently informed consensus to dictate definitive and comprehensive approaches. What can be agreed on is that the criminal justice system must provide speedy trials and that the punishment should be appropriate for the offense.

To determine appropriate punishment, most states consider the nature of the offense, its degree of severity, the defendant's past record, and the extent of the defendant's involvement in the case under consideration. (See Tables 7–1 and 7–2.) The judgment can be substantial fines or a term of imprisonment. The latter course must, however, be considered in the context of the present prison overcrowding and the high cost of incarceration. Accordingly, it is most often adopted with violent offenders—that is to say, punishment is not likely to be severe unless the offense can be defined as having as an element "the use, attempted use, or threatened use of physical force against the person or property of another, or any other offense that is a felony and that, by its nature, involves a

Table 7-1   Selected State Legislation Showing Upper Limit of Penalty

State, Statute, and Year of Passage	Term of Imprisonment	Fine
California: Sexual Exploitation of Children (1981)	6 years	$100,000
Florida: Sexual Performance of a Child (1985)	15 years	$ 10,000
Georgia: Sexual Exploitation of Children (1983)	20 years	$ 20,000
Minnesota: Sexual Exploitation of Child or Child Pornography (1982–1983)	20 years	$ 20,000
New Jersey: Endangering Welfare of Children (1984)	10 years	
New York: Sexual Performance by a Child (1977)	7 years	
Ohio: Obsenity Involving a Minor (1977)	10 years	
Pennsylvania: Sexual Abuse of a Child (1977)	10 years	
Tennessee: Use of Minors for Obscene Purposes (1985)	21 years	$ 10,000
Virginia: Production, Publication, Sale, Possession with Intent to Distribute, etc., of Sexually Explicit Items Involving Children (1986)	10 years	$ 1,000

substantial risk that physical force against the person or property of another may be used in the course of committing the offense."[22]

This approach leaves in doubt the appropriate punishment of various other offenses that lack the ingredient of violence. Child pornography, for example, is a major element of sexual trafficking, yet lacks the element of violence that would result in incarceration for even a flagrant offender. In response to this circumstance, the courts have begun exploring new options. California, for instance, has established a pilot program for treatment of offenders who have sexually abused children. Initially, an offender is required to undergo counseling in conjunction with a probationary sentence. If he continues to abuse children or declines counseling, the sentencing court removes the probationer from the program,[23] and the traditional sanction of imprisonment is imposed.

At the federal level, criteria established for fixing an appropriate sentence include:

1. Age.
2. Education.
3. Vocational skills.
4. Mental and emotional condition, to the extent that such condition mitigates the defendant's culpability or to the extent that such condition is otherwise plainly relevant.

Table 7–2   Federal Legislation

Federal Statute	Penalty
Importation of Immoral Articles Prohibited 18 U.S.C. § 1305 (1980)	Seizure and disposition, 19 C.F.R. § 12.40, 12.41.
Mailing Obscene or Crime-Inciting Matter 18 U.S.C. § 1461 (1971)	Maximum fine of $5,000 and maximum imprisonment of 5 years. Subsequent offense doubles penalties.
Offenses Committed within Indian Country 18 U.S.C. § 1153 (1986)	Penalty of state jurisdiction.
Penalty for Mailing of Sexually Oriented Advertisement 18 U.S.C. § 1735 (1970)	Maximum fine of $5,000 and maximum imprisonment of 10 years. Subsequent offense doubles penalties.
Child Sexual Abuse and Pornography Act of 1986, Pub. L. No. 99-628, Nov. 7, 1986, 100 Stat. 3510–3512 Section 2. Advertising Offenses Related to Sexual Exploitation of Children	Fined and imprisoned for any term of yrs. or life, or both.
Sexual Abuse of a minor or ward 18 U.S.C. § 2243 (1986) Chapter 109A—Sexual Abuse Aggravated Sexual Abuse (c) with Children 18 U.S.C. § 2241 (1986)	Fined and imprisoned for not more than 5 yrs., or both (minor). Fined and imprisoned for not more than 1 yr., or both (ward).
Transportation of Minors 18 U.S.C. § 2423 (1986)	Fine and maximum imprisonment of 10 years, or both.
Sexual Exploitation of Children 18 U.S.C. § 2251–2252* (1986)	Maximum fine of less than $100,000 and imprisonment up to 10 years, or both. Prior conviction: maximum fine of $200,000 and imprisonment of 5–15 years, or both. Maximum organization fine of $250,000. (See note below)*
Criminal / Civil Forfeiture 18 U.S.C. § 2253, 2254 (1986)	Forfeiture of property subsequent to seizure by federal authorities.

*Between May 1977 and November 1983, only four persons had been indicted under Section 18 U.S.C., § 2251, of whom two pleaded guilty to other charges under 18 U.S.C. § 2252 (traffic in materials portraying sexual exploitation of children), one pleaded guilty to conspiracy, and one still had proceedings pending. Report of the Judiciary Committee, House of Representatives, to Accompany H. R. 3635, Report No.98-536, at 2 (1983), 1984 U.S. CODE CONG. & ADMIN. NEWS 493. Of the 28 persons indicted during the same period for § 2252 offenses, 23 were convicted, 2 were convicted of other obscenity violations, 1 defendant committed suicide, and 2 defendants were subject to pending violations, *ibid*.

In the twenty-eight months from May 21, 1984 to Sept. 26, 1986, 274 individuals had been indicted and 214 individuals were convicted for federal sexual exploitation of children violations. Report of the Judiciary Committee, House of Representatives, to Accompany H. R. 5560, Report No. 99-910, at 5 (1986), 1986 U.S. CODE CONG. & ADMIN. NEWS 5954.

5. Physical condition, including drug dependence.
6. Previous employment record.
7. Family ties and responsibilities.
8. Community ties.
9. Role in the offense.
10. Criminal history.
11. Degree of dependence upon criminal activity for a livelihood.[24]

Careful consideration of these factors assists the sentencing court in fashioning a sentence appropriate to the circumstances and increases the likelihood of achieving the following fundamental objectives:[25]

1. Protection of the minor victim in the case at hand.
2. Protection of potential victims.
3. Separation of the offender and the victims.
4. Rehabilitation of both the victim and the offender.
5. Action to prevent reoccurrence.

This approach tends to provide alternatives to imprisonment. In 80 percent of the states and in the federal courts, the trial judge imposes sentence; jury sentencing is retained in less than a dozen jurisdictions. Under both modes, the dual objective of sentencing is apparent: the wrongdoer is punished and others are deterred from committing similar offenses.

How the System Works in Practice

As previously stated, a state's right to intervene in a minor's behalf is well-established. A point of considerable tension develops, however, when legislators and judges must balance the interests of minors against the constitutional rights of defendants. One way to measure the effectiveness of current statutory remedies is to consider how they were applied in an actual case of sexual exploitation. Clearly not all victims benefit from the remedies theoretically available. The following case is an example of what happens when legal procedures are applied in the absence of judicial advocacy. It is a mother's account of her 9-year-old son's encounter with a neighborhood pedophile and the consequences of his victimization, both within and outside the formal judicial system.

Taking the parent's point of view, the reader may answer the following questions, then evaluate the performance of the system in terms of the case's outcome:

1. What would I want the judicial system to do to ensure that my child's best interests and rights were represented?
2. What sort of penalties would I want applied to the offender?
3. What, if any, compensation would I expect for my child in the form of therapy and personal damages?
4. What consideration would I expect from the prosecutor and the judge in terms of minimizing my child's trauma during the pre-trial, trial, and post-trial phases of this case?

A VICTIM POORLY SERVED BY THE SYSTEM

Jeff was our next-door neighbor, about 36 years old and a cook at a hotel restaurant. I really trusted him—never trusted somebody so much in my life. He never seemed to have any girlfriends, but I didn't ask why 'cause it was none of my business. Jeff was good to kids, especially to Aaron. He had a yard, just a little old yard, and he'd give Aaron $10 to mow it. When I asked Aaron where he got the money, he said, "I got it from my buddy." That's what he called Jeff—"my buddy." So I called Jeff up and asked him how come he paid Aaron, a 9-year-old kid, $10. He said he liked Aaron and figured he could use some extra spending money. He kept on giving Aaron money all the time.

What a good neighbor. He'd come over, bring me the paper, take out the garbage. I've never known anybody nicer than he was. I discovered he had let Aaron drive his car. Other people had seen it. I mean, a 9-year-old driving a car? I found out about this later. Nobody told us at the time. Aaron liked him a lot. Sometimes he came over to the house to sit and talk with my husband and me about things in general. One night, around 9 p.m., Jeff stopped by to see if Aaron could spend the night at his house. I let him know that my son wasn't allowed to stay away from home. Still, we didn't think anything was really wrong. This guy would get upset, real mad, if someone else ever took Aaron out to play. Right then I should have been smart enough to figure him out, because he was always with my son. I just thought he liked him.

It's my fault for not knowing better. I was working late the day it happened. When I came home, my husband, who is disabled, met me out at the car and said, "Cathy, Aaron's sick. He's been throwing up all day, ever since he got back from Jeff's." My husband kept asking Aaron what was wrong but he wouldn't say anything. Anyways, he was just deathly sick so we took him to the hospital emergency room. The nurse told us to go sit in the waiting room while the doctors examined him. We still didn't have any idea what was wrong with our son.

Eventually the doctor came out of the examining room and told us what had happened. Jeff had had oral sex with my son. Aaron opened up to the doctors but he refused to tell us. To this day, I don't know all of the details because Aaron is too ashamed and scared to discuss it. So we don't push it. When I found out at the hospital, I just sat there in total shock. I thought, what am I going to do? After all, I trusted this guy. My next-door neighbor! I almost went crazy. Jeff of all people. For a little while my mind refused to believe it.

After the shock wore off, they told me at the hospital that I had to get a warrant for his arrest. Which I did, and they put Jeff in jail on a pretty high bond. By the way, I had to take Aaron back to the hospital the second night. He was a nervous wreck. Let me tell you what it was like for him. He wouldn't eat, was sick for days, never could get to sleep. He'd stand in a corner all day long and blame himself, repeating, "It's all my fault, all my fault." Every time the phone rings, he'll say, "Momma, is somebody asking about me?" At first he cried day and night. When he finally went back to school, word got out about what had happened, and the kids would say awful things to him— God, they were cruel. I called the teachers at the school, but that didn't help much.

When it first happened, I had a terrible time with him. You couldn't even mention the incident in the house or Aaron would burst out crying. I spent my whole paycheck to buy him a special bicycle, to help cheer him up since it was something he'd always wanted. He wouldn't play with it. Instead, he would just sit by himself and pick at his fingers. I knew what was on his mind. We took him to Baltimore for a vacation, but that didn't help. You cannot run away from something like that.

Anyways, after Jeff was arrested, there was a hearing in closed court with the prosecutor, judge, and a bunch of people (grand jury) asking questions. Aaron didn't want to go in the courtroom.

We had to practically drag him in. It broke his heart. They had questioned us one at a time, but they wouldn't let my husband or me sit in the courtroom with Aaron. Jeff had an attorney and said he was not guilty. Mr. Abbott, the prosecutor, represented us. The people in court asked me if I was a fit mother because I wanted to put my son through the pain of a trial. They actually blamed me for wanting to go to all this trouble to get the guy locked up!

There never was a trial. We were supposed to have a preliminary hearing, but the prosecutor kept putting us off. This went on for weeks. We spent a whole day sitting in his office once and he finally came out and said, "Not today. Why not drop the case?" Abbott told me that I should drop the case because Aaron would have to go through a bad time in court. At first I wouldn't do it. I told Abbott, "If I drop it, what is Jeff going to do next?" I was furious. Nobody cared if Jeff got punished.

The prosecutor called up one day and said Jeff had pleaded guilty to the charge. He was willing to do anything they wanted except go to jail. So Abbott told me that if I agreed, Jeff would be put on probation and sent to the mental health center for treatment. I was against it, but Abbott said, once again, "If you think your son went through hell at the grand jury hearing, wait till the defense gets him in open court. They'll tear him apart. Let it drop or take your chances in court." This was the choice he gave me. I still don't understand why I had to decide. Isn't a prosecutor supposed to make this decision?

I sat up all night trying to decide what to do. My husband wanted Jeff locked up. Finally, I told Abbott, okay, drop it. The only reason I agreed to probation was because he gave me so much hassle about what the defense would do to my son in open court. I didn't think Aaron could take it at the time. I gave the prosecutor my home and work phone numbers and asked him to call and notify me of the outcome of the case. He never called or let me know a damn thing. I still don't know for sure if Jeff is on probation or what they did to him. To this day no one will tell me.

The worst part is that we still run into Jeff. I've seen him. So has Aaron. About a week ago, we went to a store and Aaron suddenly took off running for the car. Jeff was in the store and Aaron saw him. My oldest son spotted this guy in town one day, jumped out of the car, and just about beat Jeff to death. Jeff tried to get a warrant issued on my son, but the prosecutor refused. When it first happened, my husband begged the police to let him go find Jeff and kill him. If the police hadn't picked up Jeff first, my husband would have killed the guy. No question about it.

Aaron has calmed down since the incident, but any little thing gets him upset. The doctors said it would take years for him to recover, but he'd never forget what happened to him. School kids still tease him and he still thinks it is all his fault. He refuses to get help at the mental health center and wants to know why he has to go there if it wasn't his fault. What did he do wrong? Aaron is 10 years old now. He cries a lot. I try not to think about it too much. My husband and I never discuss it when he's home. But I'm his mother. I know it plays on his mind. He spends a lot of time alone, just thinking. Never ever talks about the incident. I don't think he fully understands what happened to him.

I think I did wrong. I believe now I should have gone to trial, but this case just meant nothing to the prosecutor. This experience will stay with Aaron for a long time. Take it from me, and don't ever trust your next-door neighbor.

■   ■   ■

The criminal justice system in this case obviously failed to address the problem of appropriate punishment. Instead, the prosecutor accepted a plea bargain that returned a child molester immediatedly to the community. No provisions were made to place either Aaron or his family in counseling or therapy as a result of this traumatic incident. Obviously, there are a number of important peripheral issues involved in this case, including sentencing as an appropriate expression of the state's perceived interest in the welfare of a minor.

Judicial Advocacy

The rights of an underage victim of sexual molestation are sometimes incompatible with the needs of substantive due process and the application of legal remedies. In Aaron's case, the mother assumed, correctly or not, that both victim and defendant were moved through the judicial process with a minimum expenditure of effort, time, and interest by the judicial officers.

Judicial advocacy is more than just going through the motions of protecting underage victims. Alexander Lyerly, a district court judge with jurisdiction over certain types of cases involving exploited children, points out in the following case that judicial advocacy also involves the investigation, hearing, prosecution, and fair disposition of such crimes with full consideration for a victim's rights.[26] Only in such a comprehensive approach will the response be appropriate and equitable to the needs of the sexually exploited child, while still ensuring the rights of the accused.

A VIEW FROM THE BENCH

All children are potential victims of sexual abuse or exploitation. There is no minimum age: We deal with cases in which the victims are only a few days old. The significant majority of cases with which I have been involved have, however, concerned children who are in the prepubescent stage of physical/sexual development. Sexual exploitation of children may take any number of forms, from actual, definable "sexual acts" upon the persons of children, to private, traded, or commercial photographs and films, to the private or commercial prostitution of children. Victims come from all types of families. Both birth and stepparents, adoptive and foster parents are frequently the abusers. Professional caregivers in schools, group homes, day-care facilities, and even homes specifically structured to house and treat the abused child should be aware of the possibility that these places provide for staff members an excellent opportunity for exploiting children. Unfortunately the public, medical, and legal professionals, law enforcement personnel, social workers, parents, and especially the courts often lack adequate skills to deal with every level of the abused child's needs.

Children who have been sexually abused or exploited rarely fabricate the story. If anything, they tend not to relate it fully, especially if it is an isolated (rather than an ongoing) incident of abuse. Children simply lack the sexual and social sophistication to intellectualize an abusive or exploitive event. Some do, of course, but most do not. The exploiter often finds his or her encounters with kids to be more sexually and psychologically gratifying because he or she, as the abuser, can feel somehow "superior" to the child. The victim frequently has little or no sexual sophistication and generally little or no basis of comparison in sexual experiences.

Having listened to adult molesters testify in many cases, it is clear that the child may not appreciate the criminal or wrong nature of the sexual act. This gives the offender further protection from discovery. Children are also more susceptible to gifts or other forms of intimidation which insure their cooperation, confidence, or secrecy. Children almost always want to feel as if they have the approval of an individual who is usually older and perceived to be more "powerful" at the time of the abusive incident. The child will continue to seek reinforcement of this approval through continued cooperation or a bond of secrecy. The sexual abuse or exploitation of kids is usually not episodic for the abuser. It tends to become his or her regular form of sexual activity, although isolated acts of abuse do spring up from time to time.

Court resolutions of child abuse are especially difficult for the victim. In the "strange," adversarial settings of the courtroom, the child must not only relate (at some point) the incident itself but is subjected to cross-examination by adults who are fulfilling their obligatory roles, such as social worker or defense counsel. The result is that the victim finds the courtroom appearance to be an extension of the abusive act. The basic structure of the entire legal/judicial system has the added caution of not wanting to create any error at any stage which might result in that thing all judges abhor, which is reversal by an appellant court.

Over the past 15 years I have listened to, prosecuted, served as guardian ad litem in, or presided over scores of cases of child sexual abuse and exploitation. The following are four capsule summaries of some typical cases (told in the present tense).

TODD

Todd is 9 years old. He does not remember a time when he was not sexually abused by his father, mother, and even by groups of adults and other children. Todd's parents are members of "sex clubs" whose express purpose is to have sexual experiences with children, either their own or others.

He is diagnosed as being "socially retarded" because he has not been allowed to develop the usual, normal childhood relationships common for most children. Isolating abused children from their peer groups is a means used by many offenders as a form of protection from arrest. Todd is the oldest of three brothers, all of whom have been abused in a similiar fashion.

The boys were all removed from the parents several months ago; each has been in specialized care in a group home, with daily therapy sessions. After many weeks of confusion, feelings of guilt (for "putting mommy and daddy away") and some predictable incidents of sexual acting out with older youths in the group home, the boys are coming around. Everyone concerned feels it will be at least another six months before Todd and his brothers can be considered for permanent placement with adoptive parents.

CATHY

Cathy is 13. Her birth father abandoned the family nine years ago. When her mother married Jim, Cathy accepted the new family unit well. Cathy's mother is a nurse who works night duty. Jim is engaged in real estate and insurance sales, a person well thought of in the community.

Since Cathy was 10 she has slept with Jim on the nights her mother worked. At first Cathy felt "loved," "secure," and "special" sleeping in her parents' bed. The fact that Jim slept in the nude and insisted that Cathy do so did not at first seem to be of any great significance. Jim soon began to insist that she give him "rub downs" like "your mom does to people in the hospital." This request almost immediately progressed to mutual masturbation and requests by Jim for Cathy to perform oral sex on him. She was, in Jim's words, "getting to be such a beautiful woman," that he began to photograph her beginning with various stages of undress and leading eventually to nude photos.

Law enforcement agents later seized more than 220 photographs of Cathy taken over several years. Jim was prosecuted and imprisoned. Cathy's mother placed her in a group home after the trial, convinced that her daughter had somehow seduced Jim. I was Cathy's appointed guardian ad litem. She told me several times that she regretted ever having testified against Jim. His threats that "they will come and take you away" and "your mom will be upset at you" appeared, from her point of view, to have come true. Cathy felt as if she had ruined her mother's marriage and that it was she who had abandoned the family.

CHRISTOPHER

Christopher is 16. His first exposure to sexual exploitation occurred at approximately age 8 to 9. He began playing "tickling games" with his mother and two of her adult friends, a male and a female. Robb, the male, owned a photography studio. Hundreds, possibly thousands, of commercially produced photographs and films of these sessions of tickle games of three nude adults and one male child were made and sold by Robb.

When Christopher was 14, he was taken into custody by juvenile court authorities and charged with the sexual assault of a 4-year-old girl and a 17-month-old boy. He will be in a correctional facility for juveniles until he turns 18. The prognosis by his psychologist is not good. I have always wondered at the meaning of the term "correctional facility." It may well be the law's greatest misnomer, especially in dealing with exploited children.

BENJAMIN

Benjamin is 12. He was befriended by a next-door neighbor known as Uncle Steve. Uncle Steve is 47 years old, married, and the father of several children. Steve began his abuse of Benjamin by giving the boy gifts of money and trips to baseball games or the soda shop in exchange for anal intercourse and silence.

Steve is an executive with a large corporation. He also coaches junior league sports for neighborhood boys and has been active in church, a country club, and an international men's service organization. Benjamin's parents apparently knew nothing of the abuse until a school nurse noticed stains on his white tennis shorts. Benjamin was examined by an astute physician that same afternoon, who asked all of the right questions. He impressed upon the boy the importance of telling the truth so that he could be properly treated. Ultimately, Steve was prosecuted but not convicted. The foreman of the jury (six men and six women) later disclosed that they simply did not believe a man of Steve's reputation would do such a thing to a child. In their opinion, Benjamin was lying.

■   ■   ■

As these cases indicate, much remains to be done in the name of child advocacy. At both state and federal levels, it is clear that we need more uniform statutes dealing with exploitation, from the initial reporting of an incident through the disposition of the case. The courts and legislatures have made some progress—for example, permitting testimony by videotape, allowing social workers or health care professionals to testify to hearsay interviews with the children, and using anatomically correct dolls which enable children to re-enact incidents of abuse. Some states have presumptive sentencing for those convicted of child abuse or exploitation. Others have sought more meaningful regulations for child care facilities.

Three basic problems confront advocacy efforts and judicial reforms. First, the sexual exploitation and trafficking of minors remains a topic which is not sufficiently discussed. It is still an unpleasant subject for many adults and professionals and one they would, apparently, rather ignore. Second, children have little political power or influence; they are a constituency without a voice in our judicial system. And, third, the constitutional rights of the abuser, such as the right to confrontation and the standards of due process, must be addressed in a more pragmatic manner if realistic innovations are to survive judicial review. The rights of the victim, in short, must be given at least as much attention as those of the offender charged with exploitation.[26]

Conclusion

The federal response to sexual trafficking has been erratic and slowed by the lack of public awareness that the various child sex markets—private and public—constitute a major threat to the welfare of our youth. Renewed enforcement efforts by U.S. Customs and postal authorities, the passage of legislation by Congress, and the creation of a National Center for Missing and Exploited Children are the three most recent federal responses to trafficking. In addition, recent initiatives by Congress, such as amending the RICO statute (Racketeer Influenced and Corrupt Organizations) to extend coverage to sexual exploitation of children, as in the case of showing evidence of a child pornography scheme, and the passage of the Child Sexual Abuse and Pornography Act of 1986, may lead to heightened public interest in such activities.[27] What effect these measures will have on the volume of exploitive activities remains to be seen.

Most states have followed the federal example by enacting statutes that deal with exploitation outside the domain of intra-familial abuse. The common feature of these assorted efforts has been a lack of perception of the fundamental dynamics of trafficking and the failure to formulate appropriate penalties for the crimes involved.

The one connective thread between federal and state legislation is the issue of child labor, from which has sprung a profusion of statutes and amendments designed to protect minors in the work-place. Although restricted primarily to work issues, these laws have prompted improvements in peripheral areas such as child abuse and child neglect, and they have also compelled legislatures to take a broader view of the rights of minors in a variety of unrelated areas. With the introduction of juvenile courts and the slow development of a juvenile justice system, we have seen the advent of comprehensive statutory programs. These programs, while often criticized for their displacement of family rights, have at least provided the means for a state to intervene in cases of child exploitation or abuse. Such legislative actions will not eliminate the crimes of sexual trafficking, but at least they reflect a change in attitude in state government and Congress from one of compla-cency, based on gross ignorance of the problem of sexual exploita-tion of minors, to one promoting judicial advocacy for those who cannot otherwise find representation or aid within the political system.

Endnotes

1. Fair Labor Standards Act, 29 U.S.C. §§ 201 to 219 (amended 20 times since 1938), especially §§ 212, "Child Labor Provisions."
2. *Arizona Revised Statutes Annotated,* Chapter 200 (March 25, 1978).
3. McKinney's *New York Penal Law,* Title O, Article 262, "Sexual Performance by a Minor" (Commentary).
4. *May v. Anderson,* 345 U.S. 528 (1952), and *Meyer v. Nebraska,* 262 U.S. 390 (1923) (natural duty of parent to give his children education suitable to their station in life).
5. *Jackson v. Indiana,* 406 U.S. 715, 738, 32 L.Ed.2d 435, 450, 92 S. Ct. 1845 (1972).

6. *Freeman v. Commonwealth*, 288 S.E.2d 461, 465 (Sup. Ct. Va., 1982).

7. *Hammond v. Department of Public Assistance*, 142 W. Va. 208, 214 (W. Va. 1956) (cited cases omitted.)

8. See also *Ginsberg v. N.Y.*, 390 U.S. 629 640, 20 L.Ed.2d 195, 204 (U.S., 1968) (state has interest to protect the welfare of children), and *Stanley v. Illinois*, 405 U.S. 645, 552 (U.S., 1972) (state has the right and duty to protect minor children).

9. Robert E. Buckholz, Jr., ed., "Constitutional Limitations on the Scope of Child Neglect Statutes," *Columbia Law Review*, vol. 79, no. 4 (May 1979), pp. 719–732.

10. *New York v. Ferber*, 458 U.S. 747, 73 L.Ed.2d 113, 102 S.Ct. 3348 (1982).

11. *United States v. Reedy*, 632 F. Supp. 1415, 1416 (D. Okla., 1986).

12. David P. Shouvlin, "Preventing the Sexual Exploitation of Children: A Model Act," *Wake Forest Law Review*, vol. 17 (1981), p. 538.

13. Andrews Edward, ed., *Concise Dictionary of American History* (New York: Charles Scribner's Sons, 1962), p. 176.

14. 29 U.S.C., §§ 201–219. "Fair Labor Standards Act of 1938."

15. *New York v. Ferber*, 458 U.S. 747, 753, 73 L.Ed.2d 1113, 1120, 102 S. Ct. 3348 (1981).

16. *Ibid*.

17. S. Rep. No. 95–438, 96th Cong., 2d Sess. 5–6 (1984).

18. H.R. Report No. 98–536, 1st Sess. 2, reprinted 1984, U.S. CODE CONG. & ADMIN. NEWS, 492–494.

19. *United States v. Miller*, 776 F.2d 978, (11th Cir. 1985).

20. Pub. L. No. 98–473, 42 *U.S.C.* § 5771 *et. seq.*, "Missing Children's Assistance Act," (1984).

21. Fact Sheet for the Honorable Alfonse M. D'Amato, United States Senate, United States Government Accounting Office (January 5, 1986), p. 5.

22. Pub. L. No. 98–473, 18 U.S.C. § 16, "Crime of Violence Defined" (1984).

23. *Cal. Penal Code*, §§ 1000.30–1000.36 (1985).

24. 28 U.S.C. § 994(d).

25. See, for example, *Stanley v. Illinois*, 405 U.S. 645, 92 S. Ct. 1208, 31 L.Ed.2d 551 (1972); *Parham v. R.*, 442 U.S. 584, 602, 99 S. Ct. 2493, 61 L.Ed.2d 101, 119 (1979).

26. Contributed by the Honorable Lyerly, Banner Elk, North Carolina.

27. On October 18, 1986, the Senate passed S. 985, amending the RICO statute. President Reagan signed H.R. 5560, the Child Abuse and Pornography Act of 1986 (Pub.L. No. 99–628), on November 6, 1986.

Chapter 8

THE VICTIMIZATION CYCLE

Underage victims of sexual trafficking are often the targets of adults who were themselves sexually exploited as children. Thus are victims created by former victims in an unbroken regenerative cycle. Some of these exploiters are outside the family; many are within. As we have seen, victimization within the family often drives a minor to the streets, where illicit sex is one means of survival.

The intra-familial dynamics of the victimization cycle are extremely complex, and there is no completely satisfactory explanation for the tendency of underage victims to become exploiters. To some extent it may be a subconscious desire to exert power, in turn, over the weak, or to strike back in equal measure for having been victimized, or it may be a direct response to growing up in a disordered, psychologically damaging environment. Whatever the reason, the cycle of victimization perpetuates the child sex markets.

In this chapter, drawing on extensive discussions with Dr. Frank Sacco,[1] a clinical therapist of dysfunctional families, we shall examine in necessarily general terms some of the stages of the victimization cycle, as well as the significant effects exploitive parents have on minors. As we explore the dynamics of the victimization cycle, we shall find that the victim in the initial generation often becomes an exploiter in the succeeding generation. When the exploiter sexually abuses the victim, the latter—in order to adjust to this development—may adopt the exploiter's view of the acceptability of such conduct, rebel, and seek an outlet in life on the streets, or simply suffer in silence. Either way, the

181

child victim loses. The longer this conduct goes unchallenged by others in the family or by outsiders who come into contact with the victim, the more likely it becomes that the victim will undergo a transformation from victim to victimizer when she or he grows older.

The primary cause of the sexually exploited child, then, is the dysfunctional family, in which the failure to cope effectively with the uncertainties and stress of life may be expressed by some degree of abandonment of the child. Such parents take no interest in their child, make no effort to communicate with her or him, and—verbally and nonverbally—convey the message that they do not care what the child does.

Children in Dysfunctional Families

Dysfunctional families severely test even the innate resiliency of childhood. Although dysfunctional family dynamics generate both male and female victims, the minor female victim is more representative of the phenomena described below.

It is possible to trace the development of an abused infant into a parent involved in exploitation within the context of a dysfunctional family. The infant progresses through an endless series of unmet needs which create intense feelings and moods. Home is usually a very stressful place where adults treat the child in an inconsistent manner. As the baby's presence begins to interfere with the activities of the adults around her, she may be hit, burned, shaken, screamed at, or scalded. The child grows older and begins to explore her surroundings. From the child's perspective, adults are difficult to understand because conduct which is rewarded one day may serve to trigger harsh treatment on another.

As the toddler grows older, the world outside the home takes shape as a place where others are perceived to be happier and to have more of everything good. The erratic treatment which the child receives within her family becomes more difficult to tolerate when she observes others being consistently rewarded for appropriate conduct. More importantly, as the child comes into contact with other children her age, she discovers that having sexual relationships with older family members is not the norm—a discovery which gives rise to an emotional rage hard to control. As the child continues in school, her teachers notice that she "simply does not seem to care," or "just does not fit in," but they can do little more than note the presence of a troubled child.

Eventually familial damage or neglect may become so noticeable that school authorities call for intervention by the state social service system. State agencies become both villains and heroes of this scenario. Caseworkers are expected to identify and remove potential victims of child abuse. To do this, they have to make their way into a family that could at any time become violent. The abusive family member quickly identifies the human service worker as the "enemy" and a contest of wills ensues, with the child in the middle. On the one hand, the state agency social worker who questions her is kind and tries to stop abuse; on the other hand, the adults in the family continue to abuse, bribe, and threaten her.

As childhood progresses, she continues to have problems inside and outside the home. Her discomfort with school increases, dissonance grows between her and teachers, and no one at home cares about her school achievement or behavior. Her friends also tend to be in trouble. The early loss of childhood innocence and the stress of adolescence, when combined with the home's negative impact, create uncontrollable behavior ranging from crime, through depression, to suicide.

As we have noted, intervention by a social worker tends to aggravate the emotional instabilities within the family. Social workers try to protect the child through court-ordered custody fights, but when the legal system becomes overburdened, there is always the possibility that the abusive parent will be given another opportunity. Life for the child becomes a series of court-ordered programs and visits to detention centers and mental health clinics, where she is diagnosed as emotionally disturbed or found to be delinquent.

Wherever she goes, the victim accumulates lasting psychological scars and, in many cases, impulses which are exhibited as serious emotional and behavioral problems. In order to remain at home, the child must accommodate the adults around her as the price she pays for life's necessities; indeed, the instinctual connection to family may override reality. In order to survive she becomes a pragmatist and adult excesses become her norm.

With luck, someone skilled or determined in the state system may make a positive difference in the child's life. More likely, however, she will encounter situations and characters comparable to those at home. Foster parents may be transient; some are even more brutal than her own parents. Group homes or mental health clinics provide, at best, temporary stopovers during which other troubled children within the state system introduce her to new ways of making trouble.

Self-destruction becomes a life-style, because the victim has decided to accept her fate.[2] Unconsciously she feels that she is bad and that whatever harsh treatment she receives is punishment well deserved. These negative feelings are only intensified when the adolescent is introduced to sex and drugs, including alcohol. She simultaneously loses a portion of her childhood and rebels against the restraints normally placed upon one her age. Especially when sex and drugs are introduced in early adolescence, the absence of effective restraints upon her conduct may produce deadly results. If such conduct is not dealt with in a reasonable time period, effective measures to counteract the child's self-destructive impulses will be hard to implement as she grows older. Remedial programs do exist, however, and three proven methods that deal aggressively with the older adolescent are described in the succeeding chapter.

In the last stage of the victimization cycle, the young girl becomes pregnant, either within marriage or without, and finds herself a teenage parent. At first, the child is like a plaything, a toy. However, when the infant fails to stop crying and demands its mother's attention day and night, our victim—who of course lacks effective parenting skills—readily becomes a victimizer. Instead of the normal instincts to nurture and protect, this mother sees herself as entitled to self-gratification because of the injury and abuse she suffered early in life. Her baby's crying is viewed as one more source of rejection and, rather than being concerned for her child's well-being, she is mainly concerned with her own.

To complicate matters, such mothers often struggle with a variety of self-destructive life-styles involving drugs, alcohol, abusive men, or crime. The victim of many years of abuse develops a deep depression that manifests itself as suicidal behavior—a form of aggression against the self, and a known characteristic of children who are neglected and abused within the family.[3] This self-destructive mindset plays a crucial role in the behavior of mothers who fail to protect their children from sexual exploitation. Instead the children often become scapegoats for the mother's own inadequacies.

The more a mother fails in her maternal duties, the more her self-image deteriorates. Inner rage continues to build, eventually resulting in explosions of violence. As a consequence, this person often feels the need to use drugs and alcohol to make herself oblivious to her children.

Children are, of course, remarkably resilient and adept at making the best of bad situations. As the mother unsuccessfully deals with her own past miseries and present social disasters, the children look to others for help. The child's personality adjusts to its environment and she becomes tough and insensitive. Children in these situations tend to develop a "squirrel mentality"—that is, they hoard possessions—thereby revealing an insecure personality. These same juveniles often see their mothers beaten and overwhelmed, as well as indulging in overtly sexual behavior while under the influence of drugs or alcohol. A role reversal may occur in which the child attempts to protect the mother. The mother becomes the self-absorbed child and the child becomes a premature parent. The net result is a disorganized, self-perpetuating climate of selfishness, neediness, and dependency.

In short, home is not a haven for the troubled offspring of dysfunctional families. Parental reinforcement of positive conduct is generally absent, in part, because the parents come to regard the child as an unwanted intruder in their lives. The parents are also handicapped by the lack of a stable, nurturing family environment during their own childhood.

Types of Exploitive Parents

The characteristic common to all exploitive parents is a lack of empathy for others, almost to the point of total self-preoccupation.[4] Seriously neglected children learn very early to put themselves first. As adults, their selfishness becomes a private entitlement to do anything for themselves, regardless of the consequences to others. Commercial exploiters often play upon this characteristic in order to gain free reign with a child. Generally, exploitive parents fall into one of the following categories: (1) those who cooperate with the exploiter; (2) those who are "absent"; and (3) those who are seriously impaired. As prelude to further discussion of these parents, it must be made clear that, except for the sexually exploitive or abusive father, male parents are conspicuous by their absence in the majority of cases. Thus, the focus of this presentation on the role and function of mothers in the victimization process is but a reflection of our findings.

The Cooperative Parent

"Cooperative" parents participate in the commercial exploitation of their children. Such fathers and mothers fall into two categories: those who are pathologically dependent on the exploiter and become involved in the abuse of their children in order to gain the exploiter's approval, and those who are driven by pathological narcissism, or total self-absorption.

In the first instance, mental disorder is not evident. The dependent personality disorder is a psychiatric condition in which a person lives his or her life through another. The dependent person has little or no self-identity; the world is interpreted almost completely by another person. A common scenario involving such a cooperative parent occurs when a single mother brings a new mate into the home. If the man makes sexual overtures or actually abuses one or more of the children, the mother is likely to ignore her children's complaints, claiming instead that they are lying and do not appreciate all the man is doing for the family. This kind of rationalization may preserve the economic link the mother values, but the sexual abuse endured by the young victim is an unwarranted penalty extracted against the child's emotional well-being.

Whatever rationalization permits a child to be abused by a man in the child's home will also justify the participation by the same victim in pornography or prostitution outside the home. The mother's prize in the latter activity is usually not a share of the profit but rather the admiration and approval of the exploiter with whom she is cooperating. The legal culpability of such a cooperative parent is difficult to assess, because her ability to make clear choices is clouded by her mental disorder. A judge, when asked if the mother is criminally responsible for neglect, may either hold her responsible or extend leniency because of her impairment which, after all, is not so pervasive as to affect all areas of life. The question becomes: Whose well-being shall take precedence, the mother's or the child's?

The issue of responsibility is clearer in cases of the pathologically narcissistic parent, the second category of cooperative parent. This type of person is lacking in feeling for others and completely driven by self-gratification. Everyone, including their own children, is seen as merely a means of providing gratification for the self. Mothers who are complicit because of pathological narcissism are, in general, antisocial. They display disdain for society's rules and affinity for the counterculture of crime, the breeding ground of exploiters. This parent will share the profits of the exploiter or trafficker; impaired judgment is not a factor. The narcissistic parent knows that her children are being harmed, but reasons that, because she herself was once victimized as a child, it is permissible to hurt the children for her own benefit.

Sometimes these antisocial parents become active in the organization of commercial sex rings. They may distribute pornography and even participate with juveniles in sexual acts. These parents are cruel to their offspring, and physical abuse is predictable. To please the parent, the child must actively engage in the exploitation. This behavior bonds the parent and child together, propelling the victim inexorably deeper into the world of sexual trafficking.

Cooperative parents are frequently also active recruiters. Pathologically narcissistic parents often make their homes accessible to minors, then proceed to work closely with exploiters in expanding the base of a sex ring or other such activity. These parents are clearly criminally responsible for their acts.

The Absent Parent

The "absent" parent syndrome begins when the father abandons his family. The primary character is the surviving spouse.

Partially in response to the sense of abandonment created by the father's departure, the mother creates a psychological chasm between herself and her children. The children are punished and rewarded indiscriminately, causing confusion and insecurity in their minds. Both the mother's condition and the children's tend to create a situation ripe for exploitation.

During the day—while the children are in school, social services are available, and the courts are open—this mother may appear quite normal. It is the lonely nights that are her undoing. Unable to cope with her depression, she desperately seeks ways to dilute the intensity of her persistent feelings and to distance herself from a filthy, stressful, and noisy home environment of her own creation. Angry, alone, and depressed, she seeks a variety of escapes from reality, including solace in alcohol or drugs. Such a choice, of course, does nothing to alleviate the underlying causes of her insecurity, fragile self-image, and lack of control in her home.

The children, left on their own for the major part of each day and lacking any real communication with their parent, look outside the home for reassurance, especially from adults. The apparent freedom allowed the child by the mother's lack of interest and concern is the major gift of the mother to the commercial exploiter. The subsequent exploitation, of course, goes undetected by the absent parent, who attributes signs of emotional distress on the part of the child to any number of reasons other than the actual ongoing trauma of sexual exploitation. The exploiter captures the neglected child with warm attention, drugs, alcohol, money, and transportation; he may also distract the parent with offers of child care.

What is common to all absent parents is the failure to observe what is happening to their children. These parents do not necessarily lack the potential for basic love and caring; rather, they are so weak emotionally that they fail to muster the strength needed to protect their children from sexual exploiters.

The Impaired Parent

Some parents suffer serious intellectual and emotional impairments that detract from their ability to care for their children. That being the case, it is not surprising that some of them allow their offspring to be exploited. When this happens, the children become "lost sheep" and society at large becomes their shepherd—a task for which it is ill-suited.

Researchers believe that several patterns of impairment contribute to the "failure to protect" syndrome in parents of sexually exploited children. Serious psychiatric impairment, for example, is common. Unfortunately, as more state-operated institutions close in the wake of deinstitutionalization, such impaired parents are trying to care for their children without the necessary ancillary services. An example is a 32-year-old woman whose three sons (ages 8, 10, and 12) had been in foster care on and off for most of their lives, while their mother spent months at a time in the state hospital. Once she had received treatment and adjusted to her medications, she would be released and regain custody of her children. Although she would agree to stay on her medication, maintain an apartment in a federally subsidized housing project, and attend therapy sessions, she would eventually return to her old life-style of drugs, alcohol, and sexual promiscuity. During one of her at-home periods, the mother met a man at a local bar who was nice to her and the children. Soon he had become babysitter, chauffeur, and companion, and he even bought the children new bicycles and clothes. Eventually, all three boys were posing for nude photographs. The oldest subsequently ran away and became a prostitute.

Had she known about the exploiter's activities, this mother would have, in a more sober state, stopped him. She tried to kill herself when the social service department removed her children and she realized what had happened. The state won permanent custody of the remaining two boys, and she joined the ranks of the homeless. This tragic situation might have been prevented by the coordinated efforts of the state mental health department, the social service agency, and the court. Homemaker services and outreach therapy could have helped the mother care for her children, stay on her medication, and continue sessions with a psychiatrist.

A parent may also be powerless to protect by virtue of severe intellectual limitations. The problem here is not mental disturbance, bizarre behavior, or loss of contact with reality, but a built-in limit to thinking and reasoning. Such a parent does not have the mental capabilities necessary to protect her child from the influence of a commercial exploiter.

State or court intervention in the case of intellectual impairment is complicated. That a mother is intellectually limited is not sufficient cause for a child to be removed. In fact, in many instances the intellectually limited mother is very committed to her children and has a strong emotional bond with them, and her instinctual protectiveness remains intact. What is missing is the reasoning ability to discover that the child is involved in commercial exploitation. Intellectually limited parents are no match for the manipulative adult who seeks access to their children.

Once exploitation is uncovered, impaired parents need outside help to learn how to protect their children effectively. Here again is a dilemma. If the state assumes all responsibility, then the mother and juveniles do not have the chance to live together as a family; the children are placed in a foster care system and the mother drifts away. If, however, the state allows the parent to try again, without close supervision, then the children are exposed again to the threat of exploitation, including activities such as molestation and pornographic picture-taking.

Treatment for Exploitive Parents

Effective treatment for exploitive parents hinges on quick reporting of abuse and exploitation. No victim can be helped in the long term without the coordinated efforts of the criminal justice, social service, and mental health systems. But treatment for these parents is a controversial issue. Some believe that prison programs can rehabilitate exploiters, yet countless children have been the victims of supposedly rehabilitated sex offenders.

To begin with, distinctions must be made between kinds of offenders. There is a wide gap, for example, between a sex offender involved in infrequent or one-time molestation of a stepchild and one who systematically engages numerous minors, against their will, in sexual acts for money. Careful screening and multidisciplinary review by the criminal justice and mental health systems are two steps that can be taken to reduce the probability of a commercial exploiter re-entering society.

Parents who become involved in trafficking need close analysis to determine which type of response is appropriate. The case of the cooperative parent suffering from a pathologically narcissistic and dependent personality, for example, requires intervention by the judicial system, coupled with an attempt by social services to monitor the children's development. Once a mother is found to be involved with a commercial exploiter, custody of her children should be remanded to the state, pursuant to existing statutory provisions, and a contract developed between the mother, the court, social service system, and any mental health professionals working with her and the children. When initiated, this contract, or service plan, should detail exactly what kind of contact, if any, will be allowed between the mother and her offspring.

The sooner a child can be protected and given a stable living environment, the more likely recovery becomes. If an exploitive mother deceives the court or social service system and gains rights to her child without stringent conditions, the victim's progress will be in constant jeopardy. In some cases a parent involved in exploitation will profess a change of heart—often while in prison— but most such repentive parents return to their old ways.

Appearances can be deceiving. For example, a pathologically dependent mother, who is frequently unkempt, unlikable, and a poor communicator, is less of a risk than the purely narcissistic mother, who often receives better treatment than the dependent parent because of her normal appearance. Psychiatric evaluation and psychological testing can provide an understanding of the personality styles of a parent, and decisions about allowing a mother access to her children should be made only after a thorough evaluation.

Absent parents are often shocked back into a more protective stance by an investigation, although they may become suicidal or give up caring for anything, losing themselves in self-destructive life-styles. Their children are usually removed from them during the investigation. Returning a child to an absent parent should occur only under the coordinated supervision of both social service agents and therapists who are trained in recognizing signs of abuse.

If a child who is returned to an absent parent is adequately cared for, his or her development can continue despite school problems, emotional issues, or other glaring behavioral disorders. If the absent parent makes a serious effort at establishing a positive relationship, the child often shows signs of improvement. Weekly therapy can provide the structure for learning new ways of life, as well as allowing a therapist access to the family. In addition to therapy, there must be a close working relationship among the state agency, the court, and the therapist in order to produce a safe and successful strategy. Traditional office therapy without contact with social services or other social control agents increases the risk that the mother will revert to being an absent parent.

Home-based or outreach therapy is uniquely suited for this situation. Outreach therapy is, in the words of Dr. Frank Sacco, "a new application of an old idea: The victims are helped by reaching out to them in their own environment." Therapists are usually dispatched by the courts into dysfunctional homes to treat the various disorders that contribute to abuse and exploitation within the family. The court gives each family an opportunity to work directly with a professional who is cognizant of exploitation dynamics. The therapist seeks to restructure the family and remove destructive influences.

Having access to the home gives the therapist a bird's-eye view of the home climate. An absent parent who is trying to reform will follow the therapist's suggestions, change her routines, try to keep her house in better order, be more organized, and work at addressing those issues that contribute to her absentee status. Outreach therapy often requires that a therapist work with a mother to help her confront self-destructive life patterns. Alternatives to ignoring the children are suggested and small steps are constructed to help her move onto a higher level of functioning.

The outreach process may involve periods in which the children of the parent are removed to send a clear message that physical custody of the children will continue only if the mother is willing to change her behavior. Regular programming, such as after-school programs and social/recreational activities for parent and child, can make a difference in the ability of a single mother to parent safely. Loneliness and despair can be reduced through daily activities designed to relieve the pressure of 24-hour parenting by one person.

An impaired parent needs to work closely with the state departments of social services and mental health in addition to the court and individual clinicians. She must be willing to participate fully in a total treatment program. If she is not willing, the state social services agency should step in on the child's behalf and use the courts to sever parental rights. Effective treatment includes the use of home health aides, especially if the parent is intellectually limited. Services must be adequate to ensure a child's safety. Therapy must focus on helping the mother to build parenting skills, on motivating more appropriate adult behavior, and on working to set sensible limits and goals for the children. Outreach therapists can help regulate family life by strengthening a parent's decision-making abilities, assisting in daily schedules, and planning meals.

If the intellectual limitation or the psychiatric impairment is severe, the parent should be relieved of full responsibility for parenting. In such a case, a supervised cooperative apartment in which the impaired parent and the child victim receive support and regular monitoring may allow them to live safely together and avoid the trauma of breaking up the family.

Treatment for Victims

The victim's age, the duration of victimization, the parent's involvement, the extent of force used, and the nature of the exploitive acts are all factors to consider in any program of treatment. Recovery can be slow for victims if exploitation has taken place for an extended period with parental involvement. Helping victims of commercial sexual exploitation is similiar in some ways to treating prisoners of war or cultists who have been brainwashed. In these instances, the victims have repressed their experiences and buried them deep in their subconscious minds. Outward behavior may appear relatively normal until an incident triggers an emotional outburst. Self-destructive rampages are common, and safe treatment may require residential care or secure psychiatric hospitalization.

Some adolescent victims of commercial sexual exploitation try to destroy themselves, while some react to the trauma by victimizing others. In either case, the damaged adolescent is likely to disconnect from normal society and to attempt survival on the streets. All of a victim's reactions to sexual exploitation must be closely assessed before treatment begins, because the process of uncovering past victimization sometimes precipitates suicidal thoughts or psychotic regressions. A treatment continuum should start with secure hospitalization and progress to group residential care, supportive foster care, independent living, therapy, and vocational training. Victims should interact with other juveniles like themselves and become involved in a monitored process of self-revelation and image-rebuilding.

Those who treat underage victims have to be especially careful to provide a safe and protected environment, whether it be a reconstructed natural home or a foster home. Group care should be viewed as a last resort. The therapy of choice is long-term, intensive play therapy. Because child victims frequently are unable or unwilling to discuss their victimization verbally, often the best avenue of expression left is play therapy, which is a safe way for a child to explore nightmares. A play therapist tries to create an atmosphere in which the child feels comfortable, even though such an approach often is in conflict with school, foster home, or day programs that try to enforce limits to control the behavioral disorders that result from victimization. Anything is permissible as long as it is safe. The therapist must be committed to seeing a child through a complicated unraveling process. As a relationship builds between child and therapist, the weekly sessions assume the form of miniature plays, a situation which allows the young child or older adolescent to act out anger and frustration.

Conclusion

The cycle of victimization is clearly related to the sexual and psychological disorders of dysfunctional families. Through negligence, indifference, or outright complicity, an exploitive mother or father can make the values and habits of sexual exploitation an integral part of a child's learning process. No one knows how many underage victims in exploitive families grow up to become adult offenders, but most of the adult offenders we interviewed admitted to some type of sexual trauma during their childhood years. Interrupting this cycle requires a long-term, intensive commitment by local and state service and criminal justice agencies to intervene in dysfunctional families and to make a sustained effort to help and guide families susceptible to sexual trafficking so as to prevent further harm to their children.

Endnotes

1. Frank C. Sacco, Ph.D., is President of Outreach Specialists, Inc.; Director of Professional Affairs, Osborne Clinic, Agawam, Mass.; and Adjunct Professor of Psychology, American International College, Springfield, Mass.
2. Norman L. Fairberow (ed.), *The Many Faces of Suicide* (New York: McGraw-Hill, 1980).
3. Karl A. Menninger, *Man Against Himself* (New York: Harcourt Press, 1938).
4. O. F. Kernberg, *Borderline Conditions and Pathological Narcissism* (New York: Aronson, 1975).

Chapter 9

VICTIM ADVOCACY

Any plan for dealing with the complex problem of sexual exploitation should include measures to improve the victim's mental health and general welfare. Simply transferring a child to the custody of the state protective care system is not an adequate response. Social caseworkers, for example, are often unaware of the seriousness of the victim's trauma, and they tend to focus on placement and short-term therapy rather than on dealing with the long-term effects of sexual exploitation. Even members of the judiciary are sometimes unprepared to deal with charges involving child pornography, procuring, or sex rings when the principal witnesses are underage and the evidentiary strength of a case hinges upon the statements of a minor.

The plight of victimized minors is not being properly addressed today. Shuffled from agency to agency and sometimes treated more like an offender than a victim, a juvenile may well become suspicious of anyone who claims to know what is in the child's best interest. In this chapter we shall consider the issue of victim advocacy from several system and agency perspectives. The four programs described in the following pages are designed to identify the victim in the early stages of exploitation and to ease her or his entry into the criminal justice and social service systems. These programs include a comprehensive federally sponsored long-term community-based reintegration program for the juvenile prostitute, a regional sexual exploitation task force, a police-social worker team with an emphasis on pre-trial case preparation, and an interagency child service model program.

The New Connections Project: A Federal Program

A federal exemplary project originating in the fall of 1983, New Connections, was one of five projects funded at the federal level to aid sexually exploited adolescents and minors "at risk." Now a viable component of the social service network in the Charleston, West Virginia, area, New Connections has been able to identify minors at risk of being sexually exploited as well as to help those already being victimized. "Our success," according to New Connections Director Margaret Cahape, "can be measured in some very real terms. For example, in the early months of operation, the office was broken into and property destroyed, and caseworkers' cars were vandalized. We were informed by street people that these attacks were orchestrated by local pimps in retaliation for lost profits caused by our interference." A history and a description of the New Connections Program are offered by Director Cahape in the following pages.

*   *   *   *   *

During the early 1980s in the Kanawha Valley of West Virginia, several disturbing stories appeared in the media about "street kids" in the downtown Charleston area who were involved in prostitution. Apparently discouraged by inadequate help from social service and law enforcement agencies, these juveniles had resorted to drug dealing and prostitution as a way of life.

Summers Street was the center of activity, and children could be seen openly soliciting during the late evening and night-time hours. Some arrived in Charleston at the Summers Street bus station from outlying areas. If they looked pretty, lost, or vulnerable, they became easy marks for exploiters. One such victim, a young, rural Boone county girl, told how a pimp met her at the Greyhound station. He offered to help, and provided her with a room and food. Hers was not an uncommon experience, for pimps and prostitutes routinely took such young girls under their wings and introduced them to prostitution.

Staff at Patchwork, a local shelter for runaway youths, observed during this period that a growing number of their clients had resorted to prostitution before seeking help at their facility. Intervention was difficult. Many had left home with the agreement of their families. All shared lengthy runaway histories, many had been victims of child abuse, and some had criminal records. The most desirable alternative, in the eyes of the Patchwork staff, was to seek state custody and secure foster placements. This course proved to be virtually impossible, however, because most of the minors were nearing adulthood and because, in most cases, there was little tangible evidence of recent abuse or neglect to support a custody proceeding. After repeated failure to reunite children with their families or to gain foster care for them, the Patchwork staff developed its first program for teaching the skills necessary for a legal, responsible, and independent life-style.

In 1982 West Virginia's commissioner of human services and state supreme court members and staff decided to obtain an accurate estimate of the number of youths in the Kanawha Valley involved in prostitution. They also wanted to know what the community was doing to help these minors. These officials contacted a network of local agencies that served victims of child abuse and neglect to gain the information.

This network, called FACT (Families and Children Together), was charged with investigating the problem and making recommendations for its resolution. The resulting study, which surveyed all of Kanawha County's secondary school principals and youth-serving social services agencies, produced a figure of 328 youths suspected of exchanging sexual favors for money, goods, or services. Past and current prostitutes were also interviewed in order to build a profile of client characteristics and service needs. Consistent with national data, the histories of these youths included combinations of problems such as child abuse and neglect, broken homes, incest, runaway episodes, and school failure.

The FACT network reported their findings also to officials at the U.S. Department of Health and Human Services, who responded by informing FACT about an upcoming federal program that would fund a small number of demonstration projects directed at helping sexually exploited youths. The FACT network invited Daymark, Inc. (parent agency of Patchwork) to apply for these funds. A one-time 18-month grant was secured, and Daymark began its new direct services program for troubled teenagers, named New Connections, in October 1983.

New Connections arrived in downtown Charleston during the aftermath of major urban renewal efforts. Two new shopping malls had greatly changed the old downtown shopping district, including Summers Street: Many of the most popular retail stores had moved into the malls, while others had failed. Old buildings on Summers Street were abandoned or, as in the case of the Greyhound Bus Station, torn down. By then, prostitution had become so blatant on the street that city officials increased patrols, arrests soared. Soon prostitution was no longer visible in downtown Charleston, but it had spread to less centralized, less obvious locations around the city.

Initial outreach efforts were directed toward existing agencies in contact with juveniles, including the Department of Human Services, Juvenile Probation, and Patchwork. Secondary points of contact included men's and women's shelters, Covenant House (for transient adults), school social workers, health clinics, and stores where youths frequently congregated. In the first six months, 800 program cards and information sheets were distributed, and dozens of speaking engagements were conducted for community groups and service programs.

New Connections' initial program plan was to receive client referrals, prepare individual case plans, provide crisis counseling, teach life skills, and secure (through networking) shelter, job assistance, and education. Client files were prepared, including information on family background or guardianship, past and current housing, runaway history, legal involvement, sexual activities, medical and employment history, and educational background. An "attitude inventory" was conducted to profile a youth's self-image and possible need for psychiatric intervention.

It became apparent during the first two months of New Connections' existence that financial aid and support services would be essential for attracting voluntary clients and responding to their immediate needs. In November 1983 a Juvenile Justice and Delinquency Prevention grant was secured for the purpose of hiring a part-time evening counselor to offer free dinners and support groups. Financial aid was also acquired to meet medical, transportation, clothing, and housing needs. Dinner and evening group sessions rapidly became the most attractive component of the unit, offering a surrogate family environment in New Connections' small office in downtown Charleston. The staff of New Connections frequently found themselves commenting on the serious topics selected by the children for group discussion, including childbirth, love, dating, respect, stealing, sexual abuse, friendship, sexuality, nuclear war, and government. On some occasions the group would go to the park, a skating rink, or the movies.

While there is no typical New Connections client, some prevalent trends and responses were soon detected by the staff. Children were responding in a powerful way to the encouragement and support they received from the staff. With few exceptions, all youths entering the program expressed strong and sincere intentions to "change their lives, settle down, get an education, and find a job." At the same time, however, they usually lacked belief in their ability to accomplish these goals. When hard work toward a goal was not followed rapidly by the desired results, frustration often led to the youth's temporary disappearance from the program. While the staff understood the reason for this pattern, they also were convinced that successful departure from the street lifestyle requires the education and job skills necessary to compete in the labor market. This conviction was the basis upon which New Connections developed its educational learning lab and job preparation programs. Both components were created to provide short-term learning units which make provision for measurable accomplishment and flexible client attendance patterns. Funds from the Department of Human Services and Job Training and Partnership Act provided a job developer, an educator, and youth stipends for study and training hours.

During the first year of operation, the staff at New Connections learned that not all youths who exchange sexual favors for goods or services perceive themselves as juvenile prostitutes. Some consider the pimp their lover and protector, in a role not unlike that of an exploitive parent. This lack of realism has to be dealt with, for the staff was concerned lest the stigma of prostitution be attached to the program and its clients. The staff also saw a need to reach out to neglected and abused minors prior to their entry into the sex trade. As a result, New Connections extended the definition of its client population to high-risk youths.

New Connections is currently receiving financial support from state tax dollars and federal funds from the Job Training Partnership Act.[1] The program averages about three hundred students per year. Some youths participate in only one or two program components such as a learning lab or a weekly teen–parent support group. Other students have participated extensively over the long term. The staff members at New Connections have learned many valuable lessons, including, as shown in the following case of Cindy Jones (fictitious name), the need for patience and realistic expectations.

A NEW CONNECTIONS PARTICIPANT

Cindy came to New Connections six months after the program began. When she was very young, Cindy was removed from her natural family and placed with foster parents who had 11 other foster children. She does not remember her natural parents. Cindy received little parenting and told numerous tales of her runaway episodes and adventures on the street. She was a victim of both physical and sexual abuse; her current problems were school failure, substance abuse, and prostitution. She quickly became a "regular" in the learning lab and evening groups and loved to cook, sing, and entertain the other students. Cindy also loved to steal, tell sensational stories about her sexual exploits, and be disruptive in group settings.

Cindy's charms made it easy for her to obtain employment or services, but her hostility toward authority and her lack of self-discipline typically resulted in her being fired from jobs or terminated from programs. In the learning lab and evening program at New Connections, such behavior led to group chaos. The staff agonized over the policy decisions that had to be made in dealing with such behavior. Primary emphasis was given to "involvement" or "bonding" with students; knowing them as individuals and not giving up on them were other important philosophical tenets. All reasonable efforts were made to assist disruptive students in understanding how their behavior was successfully blocking the learning process for them and other students. The staff finally developed some carefully considered limits: Unreasonable students would be asked to leave the program for a brief while, usually an afternoon, but were encouraged to return when they were ready to work.

Cindy spent her first year at New Connections acting out her anger and frustrations, but progressing toward a high school equivalency degree and completing job and life skills training. At this point two important events occurred: She turned 18 and was no longer a legal responsibility of the state, and her foster mother died. Although Cindy had basically raised herself, she had no confidence in her ability to survive independently. She entered a New Connections apartment, voluntarily accepting state custody, but within one month was fired from her job and began spending nights in local bars. She was frequently drunk, but refused both therapy and help from substance abuse groups.

After an additional month of unemployment and no sign of progress or compliance, she was terminated from state custody and had to vacate the New Connections apartment. At this point Cindy became suicidal. The staff took her to a hospital, where she was admitted to the behavioral medicine unit. The next six months for her were a series of journeys between hospital settings and various foster sisters' homes—all in a state of acute depression. Whenever possible, she continued to attend group sessions, and her case manager at New Connections gave her special support and encouragement. Finally, Cindy agreed to enter a local vocational program and began to follow through with therapy at the mental health center. Because she was soon to be placed in a job and had again been evicted from a foster sister's home, the staff helped Cindy locate an apartment, paid her first month's rent, and supplied her with basic home furnishings.

Cindy has been employed for six months. She is preparing to move to a nicer apartment, which she found on her own. Her therapy and employment evaluations are good, and it is clear that, at some point during the past six months, Cindy made up her mind to live. She is calmer and seldom acts in her former disruptive fashion. She is saving money for living room furniture and other things she had never been able to own. More importantly, Cindy budgets her money appropriately and is developing patience—a new quality for her.

■　　　■　　　■

New Connections intervention with Cindy and students like her is neither brilliant nor unique, but it is persistent. Over the course of two and a half years, Cindy received training and supportive services. Equally significant, she became attached to a staff who saw her through the hard times and encouraged her not to give up. The ultimate result is that Cindy seems to be turning her life around.

The degree of hurt and anger these young people carry around with them must be remembered in the course of daily events, but thefts, angry graffati, or property destruction can test the patience of a staff. During the fall and spring, when program participation is highest, six or seven difficult children in one room can put a program to the test. At such a time, one of the students, Gary

Smith (fictitious name), taught the staff a lesson about anger and childhood survival.

GARY SMITH: A LESSON IN SURVIVAL

When he arrived in New Connections, Gary was 16, a small fairheaded child from a family of muscular boys. His pain and anger were displayed in a much more secretive and calculated fashion than Cindy's. Initially quiet and excessively compliant, Gary wanted very much to please and volunteered more than his share to do dishes or help with the office cleanup. His intelligence was readily apparent, and the New Connections' teacher found him to be an eager and rewarding student.

After a few months of daily program participation, Gary relaxed and let his wit and humor surface. He thrived on the attention of the staff and soon became the school jester. At about the same time, a rash of thefts of staff and program property occurred. Gary seemed the least likely candidate, until a note arrived in the mail a month after he secured his graduate equivalency degree, with a threat to burn the building down.

Gary told other students he had authored the letter. When staff confronted him on this and the thefts, he confessed. Gary was informed that he needed to receive counseling if he wished to continue his participation in New Connections' daytime program. His evening privileges were left intact with the intent of conveying the staff's concern and desire for him to continue coming to New Connections. During this conversation, Gary alluded to several well-kept secrets about himself, which he felt could not be shared with anyone for fear that his family would kill him. We reassured him that he was safe sharing these secrets with the staff or a counselor. During the next several weeks, however, Gary's anger became more blatant: He looked for reasons to slam doors and to act out his hostility. He began to alienate other students, and staff patience was wearing thin. After a while, Gary went to his case manager and nervously spoke of his belief that he was homosexual. He also described his history of sexual abuse at age 7 by a neighbor, as well as his infrequent but increasing homosexual acts of prostitution.

Gary received the acceptance he desperately needed and began to deal with his past. He has eagerly attended counseling for several months, while maintaining a job as an office clerk.

Gary realizes that he is somewhat amazing, having survived an abusive, alcoholic family where his role was to hold everything together, do the cleaning, and pay the bills.

■   ■   ■

Gary, Cindy, and thousands of other teenagers have suffered the devastation of sexual exploitation, but their periods of prostitution are only one tragic phase of a childhood full of trauma. National data on childhood abuse and neglect, family and teenage crises involving drugs and alcohol, school failure, and suicide attempts indicate that the number of youths who resort to prostitution is but a small segment of a much larger population of suffering juveniles. To meet the needs of children in its area, New Connections has four daytime professionals and two evening staff. One of its essential program elements is the degree of trust and friendship staff share with one another, for when cohesiveness is strong, disruptive student actions are more easily responded to.

New Connections staff members, first and foremost, like teenagers and enjoy their youthful energy. The staff is characterized by good counseling, communication, and crisis intervention skills, as well as by co-worker interaction. Indeed, talented people who lack the ability to function as team members do not make good employees for this sort of program. Such a staff must be supported and nurtured, and each member should be accorded the opportunity to be creative and to grow in his or her area of interest. The weekly meetings at New Connections for staff assignments and program discussion, recognition for a well-done job, and honest feedback on weaknesses help create the trust and cohesiveness necessary for staff unity and preservation of the program.

A final theme at New Connections is the building of positive, strong friendships with the children. The generosity and courtesy extended by the staff elicit similar acts by students. Certificates of achievement, cakes for birthdays, and announcement of GED attainment are simple but significant reinforcers. The program truly becomes surrogate parenting, creating a nurturing environment where youths get a second chance at life and an opportunity to grow.

New Connections has demonstrated a cost-effective method of providing a comprehensive array of services to high-risk and high-need youths. The cost of the program is averaging $500 per youth annually. Through continued networking, outreach, and advocacy, the staff expects to intervene more rapidly with minors either already involved in or at risk of exploitation. The concurrent delivery of supportive, educational, and intervention services is a commonsense formula that produces results.

The Anderson Special Crimes Unit: A Regional Task Force

Expanding our view of practical alternatives from the community to the regional level, it is clear that there is need for a coordinated exploitation program using the resources of criminal justice agencies. Danny Durham, Director of the Special Crimes Unit in the Office of the Solicitor in Anderson, S.C., traces below the origins and stages of development of a Special Crimes Unit in his jurisdiction. This unit investigates and prosecutes cases pertaining to the sexual exploitation of children.

*   *   *   *   *

In May 1984 a seminar was held in Charleston, South Carolina, on child pornography and missing children. The speakers discussed the problems of child pornography, child prostitution, and sexual crimes against children by pedophiles. During the course of the seminar, a U.S. postal inspector told me about a man living in my town who had been ordering and receiving child pornography through the mail. He discussed the interest of the U.S. Postal Service in arresting this suspect, but their investigation had so far not led to an arrest.

With the help of a few officers and social workers, a local investigation was begun. First, we did a thorough background check and spoke with dozens of people who knew this man over the years. We discovered that he was suspected of exploiting children for his own sexual enjoyment. It was known that the suspect was receiving child pornography, a fact indicating that he was a pedophile.

On June 14, 1984 we developed enough probable cause to arrest the suspect for distributing child pornography. Under South Carolina law, a judicial determination must be made as to whether or not the material is obscene prior to arrest for possession or distribution of pornography. After a circuit judge made a favorable determination, we obtained a search warrant for the subject's home. During the search of his residence in a middle-class neighborhood in the heart of Anderson, we seized a footlocker crammed with child pornography from Sweden, Denmark, and California. Included in the seizure were such titles as "Piccolo," "Nudist Angels," "Nudist Moppets," "Teen Moppets," "Oh Boy!" and "Wonderboy," to name but a few. We also found a list of other pedophiles with whom our subject had been corresponding for years.

Analysis of the confiscated material revealed that local children were his victims. We went to the children's parents and explained the problem. They cooperated, we prosecuted, and the man pled guilty to two counts of criminal sexual conduct on minors in the first degree and two counts of lewd and lascivious acts with children. He was sentenced to serve 20 years in prison out of a possible 80 years maximum. With the leads from that case we alerted law enforcement agencies to pedophiles in Maryland, New York, and California.

Afterward our group worked on similar cases. Sometimes the investigations did not pan out, but often we were able to make an arrest within a short time after talking with a child. What we looked for in every case was the point in time where sufficient probable cause existed for a search warrant. Experience showed that a good search is 90 percent of a case, for pedophiles love to "preserve the moment" on film and to possess child pornography.

Investigations during the summer and fall of 1984 turned up new leads, and efforts were made to create a special crimes unit. We wanted to include all appropriate parties, such as the sheriff, the chief of police, and the director of the Department of Social Services. In November 1984 at a seminar in New Orleans, we found the neccesary source of information on organizing and managing such a crime unit. Directors of such units from across the country had developed a format. We learned that if the unit is not organized in the right manner, its chances of success are minimal, for there is a clear risk of alienating the people needed to make it work. In order to be successful in apprehending and prosecuting pedophiles, all concerned agencies must work together. The personnel of a special crimes unit must be people who are motivated to rid the community of child molesters and who possess both the expertise to investigate these cases and the understanding to help victims overcome their trauma.

The members selected for our unit were a detective with the sheriff's department, a detective with the city police department, a uniformed city police officer, a state constable, two protective service workers with the Department of Social Services, and myself as a representative of the Solicitor's Office. The solicitor met with all agency heads to explain what we were doing. The director's role in the unit included assisting in investigations. The group was titled the "Special Crimes Unit," and was formally empowered on December 1, 1984.

If we are going to curb child molestation, law enforcement agencies must be creative in their investigative techniques, because pedophiles can be extremely shrewd. The seductive processes they employ can stretch over a period of several months. Advance notice, therefore, that a pedophile is in a jurisdiction can be useful to investigators. Legislation has been proposed to require a person who is a proven child molester to notify a law enforcement agency when he moves into a new jurisdiction.

By the end of December 1984, the sheriff's department had withdrawn its detective from the Special Crimes Unit, saying that a special crimes unit was not needed to investigate this type of crime and observing, furthermore, that the families of convicted child molesters might never forgive us for making an arrest. This decision by the sheriff's department is a manifestation of a large problem: Investigations often touch respectable "pillars" of the community. Some politicians are reluctant to risk political damage stemming from charges brought against such people. Because of the seriousness of the offense of child molestation, it is vital to investigate thoroughly every reported incident of child molestation before bringing charges. If lies have been fabricated against someone, a thorough inquiry will uncover the truth. In other words, it is just as important to protect an innocent person from being wrongfully accused as it is to protect kids from molestation. In this regard, it is helpful to have expert investigators from different fields to ensure that sound decisions are made.

The biggest problems that have arisen throughout the formative stages of the Anderson Special Crimes Unit are the groundless rumors circulated to divert the unit from its mission. Such rumors stir up conflicts. Individuals who do not like the idea of a special crimes unit dwell on negative possibilities while refusing to admit its positive aspects. Starting everyone in the same direction is also a major hurdle. People may differ on how to achieve a particular result or conduct an investigation, but their goals must be the same. We are now adopting a policy of active, one-on-one conversation to keep the lines of communication open between agencies. The key ingredient is to reach a common ground between departments. Treading on another agency's jurisdiction must be avoided. Agencies not a part of your unit must be involved as soon as possible.

A situation arose, for example, where the initial investigation of a pedophile began within the jurisdiction of an agency participating in the Special Crimes Unit. The unit monitored this man for about five months. From his prior record he was a known pedophile who associated with other pedophiles. Before long he was bringing underage males to his home for overnight stays. We acquired enough probable cause to obtain a search warrant for his residence and an arrest warrant for him on criminal conspiracy charges. On the basis of that arrest we were able to talk with the victims, ages 10 through 14, and to later charge the man with four counts of criminal sexual conduct. Information gathered in the search pointed to another man in the conspiracy who lived in a different jurisdiction. The case was discussed with that agency's supervisor, whose department extended its full cooperation in the investigation.

To minimize political criticism, a unit may seek federal grants for purchasing equipment, personnel training, and overtime compensation. Local government officials concerned about expenditures should be informed that after the initial start-up costs, a unit's operating costs are minimal. A crimes unit may also improve its credibility and acceptance by speaking to civic organizations and participating in public forums that promote awareness of child sexual abuse. Educating the community and law enforcement personnel should be a major goal of the unit; this can be achieved through seminars, lectures, and workshops. In short, the unit should not be kept a secret; the community should be involved. Once people understand what is being done, they will be supportive. The news media can be helpful in this regard. In their coverage, they can attest to the unit's procedures and success. Press releases should be drafted so as not to be overly prejudicial or reveal investigative techniques.

The director will typically act as spokeperson for the unit. Each agency involved should receive ample credit for its efforts. To avoid jealousy over publicity, the sheriff or chief of police, depending on jurisdiction, should be afforded the opportunity to speak to the press after a news release. In return, he may realize that, by cooperating with the unit, he can increase his popularity.

The director's role is that of overall manager of investigations. He orchestrates a unit's activities without encroaching on decisions or actions that fall within the domain of the investigators. In addition, he must be aware of potential conflicts within the unit and be prepared to resolve diplomatically such issues as they arise. Careful groundwork and thorough planning will insure the successful creation and operation of a special crimes unit, and its experts can deal a major blow to those who sexually abuse minors.

The Police–Social Worker Team: A Coordinator Approach at the Local Level

Another approach to victim advocacy involves the careful management of limited agency resources and investigative manpower at the local level. Lieutenant Thelma Milgrim of the Wytheville, Virginia, Sheriff's Department was a catalyst in the creation of a police–social worker team. Below she outlines the basic stages that led to the implementation of this unit.

*   *   *   *   *

Small police departments often believe that none of the approaches used by specialized units of larger departments can be effectively applied by them, but this need not be the case. The Wytheville Department, for example, has 32 sworn officers. Despite this small number, we have successfully implemented the police–social worker team approach. To assist the team, other officers are trained to know the basic facts and to recognize the signs of child sexual abuse and exploitation.

In the past, cooperation between police and social workers here was hampered by preconceived ideas and attitudes. Police officers, as a general rule, felt the social worker was too easy on the abuser, whereas the social worker believed the police were too hard. By discussing these issues in depth with local social workers, we were able to resolve our differences of opinion. As a result of adequate communication and planning, a police–social worker team was started in our county.

The team investigates all sexual abuse incidents. If the case is founded on fact, prosecution usually occurs. Most offenders are convicted, but not all are sentenced to prison. Probation, with intense counseling, can occur. Our commonwealth attorney is aware of the team and cooperates fully with it. One of the greatest advantages to this approach is that it does benefit the victim. The following steps demonstrate how such a team can be implemented:

1. Survey the problem of sexual abuse and exploitation in the police department's jurisdiction.
2. Select one or two people from the police department and from the social service agency to form the nucleus of a team.
3. Review existing departmental policies to identify obstacles in coordinating resources. Secure executive approval for the team from both departments. Be prepared to deal with attitude problems (intradepartmental and public) in the formation of a team.
4. Set operating guidelines regarding such matters as hours, case load, and lines of communication to improve coordination. Decide, for instance, when and how the members will meet, share leads or information, and perform follow-up work.
5. Identify official and community resources that may be of value or assistance, such as the prosecutor's office, crime prevention councils, and juvenile counselors.
6. Keep the departments and community posted as to the team's activities and accomplishments. Good public relations are an essential ingredient of a successful team. Initiate community awareness programs to help educate the public regarding child sexual abuse and create grassroots support for the team.

The Police–Social Worker Team in the Pretrial Phase

As it has in Wytheville, a police–social worker team can significantly improve the level and quality of services and resources applied to the investigation and prosecution of cases involving sexual exploitation. In the following discussion, Kurt Stakeman, a former police attorney, discusses case preparation as an extension of the efforts of the police–social worker team. He points out the urgency of adhering to a series of fundamental steps in developing information and building a strong case prior to prosecution.

*   *   *   *   *

Time is of the essence in preparing a case: Every day of delay is one more day in which the child can be pressured into silence. In the interest of moving swiftly one may assume, when preparing cases of exploitation for prosecution, that the following generalizations hold true:

- The typical offender has used the child victim sexually in every way possible that was not too physically painful for him or her.
- The offender has had fantasies about having sex with children prior to the act, and he has supplemented the act with erotic books, films, or photographs depicting sex with children.
- The offender probably has had more than one victim, which makes it important to interview the children he had access to.

Often commercial aspects of child sexual exploitation are involved. In one small town, for instance, the police had a suspect and one victim. The police investigated the possibility of other victims by going door to door in the neighborhood. Their efforts uncovered a sex ring which included another adult and more than ten children and involved pornography and the use of aphrodesiac chemicals.

At the first meeting with the victim, he or she should be encouraged to tell about the event in her or his own words. Two to three hours should be allowed for this meeting. The child should be asked to draw a picture of herself/himself and the suspect naked, identifying the touching parts: Even a drawing of stick people will help clarify what happened. Such a drawing can be entered as an exhibit in a trial. Anatomically correct dolls can also be helpful. It is important not to lead the child, particularly early in the conversation: The state's case can be helped by the victim's detailed knowledge of sexual acts and parts, whereas the defendant's case can be helped by the depiction of an investigator or prosecutor who has put words into the child's mouth. Questions should be open-ended. For example, the interviewer might point to his head and ask, "Did he touch you here?" "With what?" The survey can continue with other parts of the body.

The child should be asked whether she or he has ever been shown any pictures of naked people and whether anyone has taken pictures of her/him. If pictures were taken, what was she or he doing? Were the victim's clothes on or off? The victim should understand that the questions pertain to any time, not just one particular incident or period. The answers can form the basis for a legal search of the offender's premises; in some cases it can even prove to be the key in identifying a sex ring. It is important to question the child about every detail of the sex act(s). After the interview, details can be corroborated, with the objective of proving the child's story so detailed, so informed, that it must be true.

At the first meeting, some questions should be aimed at qualifying the child as a court witness—for example, is she or he able to tell the difference between truth and falsehood, between reality and fantasy? This can be done informally and as a preliminary step for future conversation. It will help prepare the child for court and provide more information about the victim.

A polygraph should be available for the suspect at the first interview. Records show that, during the first contact with officials, many defendants request a polygraph test to back up their protestation of innocence. The test should be given as soon as possible, even if the results are not admissible in court. A surprising number of molesters agree to undergo a test, then tell the truth prior to or at the time of the test.

A search of the offender's premises may well be the most important step in building a strong case, for virtually every offender owns some type of child or adult pornography. Objects of the search include evidence of the crime itself—for example, a vibrator used on the victim—or evidence concerning the identity, motive, or knowledge of the offender. A search of the offender's premises can be the most critical pretrial action for the prosecution for the simple reason that most cases turn into a contest between the child victim's statements and those of the adult offender. Because the state must prove its case beyond a reasonable doubt, corroborative evidence can be crucial.

A close pretrial relationship between the victim and the interviewer is essential to encourage the child to testify in court. From the child's point of view, there are few good reasons to testify and many good reasons to recant. If the child is not fully prepared to testify in front of several people, the search for truth will be unsuccessful. The victim's fear of the unknown must be overcome through adequate preparation by the police, the social worker, and the prosecutor in a joint effort. It should be possible to clear up any misconceptions that she or he might have about what will happen during or after the trial.

The Child Service Model: A Strategy for Prevention

Only long-term, sustained efforts—including preventive measures—can effectively arrest the development of sexual trafficking in minors. Such a program may be constructed from the elements of the child service model presented below. In this model, social service and criminal justice professionals work with others to effect a coordinated and comprehensive program designed to interrupt the cycle of victimization.

The services of many practitioners can be coordinated toward a common goal. The following outline illustrates the basic development of a multidisciplinary program suited for both local and regional application. This model offers a foundation for coordinating resources, expertise, and services within a limited budget and seeks to create a nucleus of local practitioners who are dedicated to the elimination of sexual trafficking. It is assumed that this nucleus will consist of a few committed people, exist on a meager budget, and succeed as a result of the preparation and organization that its participants bring to the programs.

OUTLINE OF CHILD SERVICE MODEL

In stage one, various agencies and individuals found in most communities should be identified and contacted for assistance in formulating a local or regional program.

Stage 1: Resource Identification
A. Regional agencies or persons with a legal mandate or interest in the status of victimized minors
   1. Investigation
      (a) Social service agency
      (b) Municipal and county police departments
   2. Prosecution by district attorney
   3. Victim aid and aftercare
      (a) Juvenile court counselor
      (b) Welfare and family services

     (c) Mental health center

     (d) Medical examiner, pediatricians, and nurses

     (e) Outreach therapists

     (f) Youth service agencies (public and private sector)

     (g) Community action groups

     (h) Elementary and high school counselors and teachers

B. Types of resources required

    1. Liaison person representing each agency or group

    2. Funding (local, state, or grants)

    3. Program site

    4. Community support

    5. Operating materials, supplies, and equipment

In stage two, steps should be taken to create an effective program at the grassroots level, including the selection of liaison persons and the drafting of interdepartmental protocols.

Stage 2: Creation of a Child Service Program

A. Selection of agency and group liaison persons

B. Pooling of identified resources and services

C. Division of responsibilities

D. Drafting of intra-agency protocols

E. Design of rudimentary data bank

    1. Case status reports

    2. Program meeting notes

    3. Work assignments for members

    4. Financial records

F. Identification of program clientele

G. Training workshops for program members

    1. Dynamics of sexual trafficking crimes

    2. Streamlined techniques for case building

    3. Victim assistance during prosecutorial phase

    4. Delivery of support and aftercare services for victim

In stage three, program implementation is outlined in three areas: investigation, prosecution, and aftercare for the victim:

Stage 3: Implementation of a Program

A. Bi-monthly meetings

B. Investigation by law enforcement and social services

    1. Routine review of pending and unsolved cases

    2. Sharing of street and intelligence data or leads

C. Prosecution

    1. Collaboration with police and social services regarding case building

       2. Assignment of single prosecutor to follow a case and help a victim through the entire judicial proceeding
       3. Provision of a battery of support services to victim during prosecutorial phase, including a witness protection program

D. Aftercare
   1. Post facto assistance
     (a) Outreach therapy
     (b) Mental health and clinical services
     (c) Foster or group home placement
     (d) Counseling for parents of victim
     (e) Legal advice
   2. Street-level assistance for sexually exploited child program
     (a) Directed toward current or former victims of sexual trafficking under age 18
     (b) Location in a sheltered, secure setting in a community
     (c) Program resources and facilities reserved exclusively for sexually exploited minors
     (d) Victims attracted to program by offer of immediate services such as food and housing
     (e) Intensive evaluation performed to determine victim's needs and services
     (f) Training and education provided, with an emphasis on life skills necessary to prepare a juvenile for independent living

In the fourth part of the model, the primary goals of a child service program are formulated.

Stage 4: Program Goals
A. Identify and intercept children at risk.
B. Provide long-term support services and treatment for victims.
C. Develop and implement reactive strategies for the abolition of sexual trafficking.
D. Simplify and upgrade the case-building process between departments.
E. Serve as advocates on behalf of victimized minors.
F. Increase public awareness to gain support for efforts to prevent sexual exploitation.
G. Create a data bank on local traffickers.

Evaluation is important to the success of any program. Stage five identifies the evaluative criteria most appropriate for this model.

Stage 5: Program Evaluation
A. Periodic reviews and critiques of program efforts
B. Number of victims assisted
C. Convictions as a percentage of arrests

D. Expansion or diminution of services to victims
E. Efficient allocation of limited resources and manpower
F. Program acceptance by juveniles at risk

Conclusion

Victim advocacy requires the implementation of practical programs that specifically address the crimes of sexual trafficking and the needs of minors subjected to exploitation. It also must deal with questions of judicial equity, compensation, due process, and the quasi-legal status of minors within the criminal justice system. Well-conceived programs and service models can positively affect the way underage victims are treated in the judicial process. The fact that few such programs exist throughout the country is not surprising. Because programs dealing with sexually victimized children must be innovative, they inevitably meet widespread opposition. Also, their goals and funding needs often conflict with those of established bureaucracies, such as social service and law enforcement agencies.

To avoid this impasse, we recommend integration of existing services and personnel into a cohesive program or task force. As noted in this chapter, a comprehensive approach to victim advocacy is practical, especially at the regional or local level. Community-based, grassroots programs are the keys to providing investigative, prosecutorial, and treatment services that either reduce the level of trafficking or extend direct and immediate assistance to its victims.

Sexually exploited minors constitute a unique segment of the juvenile population. Providing for their needs while engaging in rehabilitation is a multidisciplinary challenge that too often is not met by conventional judicial and human service agencies. The crimes of sexual trafficking are unusual in that they often occur at a point beyond the sight of traditional law enforcement agencies. Alternative programs should be established to intercept exploiters as a way of compensating for the inherent shortcomings of local agencies. Federal child sexual exploitation programs, special crimes units, and police–social worker teams are effective options that can minimize the effects of victimization and make progress in the abolition of the child sex markets.

Endnote

1. When enacted in 1982, the intended purpose of J.T.P.A. was "to establish programs to prepare youths and unskilled adults for entry into the labor force. . . . " [29 USC 1501 (P.L. 99–300)]. In October 1986 Congress added Section 1630, Summer Youth Employment and Training Programs, whose "purpose of programs assisted under this part to: (1) enhance the basic educational skills of youth: (2) encourage school competition, or enrollment in supplementary or alternative school programs; (3) provide eligible youth with exposure to the world of work." [29 USC 1630, (PL 99–496), § 8 (a) (2)].

Chapter 10

STRATEGIES FOR CHANGE

Beyond sexual trafficking's pale of misery lies the potential for a reshaped future for underage victims. Fulfilling this potential, however, will depend on how well we plan strategies for change. Extricating a victim from an exploitive situation requires a substantial expenditure of scarce tax dollars, but what higher priority have we than the welfare of our children? Vigorous efforts must be made to prevent exploitation and to prosecute exploiters.

In this chapter we review some options. No single action will, by itself, solve the problem of trafficking, but each can contribute to the solution. Each recommendation addresses a specific aspect of these crimes and is considered, accordingly, from one of three perspectives: (1) prevention, (2) investigation and prosecution, and (3) victim's rights. In the final analysis, of course, the permanent abolition of sexual trafficking can result only from a nationwide commitment on behalf of sexually victimized minors in all three areas. We must, in short, reallocate traditional law enforcement and judicial resources and reorder our priorities to address properly the issue of sexual trafficking.

Recommendations for Action

National Symposia on Trafficking   Judicial, social, and human service practitioners should be brought together for open exchange of ideas and research findings and a search for solutions. In such an arena, the various participants can set priorities, arrive at a common language for discussion of sexual trafficking, introduce new research ideas, and plan courses of action.

Training of Practitioners System practitioners must be kept informed of agency protocols, legislative changes, and successful enforcement techniques.

Research Funding The literature on sexual exploitation is rich with hypotheses but short on practical solutions. Available federal and state funds should be allocated to projects that offer the greatest prospects for improving the plight of victims and preventing sexual trafficking crimes.

Public Awareness Campaigns The issue of child sexual exploitation must be brought before the public in order to stimulate community-based support.

Education in the Schools Administrators and teachers should be taught how to identify, report, and treat victims, and students should be made aware of sexual exploitation as a peril.

Legislative Review Federal and state legislatures should reevaluate laws regarding sexual trafficking in the areas of criminal sanctions, definitions, victim compensation, and child advocacy. Efforts should be directed toward clarity of purpose, streamlining of existing laws, and uniformity of language.

Outreach Therapy Because it is one of the more cost-effective methods for treating exploitive families and victims on a comprehensive basis, outreach therapy should be widely employed in judicial dispositions as an alternative to imprisonment and the permanent dissolution of potentially salvageable families. Outreach therapy can be used as preventive medicine to stem the spread of exploitation within a dysfunctional family, while also being of therapeutic value to victims.

Crime Data The Uniform Crime Reports require a revised classification format to incorporate the crimes of sexual trafficking at the national level. Such information would prove invaluable in identifying the extent, flow, and patterns of these offenses. On October 12, 1984, Congress passed Public Law 98–473, directing the Administrator of Juvenile Justice and Delinquency Prevention to compile information emphasizing (1) effective programs to prevent the abduction and sexual exploitation of children, and (2) effective program models to provide treatment, counseling, or other aid to parents of missing children, or children who have been the victims of abduction or sexual exploitation (42 U.S.C., 5773).

Offender Tracking   Adults convicted of a crime of sexual trafficking should be required to register upon relocation to a new
residence. In August 1986 the Illinois General Assembly enacted
Senate Bill 2292, or Public Act 84–1279,[1] which requires a habitual
child sex offender, defined as an individual who has been convicted
for a second time of committing, or attempting to commit, criminal
sexual assault, aggravated criminal sexual assault, or criminal or
aggravated criminal sexual abuse against a victim under the age of
18, to register with the law enforcement authorities of a community in which he resides for more than thirty days. (See *Ill. Ann.
Stat.*, ch. 127, 55a–3.) The principle behind such a requirement is
analogous to that establishing central registries for reported cases
of child abuse and neglect for use by state departments of social
service.

While a general provision would require registration of all
former offenders, an exemption should be available to those who
can demonstrate that they are rehabilitated. Under New York
statutes, for example, an offender who goes five years without any
misdemeanors or felonies related to sexually exploitative activities
is exempt from reporting requirements."[2]

Parental Training   Providing vocational training and primary
education to parents of dysfunctional families could help disrupt
the generational cycle of abuse and exploitation by supplanting
abusive habits with effective work skills. Indeed, social scientists
have established a high correlation between child abuse and unemployment. As observed in Chapter 8 and in case studies
throughout this book, child abuse is frequently an antecedent
condition of sexually exploitive activities. While other environmental factors, such as the absence of a supportive network of extended
family and friends, may aggravate an exploiter's poor self-image,
he—like everyone—will commonly describe himself in terms of
his job. Steady, satisfying work not only increases an individual's
positive self-esteem but lessens the probability of sexual abuse and
related activities.

Mandatory Reporting   Because intra-familial sexual and physical abuse are often the antecedents to more commercially exploitive activities, all jurisdictions should require reciprocal and immediate reporting of known incidents of abuse to law enforcement
and social service departments.

Federal Priorities   The National Center for Missing and Exploited Children is, because of its legislative mandate, a function-

ally limited organization. We propose that its charter be revised to focus the center's resources on sexual exploitation. Its programs should include national training of human service workers by competent practitioners, development of a central data bank to house information germane to trafficking, and a two-way exchange of information between participating state and local agencies.

Alternative Sentencing Options   In light of the acute shortage of cell space in most of the nation's correctional facilities, a wider range of sentencing options should be made available to judges. These options, as noted in Chapter 7, can be reserved for inchoate offenses, noncoercive or noncontributory acts, and those situations in which the offender could benefit more from intensive supervision with therapy rather than incarceration. As long-term participants in the sentencing process, judges rather than petit juries are better situated to make sentences appropriate to the offense.

Probation is an acceptable alternative to imprisonment when the hazard posed to the community can be effectively minimized by intensive supervision. Fines, in addition to probation, could serve a purpose beyond depriving the accused of pecuniary gain: The proceeds could be used to defray the costs of investigation and probation, as well as to provide restitution for the victim.

Investigative and Prosecutorial Strategies

Many law enforcement agencies and district attorneys do not assign a high priority to cases involving sexual trafficking in children, and the manpower and resources devoted to the interdiction of these crimes are often minimal. It is important, therefore, that existing, limited resources be used effectively. The recommendations in this section seek to increase the level of effectiveness for agency practitioners who wish to identify sexually exploitive activities within their jurisdictions.

Pimp File   In areas of heavy prostitution, the identities of pimps can usually be established. A pimp file could help identify and locate procurers who recruit juveniles, by providing a means of exchange of current information among law enforcement agencies within a region.

Pornography Index/Data Bank   A file of active pornographers and pornographic photographs can be useful in spotting current

victims of child pornography, especially since it is rare for a
pornographer to limit his activities to one child.

Criminal History Review Agencies, firms, and organizations
that work with minors (such as day-care centers and school boards)
should check the background of applicants to screen out pedophiles. Kentucky and California, for instance, prohibit boards of
education and child care centers from employing anyone convicted
of a sex crime, drug crime, or crime of violence in positions which
entail supervisory or disciplinary authority over minors. (See *Ky.
Rev. Stat.*, Ch. 17, 1986, and *Calif. Penal Code*, § 11105.3, 1986.)

Sexual Exploitation Units/Task Forces Appearing in growing
numbers throughout the nation, these groups are a practical
solution for departments lacking funds and manpower. Examples
of the various types of programs that can be constructed at the
grassroots level are described in Chapter 9.

Intra-Agency Cooperation A recurrent theme of this book has
been the overriding need for cooperation among agencies at the
three levels of government. Such a cooperative effort means the
sharing of leads, mutual trust, and a multi-departmental approach
to the location, investigation, and recovery of sexually victimized
children. To ensure the continuity of an investigation across jurisdictions, we recommend that one liaison officer or coordinator be
used to expedite such cases.

Sting Operations A carefully formulated sting operation can be
an excellent proactive tool for investigators of trafficking activities.
This tactic is most useful in areas where officials are aware of a
concentration of pornographers or locales where juvenile prostitutes and pimps are known to work.

Child Witness Protection—Sanctuary Child victims are, in
many cases, put into a state of jeopardy because of their critical
role in the adversarial process. A juvenile hustler, for example,
who is willing to testify against her pimp puts her life in the court's
hands. Frequently, a prosecutor's case rest entirely on the testimony of the victim without other corroborative evidence. These
child witnesses should receive physical protection during and after
prosecution. A series of safe houses should be made available for
exploited minors in immediate danger because of their involvement in trafficking or knowledge of offenders. These sanctuaries
should incorporate a secure, structured environment that provides
for the victim's daily needs, safety, and well-being.

Revised Question Inventories The question inventories used during interrogation of an offender or during an interview with a victim should be expanded to include crimes of sexual trafficking. If, for instance, the initial report indicates familial sexual abuse, the interviewer should ask the offender and the victim if the act included the taking or showing of "questionable" photographs or films, whether other adults contributed directly or peripherally to the event, and whether other minors were exposed to the same activity.

Polygraph Examination   In the absence of physical evidence and corroborating witnesses, the polygraph is an important investigative tool. As Elaine Surma, a special investigator for the Pennsylvania Attorney General's Office and a certified polygraph examiner who has interviewed numerous adult exploiters, explains in the following observations, it can be an effective method for answering unsolved questions of trafficking:

> *An investigator may suggest to a suspect that the examination would help prove his innocence. The fact that a polygraph has cleared many people accused of crimes is an important point that should be brought to the subject's attention. Except in rare instances, most people will claim that they have told the investigator the truth. One inducement to convince a reluctant suspect to talk to a polygraphist is when the opposing party or complaining witness agrees to take the examination.*
>
> *Whenever possible, a polygraph examination for the accused should be scheduled as soon as an alleged incident is discovered. A person who is sick, overtired, or who has been severely interrogated should not be examined. The same is true for a person who suffers from a heart condition or is under medical supervision. Most minors under the age of 12 should not be tested, but this decision depends on the child's intellectual capacity. Persons under the age of 18 as a general rule require written permission from a parent or guardian. The victim is typically questioned last in order to ease the strain of having a minor relive the offense. This procedure enables the investigator to limit the questions to essential points and, if successful, improves the chances of completing a profitable interview about the allegedly exploitive activity.*

Case Managers   Once an exploitive situation has been identified by social service or law enforcement authorities, a specially trained case manager operating out of the prosecutor's office should be assigned to coordinate efforts, aid the victim, and supervise judicial processing. Whenever possible, the prosecutor who makes the initial appearance should handle the case from initiation to sentencing. The case manager must be capable of reducing the judicial process down to human proportions in a manner that is not threatening to the victim or prejudicial to the constitutional guarantees of the defendant.

During the pretrial phase, this resident expert on sexual exploitation should help the victim alleviate his or her fear of the potential consequences. A victim's emotion-based defense of the offender must also be overcome. Apprehension induced by the judicial setting can be reduced by various measures, such as dispensing with the use of judicial robes when such formal attire might intimidate the minor and using smaller facilities for the proceedings. Another proposal is that underage victims be examined in a "child's courtroom," with the defendant located behind a one-way mirror.[3] Videotaped depositions and a court closed to all persons not essential to the proceedings have also been recommended.

Revised Agency Guidelines   Law enforcement departments that lack specific expertise in the area of child sexual trafficking should consider revising their internal policies and procedural guidelines in order to improve the quality of their investigations. As Hal Nees, Chief of Detectives in Boulder, Colorado, points out, these goals can be achieved in a number of ways.

Much has been written lately in national publications about the sexual exploitation of children, with an emphasis on a few well-known incidents where the criminal justice system failed to react properly. Law enforcement administrators and supervisors can learn from these incidents by reviewing the operational and written practices of their own agencies to see if they might be prone to similiar errors. Following are some effective implementation standards and guidelines that can be adopted by law enforcement agencies:

A. Training: Agencies need to provide pre-service and in-service training for law enforcement officers. They need specific information about the broad range of methods/techniques common to sexual exploitation as well as about policies and procedures for carrying on active investigations. At least 80 hours of basic training should be provided to all incoming youth officers/juvenile detectives in these areas:

1. General investigative skills
2. Interview/investigative techniques
3. Legal status of children
4. Available services/resources for youths
5. Delinquency causation and prevention

6. Counseling skills

7. Child development and abuse

B. Sources of Information/Intelligence: Agencies should collect facts and information about groups or individual adults with a sexual interest in youths. Local outlets for pornography can be monitored for their compliance with local, state, and federal laws. Local newspaper/magazine personal advertisements should also be reviewed for leads to pedophiles operating in the area.

C. Inter-Agency Cooperation: A close working relationship with the U.S. Customs and postal authorities is needed to determine who is receiving child pornography from abroad. Local and regional agencies must keep lines of communication open about sexual exploitation within their jurisdictions, particularly since many cases involving pedophiles cross jurisdictional boundaries.

D. Coordination with School and Youth Service Agencies: Agency officials should meet on a regular basis with the above agencies. Such meetings can help promote greater public awareness and may produce useful leads of any potential exploitation in the area.

E. Prevention Programs: If a sexual exploitation prevention program does not exist in a community, one should be started. With periodic reviews and evaluations to insure the program's overall effectiveness, available resources can be directed toward prevention and identification.

F. Agency Policies: A law enforcement agency can draft written policies on how to deal with youths, both as victims and suspects. To that end, officers specifically trained in child sexual abuse should be given responsibility for investigation; the quality of investigation can be enhanced by the assignment of such highly qualified investigators. Also, reducing the workload of investigators who handle sexual exploitation cases often will encourage specialization and speed up the investigative process—especially important in instances of missing and runaway children, where reports need to be acted on without delay.

G. Community Response: An administrator should examine the response of his community to the problem of sexual exploitation in terms of (1) facilities that are available for runaways, (2) coordination among youth/social service agencies, and (3) prevention and education programs.

Victim Rights: Assistance and Support

Traditionally the victim of crime has been uninvolved in the sentencing process after a verdict of guilty. Some jurisdictions, however, now actively solicit the victim's opinion on an appropriate sentence. In June 1982 California approved a decision to give victims of crime the right to attend all sentencing proceedings in person or by counsel and to express their views about the crime or the need for restitution (Calif. Penal Code 1191.1). We believe that the criminal justice system must also prepare in advance to help underage victims of sexual trafficking. Our recommendations include victim restitution and treatment, victim trust funds, community-based victim aid, youth service licensing, and international victim advocacy.

Victim Testimony Recommendations for victim testimony include: (1) examining minors who testify to establish competency; (2) allowing out-of-court statements made by a child victim in the record as an exemption to the hearsay rule; (3) allowing videotaped testimony from minors; and (4) maintaining a closed court when the child victim is testifying. All of these recommendations are currently being tried, tested, or modified in various states.

The Massachusetts Legislature, for example, has enacted legislation which permits the presentation of a child victim's testimony by videotape or film whenever the trial court determines by a preponderance of the evidence that the child is likely to suffer psychological or emotional trauma in the open court or in the presence of the defendant. (See *Mass. Gen. Laws, Ann.* ch. 278, § 16D.) A similar procedure was successfully challenged in the Kentucky Supreme Court, where a statute authorizing a videotaped interview with a child victim (*Ky. Rev. Stat.* 421.350(2)) as declared unconstitutional, but the Kentucky statute did not require a judicial determination of the child's competency to testify. (See *Gaines* v. *Com.* 728. S.W. 2d 525 (Ky. 1987)). And, a Washington statute permits testimony by an under-10-year-old victim of sexual contact with an adult to be admissible within certain guidelines and in accordance with specific criteria.[4]

In short, an enlightened approach to victim testimony, when combined with elimination of the husband-wife evidentiary privilege stating that one may not be compelled to testify against one's spouse, can be of benefit to the underage victim in an exploitive family.

Victim Restitution and Treatment Uniform legislation, surely one of the most neglected areas of sexual exploitation, is needed to extend the rights of financial restitution, guaranteed treatment/ rehabilitation, and long-term aftercare to victimized minors.

Victim Trust Funds A fixed amount should be deducted from every civil fine imposed and rerouted to a victims' trust fund. This fund would be used to provide some financial compensation for psychological or physical injuries sustained by a victim. In addition, it could be used to defray other supplementary costs, such as medical care, lost income, and relocation expenses.

Community-Based Victim Aid   Civilian youth service agencies, such as runaway shelters and church-sponsored programs, should pool their resources to offer street-level assistance to minors currently active in the child sex markets. Coordination of efforts should also result in more intensive, specialized counseling for exploited minors.

Youth Service Licensing   All foster and group homes and day-care centers should be licensed according to appropriate state standards and routinely monitored by state licensing investigators for violations involving the sexual or physical mistreatment of children.

International Victim Advocacy   The U.S. government should honor and abide by existing international treaties, covenants, and declarations regarding the global traffic in child sex. At present, the United States does not uphold or uniformly enforce these various obligations (see Chapter 6), nor has it given any indication that it intends to participate as an advocate for victimized minors subjected to international trafficking. Official policy statements notwithstanding, there is little reason to believe that the international status of sexually exploited children will change for the better in the near future.

Conclusion

A society that can place a man on the moon can surely supply and coordinate the resources needed to end the sexual trafficking in children. We must, however, divorce ourselves from the notion that any one measure will achieve that end. In this regard, we endorse the interdisciplinary task force approach, which enables concerned professionals to take the steps required to stifle sexual trafficking in minors. Social service workers and law enforcement officials have different skills and perspectives; each benefits when information and expertise are shared. The Anderson, South Carolina, program need not be an isolated instance; it can be replicated and modified to meet concerns in other places.

No child knowingly volunteers for the role of victim in a sexually exploitive situation. The circumstances are complex. Exploiters take advantage not only of the victim's weakness, ignorance, and distress but also of certain characteristics of our society. Sexual exploitation within a family, for example, is difficult to detect because of our emphasis on family privacy. While we must proceed with caution when dealing with dysfunctional families, we must not extend the tolerance we have for various parenting practices to sexual abuse and exploitation. As we have seen in preceding chapters, sexually exploitative practices in the home often produce runaway children, child prostitutes, and other victims.

The activities of the various professionals dealing with sexual exploitation are governed by laws and administrative regulations. The latter should be fashioned with the advice of professionals, for, in the final analysis, the victims depend on them to redress the balance between victim and exploiter.

And, finally, the victim must be provided with a choice. When real alternatives exist, the vast majority of victims choose the positive situation of an independent, yet nurturing and supportive environment, thereby breaking the vicious cycle of victimization. Therein lies our best hope for the future.

Endnotes

1. *West's Criminal Law News*, Vol. 3, No. 23, 10–01–86 (St. Paul, Minn.: West Publishing Co., p. 53).
2. Some would argue that such a registry constitutes an infringement upon the felon's right to privacy. A viable alternative would be to require the systematic exchange of information among law enforcement and correctional agencies, as presently occurs under the Interstate Compact on Juveniles (*In Re D.B.*, Vt., 1981, 431 A. 2d 498), the Interstate Agreement on Detainers Act (Public Law 91–538, Title 18, U.SC., App.), and the New England Interstate Corrections Compact (*Breest v. Moran*, 571 F. 343 (D.R.I., 1983).
3. Gary B. Melton "Procedural Reforms to Protect Child Victim/Witnesses in Sex Offense Proceedings," *Child Sexual Abuse and the Law* (Washington, D.C.: National Legal Resource Center for Child Advocacy and Protection, 1981), pp. 184–193.
4. Washington Revised Code Annotated, 9A, 44, 120 (1985).

AGENCY RESOURCE DIRECTORY

Following is a list of agencies and persons who have resources or services germane to the issue of child sexual trafficking. To identify specific programs in your area, write or call:

- National Directory of Children and Youth Services
CPR Directory Services Co.
1301 20th Street, N.W.
Washington, D.C. 20036
- National Center for Missing and Exploited Children
1835 K. Street, N.W.
Suite 700
Washington, D.C. 20006
- Governor's Crime Control Commission in your state.

NATIONAL AGENCIES

1. Adam Walsh Child
   Resource Center
   Suite 306
   1876 N. University Drive
   Ft. Lauderdale, FL 33322

2. Adults Molested as
   Children United
   P.O. Box 952
   San Jose, CA 95108

3. C. Henry Kempe National Center
   for the Prevention of Child Abuse
   and Neglect
   1205 Oneida Street
   Denver, CO 80220

4. Child Find, Inc.
   P.O. Box 277
   New Paltz, NY 12561

5. Child Welfare League of
   America, Inc.
   67 Irving Place
   New York, NY 10003

6. Children of the Night
   1800 N. Highland Ave.
   Suite 128
   Hollywood, CA 90028

7. Children's Legal Rights
   2008 Hillyer Place, N.W.
   Washington, DC 20009

8. Children's Rights, Inc.
   3443 17th Street, N.W.
   Washington, DC 22210

9. Children's Rights of Florida, Inc.
   P.O. Box 173
   Pinellas Park, FL 33565

10. Children's Rights of
    New York, Inc.
    19 Maple Street
    Stony Brook, NY 11790

11. Children's Rights of Pennsylvania
    P.O. Box 2764
    Lehigh Valley, PA 18001

12. Committee to Find Etan Patz
    760 Pompton Avenue
    Cedar Grove, NJ 07009

13. Covenant House
    P.O. Box 731
    Times Square Station
    New York, NY 10108

14. Dee Scofield Awareness Program
    4418 Bay Court Avenue
    Tampa, FL 33611

15. Defense for Children
    International—U.S.A.
    534 Eighth Street
    Brooklyn, NY 11215

16. Detroit Transit Alternatives
    2211 Woodward
    Suite 1208
    Detroit, MI 48204

17. Exploited and Missing Child Unit
    216 South 5th Street
    Louisville, KY 40202

18. Family and Friends of
    Missing Persons
    P.O. Box 21444
    Seattle, WA 98111

19. Find-Me, Inc.
    P.O. Box 1612
    Lagrange, CA 30241

20. Find the Children
    11811 Olympic Blvd.
    Los Angeles, CA 90064

21. Focus Youth Services
    1916 Goldring
    Las Vegas, NV 89106

22. Formerly Abused Children
    Emerging Into Society
    Manchester Memorial Hospital
    Child Life Dept.
    71 Haynes St.
    Manchester, CT 06040

23. Foundation for America's Sexually
    Exploited Children
    Bin 5—B
    Bakersfield, CA 93385

24. Georgia Baptist Children's Home
    2930 Flowers Road
    Atlanta, GA 30341

25. Governor's Task Force on
    Missing Children
    512 North Salisbury Street
    Raleigh, NC 27611-7687

26. Help Find Johnny Gosch, Inc.
    P.O. Box 65332
    West Des Moines, IA 50265

27. Huckleberry House, Inc.
    1421 Hamlet Street
    Columbus, OH 43201

28. Identi-Find-A-Child
    Data Center
    P.O. Box 4368
    Albuquerque, NM 87196

29. International Association of Chiefs
    of Police
    13 Firstfield Road
    P.O. Box 6010
    Gathersburg, MD 20878

30. International Juvenile Officers
    Association
    Lt. Frank Schafer, President
    c/o Ferguson Police Dept.
    222 South Florisant Road
    Ferguson, MO 63135

31. Legal Services for Children
    149 Ninth St., Top Floor
    San Francisco, CA 94103

32. Mercy Boys Home
    1140 W. Jackson Blvd.
    Chicago, IL 60607

33. Missing Children Help Center
    Suite 715
    410 Ware Blvd.
    Tampa, FL 33619

34. Mt. Plains Youth Services
    Coalition
    P.O. Box 1242
    Pierre, SD 57501

35. National Center for Missing and
    Exploited Children
    1835 K Street, N.W.
    Suite 700
    Washington, DC 20006

36. National Center on Child Abuse
    and Neglect
    P.O. Box 1182
    Washington, DC 20013

37. National Committee for
    Prevention of Child Abuse
    332 South Michigan Ave.
    Suite 1250
    Chicago, IL 60604-4357

38. National Crime Prevention
    Council
    805 15th St., N.W.
    Washington, DC 20005

39. National Fraternal Order of Police
    8035 Northwest 185 Terrace
    Hialeah, FL 33015

40. National Legal Resource Center
    for Child Advocacy and Protection
    1800 M. Street, N.W.
    Washington, DC 20036

41. National Missing/Abducted
    Children
    Criminal Justice Center
    Sam Houston State University
    Huntsville, TX 77341

42. National Network of Runaway and
    Youth Services, Inc.
    905 6th Street, S.W.
    Suite 612
    Washington, DC 20024

43. National Runaway Switchboard
    2210 N. Halstead
    Chicago, IL 60614

44. National Sheriff's Association
    1250 Connecticut Ave., N.W.
    #320
    Washington, DC 20036

45. New Connections
    214 Brook Street
    Charleston, WV 25301

46. New York City Runaway Hotline
    2 Lafayette Street
    New York, NY 10001

47. Office of Juvenile Justice and
    Delinquency Prevention
    Department of Justice
    633 Indiana Ave., N.W.
    Washington, DC 20531

48. Parents of Murdered Children
    1739 Bellavista
    Cincinnati, OH 45237

49. Parents United, Inc.
    P.O. Box 952
    San Jose, CA 95108

50. Martin House
    1020 S. Main Street
    Rockford, IL 61101

51. San Diego Youth and Community
    Services
    1214 28th Street
    San Diego, CA 92102

52. Society for Young People
    29 Thurston Avenue
    Newport, RI 02840

53. Stolen Child Information Network
    P.O. Box 465
    Anaheim, Ca 92805

54. Texas Child Search
    P.O. Box 8122
    San Antonio, TX 78208

55. The American Humane
    Association
    Children's Division
    P.O. Box 1266
    Denver, CO 80201

56. The Bridge, Inc.
    3151 Redwood Avenue
    San Diego, CA 92104

57. The Family Link
    P.O. Box 40437
    Memphis, TN 38104

58. The Shelter
    1545 12th Ave., South
    Seattle, WA 98144

59. Tumbleweed
    505 N. 27th Street
    Billings, MT 59101

60. Voyage House, Inc.
    311 S. Juniper Street
    Philadelphia, PA 19107

61. West Virginia Criminal Justice
    Institute
    5 Park Road
    Wheeling, WV 26003

62. Youth Development Bureau
    400 6th Street, S.W.
    Washington, DC 20201

63. Youth in Crisis
    3030 Park Avenue
    Bridgeport, CT 06604

INTERNATIONAL AGENCIES

1. Defence for Children
   International
   Case Postale 359—1211 Geneve 4
   Switzerland

2. National Sections of DCI:

   (a) Mr. Jaime Diaz
       DCI-Colombia
       c/o CODECAL
       Apartado Aereo 20439
       Bogota, Colombia

   (b) Ms. R. Bruning
       DCI-the Netherlands
       Postbus 90492
       1006 BL Amsterdam
       The Netherlands

   (c) Claudia Calvaruso
       DEI-Italia
       Via Vittoria 24

   (d) Mme. Marie-Paule Etsete
       DEI—France
       c/o Me. Yvonne Tolman-
       Guillard
       9, bd Saint-Martin
       75003 Paris, France

   (e) DCI—UK
       Children's Legal Centre
       20 Compton Terrace
       London N1 1UN
       England

3. The Anti-Slavery Society for the
   Protection of Human Rights
   Peter Davies, O.B.E.
   180 Brixton Road
   London SW9 6AT, England

4. LAWASIA
   170 Phillip Street
   Sydney, NSW 2000
   Australia

5. J.N. Kaul; Secretary General
   SOS Children's Villages of India
   50 Vishal Bhawan, 95 Nehru Place
   New Delhi, India
   110019

6. Sr. Mathilde Van Kerckhoven
   General Coordinator Asi-Senden
   Home
   2422 Pedro Gil Santa Ana-Manila
   P.O. Box 2508
   Manila, Philippines

7. Ms. Rangisma Limpisawas
    The Foundation for Children
    1492 Banglumpoo Lang
    Chareon-Nakorn Road
    Klongsarn
    Bangkok 10600, Thailand

8. Peter Tacon
    Regional Advisor on Abandoned
    Children
    UNICEF
    Apdo. Aero, 7555
    Bogota, Columbia

9. Mr. Tsegaye Chernet
    c/o National Children's
    Commission
    P.O. Box 1133
    Addis Adaba
    Ethiopia

10. Ng Shui Lai; Deputy Director
    Hong Kong Christian Service
    33 Granville Road
    Kowloon, Hong Kong

11. Sr. Moises Vidales
    Hogares Providencia
    Mexico City, Mexico 01300

12. Fr. Thomas Gaffney, S.J.
    Director
    St. Xavier's Social Service Centers
    G.P.O. Bx. 450
    Kathmandu, Nepal

BIBLIOGRAPHY

JUVENILE PROSTITUTION

ALLEN, DONALD M. "Young Male Prostitutes: A Psychosocial Study," *Archives of Sexual Behavior,* v. 9, n. 5 (1980): 399–426.

BAIZERMAN, MICHAEL, JACQUELYN THOMPSON, and KINAKA STAFFORD-WHITE. "Adolescent Prostitution," *Children Today* (September/October 1979): 20–24.

BARCLAY, KATHRYN, and JOHNNY L. GALLEMORE, "The Family of the Prostitute," *Corrective Psychiatry and the Journal of Social Therapy,* v. 18, n. 4 (1972): 10–16.

BELL, ROBERT R. "Prostitution," in *Social Deviance: A Substantive Analysis* (Homewood, Ill.: Dorsey Press, 1971).

BENJAMIN, HARRY, and R. E. L. MASTERS. "Homosexual Prostitution," *Prostitution and Morality* (New York: Julian Press, 1964).

BOYER, DEBRA K., and JENNIFER JAMES. "Prostitutes as Victims," in DONALD E. J. MACNAMARA and ANDREW KARMEN (eds.), *Deviants: Victims or Victimizers?* (Beverly Hills: Sage, 1983).

BRACEY, DOROTHY H. "Baby-Pros," *Preliminary Profiles of Juvenile Prostitutes* (New York: John Jay Press, 1979).

BREE, MARLIN. "Obsessed with Faith: The Minnesota Connection," *The Saturday Evening Post* (March 1979): 30–31.

BROWN, MARJORIE E. "Teenage Prostitution," *Adolescence,* v. 14, n. 56 (Winter 1979): 665–679.

BRYAN, JAMES H. "Apprenticeships in Prostitution," *Social Problems,* v. 12, n. 3 (Winter 1965): 287–297.

BUTTS, WILLIAM M. "Boy Prostitutes of the Metropolis," *Journal of Clinical Psychotherapy,* v. 44, n. 5 (1974): 441–451.

CAPLAN, G. M. "Facts of Life About Teenage Prostitution," *Crime and Delinquency,* v. 30, n. 1 (January 1984): 69–74.

CAUKINS, SIVAN E., and NEIL R. COOMBS. "The Psychodynamics of Male Prostitution," *American Journal of Psychotherapy,* v. 30, n. 3 (July 1976): 441–451.

COOMBS, NEIL R. "Male Prostitution." *American Journal of Orthopsychiatry,* v. 44, n. 5 (October 1974): 782–789.

234

COONEY, CLAIRE H., and JANET QUINT. "Prostitution in New York City: Answers to Some Questions," *New York Women in Criminal Justice*, (June 1977).

CRAFT, MICHAEL. "Boy Prostitutes and Their Fate," *British Journal of Psychiatry*, v. 112, n. 492 (November 1966): 1111–1114.

DAVIDSON, MICHAEL. *Some Boys* (London: David Bruce, 1970).

DAVIS, KINGSLEY. "The Sociology of Prostitution," *The Sociological Review*, v. 2, n. 5 (October 1937): 744–755.

DEISHER, ROBERT W., VICTOR EISNER, and STEPHEN I. SULZBACHER. "The Young Male Prostitute," *Pediatric Annals*, v. 43, n. 6 (1967): 936–941.

DEISHER, ROBERT W., GREG ROBINSON, and DEBRA BOYER. "The Adolescent Female and Male Prostitute," *Pediatric Annals*, v. 11, n. 10 (1982): 819–825.

DOSHAY, LEWIS J. *The Boy Sex Offender and His Later Criminal Career* (New York: Grune and Stratton, 1943).

DREW, DENNIS, and JONATHAN DRAKE. *Boys for Sale: A Sociological Study of Boy Prostitution* (New York: Brown Books, 1969).

ENABLERS. *Juvenile Prostitution in Minnesota: The Report of a Research Project* (St. Paul: The Enablers, 1978).

GANDY, PATRICK, and ROBERT DEISHER. "Young Male Prostitutes: The Physician's Role in Social Rehabilitation," *Journal of the American Medical Association*, v. 212, n. 10 (1970): 1661–1666.

GIBBENS, T. C. N. "Juvenile Prostitution," *British Journal of Delinquency*, v. 8, n. 1 (July 1957): 3–12.

GINSBURG, KENNETH N. "The Meat Rack: A Study of the Male Homosexual Prostitute," *American Journal of Psychotherapy*, v. 21:2 (April 1967): 170–185.

GRAY, DIANA. "Turning-Out: A Study of Teenage Prostitution," *Urban Life and Culture*, v. 1, n. 4 (1974): 401–425.

HARLAN, SPARKY, LUANNA L. RODGERS, and BRIAN SLATTERY. *Male and Female Adolescent Prostitution: Huckleberry House Sexual Minority Youth Service Project* (Washington, D.C.: Youth Development Bureau, U.S. Department of Health and Human Services, 1981).

HARRIS, M. *The Dilly Boys: The Game of Male Prostitution in Picadilly* (Rockville, Md.: New Perspectives, 1973).

JAMES, JENNIFER. "Motivations for Entrance into Juvenile Prostitution," LAURA CRITES (ed.), *The Female Offender* (Lexington, Mass.: Lexington Books, 1976).

JAMES, JENNIFER, and JANE MEYERDING. "Early Sexual Experience and Prostitution," *American Journal of Psychiatry*, v. 134, n. 12 (December 1977): 1381–1385.

LLOYD, ROBIN. *For Money or Love* (New York: Vanguard Press, Inc., 1979).

MacLeod, Celeste. "Street Girls of the 70's," *The Nation* (April 20, 1974): 486–488.

MacVicar, Katherine, and Marcia Dillon. "Childhood and Adolescent Development of Ten Female Prostitutes," *Journal of the American Academy of Child Psychiatry*, v. 19,n. 1 (1980): 145–59.

Marlowe, Kenneth. "The Life of the Homosexual Prostitute," *Sexology*, 31 (1974): 24–27.

Morgan, Ted. "Little Ladies of the Night," *New York Times Magazine* (November 16, 1975): 34–50.

Nelson, D. *Juvenile Prostitution in Minnesota* (Minneapolis: Enablers, Inc., 1978).

Newman, Frances, and Paula J. Caplan. "Juvenile Female Prostitution as a Gender-Consistent Response to Early Deprivation," *International Journal of Women's Studies*, v. 5, n. 2 (1981): 128–137.

Pittman, David J. "The Male House of Prostitution," *Trans-Action* 8 (March–April 1971): 21–27.

Reiss, Albert J., Jr. "The Social Integration of Peers and Queers," *Social Problems*, v. 9, n. 2 (Fall 1961): 101–121.

Roberts, Robert E., Laurence Abrams, and John R. Finch. "Delinquent Sexual Behavior Among Adolescents," *Medical Aspects of Human Sexuality*, n. 1 (1973): 162–183.

Russell, Donald H. "From the Massachusetts Court Clinics: On the Psychopathology of Boy Prostitutes," *International Journal of Offender Therapy* 15 (1971): 49–52.

Silbert, Mimi H., and Ayala M. Pines. "Sexual Child Abuse as an Antecedent to Prostitution," *Child Abuse and Neglect*, v. 5, n. 4 (1981): 407–411.

Sonenschein, David. "Hustlers Viewed as Dangerous," *Sexual Behavior* 2 (1972): 20.

Sereny, Gitta. *The Invisible Children* (New York: Alfred A. Knopf, 1985).

Tassel, Joan Van. "From Street Life to Straight," *Big Valley*, v. 7, n. 8 (August 1982): 36–41.

Urban and Rural Systems Associates. *Adolescent Prostitution: A Study of Sexual Exploitation, Etiological Factors, and Runaway Behavior with a Focus on Adolescent Male Prostitutes* (San Francisco: Urban and Rural Systems Associates, 1982).

Vitaliano, Peter P., Jennifer James, and Debra Boyer. "Sexuality of Deviant Females: Adolescent and Adult Correlates," *Social Work*, v. 26, n. 6 (1981): 468–472.

Weisberg, D. Kelly. *Children of the Night* (Lexington, Mass.: Lexington Books, 1985).

———. "Children of the Night—The Adequacy of Statutory Treatment of Juvenile Prostitution," *American Journal of Criminal Law*, v. 12, n. 1 (March 1984): 1–67.

WILSON, V. W. "A Psychological Study of Juvenile Prostitutes," *International Journal of Social Psychiatry*, v. 5, n. 1 (Summer 1959): 61–73.

WINICK, CHARLES, and PAUL M. KINSIE. *The Lively Commerce* (Chicago: Quadrangle Books, 1971).

CHILD PORNOGRAPHY

BAKER, C. DAVID. "Preying on Playgrounds: The Sexploitation of Children in Pornography and Prostitution," *Pepperdine Law Review*, v. 5, n. 3 (1978): 809–846.

BROWN, SANDRA Z. "First Amendment—Nonobscene Child Pornography and Its Categorical Exclusion from Constitutional Protection," *Journal of Criminal Law and Criminology*, v. 73, n. 4 (1982): 1337–1364.

BURGESS, ANN W., and MARIEANNE L. CLARK (eds.). Child Pornography and Sex Rings (Lexington, Mass.: D. C. Heath and Company, 1984).

CASO, A. T. "Free Speech and Self-Incrimination—The Constitutionality of California's New Child Pornography Laws," *Pacific Law Journal*, v. 10, n. 1 (January 1979): 119–140.

D'AGOSTINO, R. B., et. al. "Investigation of Sex Crimes Against Children: A Survey of Ten States," *The Police Chief* (February 1984): 37–50.

DAUBER, ERIC L. "Child Pornography," *Florida State University Law Review*, v. 10, n. 684 (1983): 684–701.

DENSEN-GERBER, JUDIANNE, and STEPHEN F. HUTCHINSON. "Developing Federal and State Legislation to Combat the Exploitation of Children in the Production of Pornography," *Journal of Legal Medicine* (September 1977).

DUDAR, HELEN. "America Discovers Child Pornography," *Ms.* (Magazine) (August 1977): 45–47, 80.

"First Amendment—Child Pornography," *The Criminal Law Reporter: Court Decisions*, v. 37, n. 13, (June 26, 1985): 2244–2245.

GUIO, MICHAEL V. "Child Victimization: Pornography and Prostitution," *Journal of Crime and Justice*, v. III (1980): 65–81.

HEINRICH, B. "Extent of Child Pornography in Texas," Texas House Select Committee on Child Pornography, Interim Report (66th Legislative Session, 1978).

HOUSTON, JUDITH, SAMUEL HOUSTON, and E. LA MONTE OHLSON. "On Determining Pornographic Material," *The Journal of Psychology* 88 (1974): 227–287.

KUTCHINSKY, BERL. "The Effect of Easy Availability of Pornography on the Incidence of Sex Crimes: The Danish Experiment," *Journal of Social Issues*, v. 29, n. 3 (1973): 163–181.

McKINNON, ISAIAH. "Child Pornography," *F.B.I. Law Enforcement Bulletin* (February 1979): 18–20.

MOORE, JAMES W. "Child Pornography, The First Amendment and the Media: The Constitutionality of Super-Obscenity Laws," *Comm./Ent.*, v. 4, n. 1 (1982): 115–139.

O'BRIEN, SHIRLEY. *Child Pornography* (Dubuque, Iowa: Kendall Hunt, 1983).

PAYTON, JENNIFER M. "Child Pornography Legislation," *Journal of Family Law*, v. 17, n. 3 (1978–1979): 505–543.

ROONEY, RITA. "Innocence for Sale: A Special Report on Child Pornography," *Ladies Home Journal* (April 1983): 79–81, 127–132.

SCHOETTLE, ULRICH C. "Treatment of the Child Pornography Patient," *American Journal of Psychiatry*, v. 137, n. 9 (September 1980): 1109–1110.

SMITH, ARLO E., and ALVIN J. KNUDSON. Report to the Attorney General on Child Pornography in California (California Attorney General's Advisory Committee on Obscenity and Pornography, August 16, 1977).

TAMBORLANE, THEO A. "A Study of State and Federal Child Pornography Statutes," *Advocate Criminal Law* (May 1982).

"Tightening the Reins on the Child Pornographer," in GOTTESMAN, R. (ed.), *Children's Legal Rights Journal*, v. 5, n. 3 (Summer 1984): 2–9.

WALLACE, PAUL S., JR. "The Evolution of Censorship Through the Judicial Process." *Congressional Research Service* (May 3, 1977): 3976–4007.

WARD, J. "Federal Court Sees Constitutional Problems in Child Pornography Law," Criminal Law Reporter. 22 CRL 2282–2283, (December 28, 1977).

PEDOPHILIA

BERNARD, FREDERIC. "An Enquiry Among a Group of Pedophiles," *The Journal of Sex Research*, v. 11, n. 3 (August 1975): 242–255.

COOK, MARK, and KEVIN HOWELLS (eds.) *Adult Sexual Interest in Children* (New York: Academic Press, 1981).

FREUND, KURT, et al. "The Female Child as a Surrogate Object," *Archives of Sexual Behavior*, v. 2, n. 2 (1972): 119–133.

FREUND, KURT. "Erotic Preference in Pedophilia," *Behavior Research and Therapy* 5 (November 1967): 339–348.

FREUND, KURT, and R. LANGEVIN. "Bisexuality in Homosexual Pedophilia," *Archives of Sexual Behavior*, v. 5, n. 5. (1976): 415–422.

GIGEROFF, ALEX K., J. W. MOHR, and R. E. TURNER. "Sex Offenders on Probation: Heterosexual Pedophiles," *Federal Probation* (December 1968): 17–21.

GROTH, A. NICHOLAS, and JEAN H. BIRNBAUM. "Adult Sexual Orientation and Attraction to Underage Persons," *Archives of Sexual Behavior,* v. 7, n. 3 (1978): 175–181.

JONES, GERALD P. "The Social Study of Pederasty: In Search of a Literature Base," *Journal of Homosexuality,* v. 8, n. 1 (Fall 1982): 61–95.

MARSHALL, W. L., and M. M. CHRISTIE. "Pedophilia and Aggression," *Criminal Justice and Behavior,* v. 8, n. 2 (June 1982): 145–158.

NEWTON, DAVID E. "Homosexual Behavior and Child Molestation: A Review of the Evidence," *Adolescence,* v. 13, n. 49 (Spring 1978): 29–41.

O'CARROLL, TOM. *Paedophilia: The Radical Case* (London: Peter Owen, 1980).

PETERS, JOSEPH J., and ROBERT L. SADOFF. "Clinical Observations on Child Molesters," *Medical Aspects of Human Sexuality* 4 (November 1970): 20–32.

ROOTH, GRAHAM. "Exhibitionism, Sexual Violence and Paedophilia," *British Journal of Psychiatry* 122 (1973): 339–348.

ROSSMAN, PARKER G. "Literature on Pederasty," *The Journal of Sex Research,* v. 9, n. 4 (November 1973): 307–312.

ROSSMAN, PARKER G. *Sexual Experience Between Men and Boys* (New York: Association Press, 1976).

SANDFORT, THEO. The Sexual Aspects of Pedophile Relations (Netherlands: Spartacus, date unknown).

SWANSON, DAVID W. "Who Violates Children Sexually?" *Medical Aspects of Human Sexuality* 5 (January 1971): 184–197.

TARNOWSKY, BENJAMIN. *Pederasty in Europe* (New York: Anthropological Press, 1933).

TINDALL, RALPH H. "The Male Adolescent Involved with a Pederast Becomes an Adult," *Journal of Homosexuality,* v. 3, n. 4 (Summer 1978): 373–382.

TSANG, DANIEL (Ed.). *The Age Taboo* (Boston: Alyson Publications, 1982).

UNGARETTI, JOHN R. "Pederasty, Heroism, and the Family in Classical Greece," *Journal of Homosexuality,* v. 3, n. 3 (Spring 1978): 291–300.

VANGGAARD, THORKIL. *Phallos* (New York: International University Press, Inc., 1972).

VIRKKUNEN, MATTI. "Victim-Precipitated Pedophilia Offenses," *British Journal of Criminology,* v. 15, n. 2 (April 1975): 175–180.

WILSON, GLENN D., and DAVID N. COX. *The Child Lovers* (London: Peter Owen, 1983).

SEXUAL EXPLOITATION / ABUSE

BALES, RICHARD H. "Sexual Exploitation as a Form of Child Abuse," *The Police Chief* (April 1979): 34–35.

BRANT, RENEE S. T., and VERONICA TISZA. "The Sexually Misused Child," *American Journal of Orthopsychiatry*, v. 47, n. 1 (January 1977): 80–90.

BROWN, SELMA. "Clinical Illustrations of the Sexual Misuse of Girls," *Child Welfare* (July/August 1979): 435–443.

BURGESS, ANN W., et al. *Sexual Assault of Children and Adolescents* (Lexington, Mass.: D. C. Heath and Company, 1978).

CAMPAGNA, DANIEL S. "Sexual Exploitation of Children: Resource Manual" (Wheeling: West Virginia Criminal Justice Institute, 1985).

DAVIDSON, HOWARD A. "The Sexual Exploitation of Children," *The Prosecutor* 16 (Summer 1982): 6–11.

DE YOUNG, MARY. "Counterphobic Behavior in Multiply-Molested Children," *Child Welfare*, v. 63, n. 4 (July/August 1984): 333–339.

————. *The Sexual Victimization of Children* (Jefferson, North Carolina: McFarland and Company, 1982).

FINCH, STEWART M. "Adult Seduction of the Child: Effects on the Child," *Medical Aspects of Human Sexuality* 7 (1973): 170–187.

FINKELHOR, DAVID. "Sexual Abuse of Children: A Sociological Perspective," *Child Abuse and Neglect*, v. 6, n. 1 (1983): 95–102.

————. "What's Wrong with Sex Between Adults and Children?" *American Journal of Orthopsychiatry*, v. 49, n. 4 (October 1979): 692–697.

————. "Risk Factors in the Sexual Exploitation of Children," *Child Abuse and Neglect* 4 (1980): 265–273.

FONTANA, VINCENT J. "Finding the Hidden Signs of Child Sexual Abuse," *Medical Aspects of Human Sexuality* (January 1985): 156–158.

GEISER, ROBERT L. *Hidden Victims* (Boston: Beacon Press, 1979).

GERBER, JUDIANNE D., and S. F. HUTCHINSON. *Maltreatment of Children* (Baltimore: University Park Press, 1978).

GROUSE, LAWRENCE D. "The Chlamydia Epidemic," *JAMA*, 245 (May 1, 1981): 1718–1723.

GRUBER, KENNETH. "The Child Victim's Role in Sexual Assault by Adults," *Child Welfare*, v. 60, n. 5 (May 1981): 305–310.

INGRAM, DAVID, et al. "Vaginal Chlamydia Trachomatis Infection in Children with Sexual Contact," *Pediatric Infectious Disease*, v. 3, n. 2 (March 1984): 97–99.

JONES, ROBERT J., et al. "Reactions of Adolescents to Being Interviewed About Their Sexual Assault Experiences," *The Journal of Sex Research*, v. 19, n. 2 (May 1983): 160–172.

LEWIS, KEN. "On Reducing the Child-Snatching Syndrome," *Children Today* (November/December 1978): 19–35.

LINEDECKER, CLIFFORD L. *Children in Chains* (New York: Everest House, 1981).

MC CALL, CHERYL. "Runaway Kids Eke Out a Mean Life in Seattle," *Life Magazine* (August 1983).

National Legal Resource Center for Child Advocacy and Protection. *Child Sexual Exploitation: Background and Legal Analysis*, rev. ed. (American Bar Association, April 1983).

PETERS, JOSEPH J. "Children Who Are Victims of Sexual Assault and the Psychology of Offenders," *American Journal of Psychotherapy*, v. 30, n. 3 (July 1976): 398–421.

SARAFINO, EDWARD P. "An Estimate of Nationwide Incidences of Sexual Offenses Against Children," *Child Welfare*, v. 58, n. 2 (February 1979): 127–134.

SCHULTZ, LEROY G. (Ed.) *The Sexual Victimology of Youth* (Springfield, Ill.: Charles C. Thomas, 1980).

——— and PRESTON R. JONES, JR. "Sexual Abuse of Children: Issues for Social Service and Health Professionals," *Child Welfare*, v. 62, n. 2 (March/April 1983): 99–107.

SGROI, SUZANNE M. "Childhood Gonorrhea," *Medical Aspects of Human Sexuality*, v. 16, n. 7 (July 1982): 118–141.

———. *Handbook of Clinical Intervention in Child Sexual Abuse* (New York: McGraw-Hill, 1981).

SHOUVLIN, DAVID P. "Preventing the Sexual Exploitation of Children: A Model Act," *Wake Forest Law Review* 17 (1981): 535–555.

SUMMIT, ROLAND C. "The Child Sexual Abuse Accommodation Syndrome," *Child Abuse and Neglect* 7 (1983): 177–193.

——— and JO ANN KRYSO. "Sexual Abuse of Children: A Clinical Spectrum," *American Journal of Orthopsychiatry*, v. 48, n. 2 (April 1978): 398–421.

United States General Accounting Office. "Sexual Exploitation of Children—A Problem of Unknown Magnitude" (GAO Report, April 20, 1982).

INDEX